Staging the Jew

Staging the Jew

THE PERFORMANCE OF AN AMERICAN ETHNICITY, 1860–1920

HARLEY ERDMAN

Rutgers University Press
New Brunswick, New Jersey, and London

Library of Congress Cataloging-in-Publication Data

Erdman, Harley, 1962–
    Staging the Jew : the performance of an American ethnicity,
    1860–1920 / Harley Erdman.
        p. cm.
    Includes bibliographical references and index.
    ISBN 0-8135-2413-X (cloth : alk. paper). — ISBN 0-8135-2414-8
    (pbk. : alk. paper)
        1. American drama—19th century—History and criticism.   2. Jews
    in literature.   3. American drama—20th century—History and
    criticism.   4. Ethnic groups in literature.   I. Title.
    PS338.J4E73   1997
    791'.089924073—dc22   97-6968
                                                       CIP

British Cataloging-in-Publication data for this book is available from the British Library

Manufactured in the United States of America

This book is dedicated to the memory of Audrey Lesser Erdman, my Jewish mother, who spoke out with courage, humor, and chutzpa throughout the stages of her life.

CONTENTS

Illustrations   *ix*
Preface   *xi*

Introduction: "The Memory of That Agony"   *1*

PART I *The Burden of the Dominant*

1 *Making the Jewish Villain Visible:*
American Approaches to Shylocks and Sheenies   *17*

2 *Taming the Exotic Jewess: The Rise and Fall*
of the "Belle Juive"   *40*

PART II *Emerging Encounters*

3 *Becoming a Jolly Good Fellow:*
The First Wave of Jewish Comedians   *63*

4 *Managing Power: The Entrance of Jews*
into the Show Business Mainstream   *93*

5 *Breeding New Generations: Race, Sexuality, and*
Intermarriage in Progressive Era Performances   *118*

6 *Getting Reformed: The Transition toward*
Jewish Invisibility in Popular Performance   *144*

Appendixes
A. *Selected Shtick from Comic Performances
    Featuring Jewish Characters   163*
B. *American Productions of Plays with Jewish
    Characters, 1860–1920   173*
Notes   *183*
Select Bibliography   *201*
Index   *213*

ILLUSTRATIONS

1. Edwin Booth as Shylock, 1870   *24*
2. Henry Irving as Shylock, 1879   *30*
3. Kate Bateman as Leah, c. 1870   *47*
4. Sarah Bernhardt as Leah, 1892   *50*
5. "Hints for the Jews—Several Ways of Getting to Manhattan Beach." Cartoon from *Puck*, July 30, 1879   *69*
6. Frank Bush in character, c. 1890   *77*
7. Cover to Frank Bush's "Pesock the Pawnbroker Songster," c. 1880   *79*
8. Poster for *Sam'l of Posen, as The Drummer on the Road* (*Spot Cash*), c. 1885   *85*
9. "The Drama in New York." Cartoon from *Life* magazine, May 12, 1898   *95*
10. Joe Welch in *Cohen's Luck*, 1904   *103*
11. David Warfield in *The Auctioneer*, 1901   *109*
12. Cover to Harry Lee Newton and Aaron Hoffman's *Glickman the Glazier*, 1904   *119*

PREFACE

The initial impetus for this book came during the summer of 1990, when I was taking a playwriting workshop taught by David Cohen at the University of Texas. I was working on a play about immigrant life in turn-of-the-century New York that incorporated interplay between my characters' material "reality" and the stereotyped way they were represented on popular stages of the day. My play was not inspired by objective social history as such but rather by traditions of performance. In other words, it was a fantasia on the conflicts that resulted when "stage Irish," "stage Jews," and others encountered each other in the dramatic landscape I was fashioning for them.

Writing the play meant researching old comedy routines. I found that, while it was relatively easy to come across old vaudeville and variety sketches written for Irish, German, and African-American characters, the Jewish materials were few and far between—a few pages in a book on vaudeville there, a section in an unpublished dissertation there—in spite of the fact that I had a nagging sense that there must have been a rich tradition of Jewish-American shtick that predated the age of sound recording and film. My research only confirmed this hunch but gave me few specifics as to the nature of this old staging tradition and how it had evolved over the years. I sensed that there was a story out there that had never fully been told. This book, then, represents my attempt to tell that story.

Popular culture of more recent vintage has also spurred my interest in excavating and assembling this history. I've been struck in recent years by the number of openly or clearly coded Jewish characters who have taken leading roles in television shows, movies, and plays, that have been seen by large audiences. This new trend is reflected in popular television shows like

"Northern Exposure" and "Seinfeld," successful films like *Quiz Show*, and important plays like *Angels in America*. Two issues strike me as notable about this 1990s "uncloseting" of the Jew. One has been that most of these performances have come out of scripts not specifically focused on Jewishness as overriding subject matter or theme; Jewish identity has been *an* issue without being *the* issue. Second, the vast majority of these Jewish protagonists have been male. Female Jewish characters for the most part remain excluded or marginalized.

The exclusion of compelling female Jewish characters, while disturbing, comes as little surprise, given the fact that the show business industry remains overwhelmingly a male domain. More striking to me has been the fact that it has taken so long for a variety of openly Jewish characters of either gender to emerge in popular culture, given that male Jewish writers, producers, directors—and, less frequently, performers—have for decades been a major force in shaping the stories, images, and performances that now are marketed internationally. Too often, Jewish presence and visibility behind the scenes has resulted in a curious absence or invisibility in front of the cameras or footlights. This irony is not unique to the entertainment industry; academia is arguably another stage where Jewish women and men are plentiful, but where our objects of study have more frequently been Others rather than ourselves, even if our work on these Others has been heavily inflected with our own *yiddishkeit*.

To understand why this dichotomy in Jewish representation may finally be disappearing (some would argue that it has gradually been disappearing since the 1960s), it is important to understand the reasons why it emerged in the first place, which means telling the story of that earlier era when Jewish characters and their shtick were plentiful—a staple of urban popular culture. By telling this story, I hope Jewish men in positions of cultural power will reexamine our performances of others, and more to the point, ourselves, in the belief that the self-critique that this sort of history offers represents the necessary first step toward a visibility which is progressive and empowering.

My story, then, is the interplay of the Jew as both subject and object in American popular culture: both as somebody who shaped the performances that influenced all Americans' understanding of this ethnicity, and as a fictional stage character who appeared in these influential performances. To tell either of these stories without its complement—to look at the characters who appeared on America's stages without understanding the artists and audiences who shaped and responded to them—is to construct an incomplete theory of the abiding Jewish presence in the American performing arts.

The implications of this work hold deep personal meaning for me. As a Jewish-American man who has been a creator, scholar, and teacher of these performances, I am proud to situate myself in an established tradition of Jews in the performing arts. I also follow others of my generation in resisting any notion of an "authentic" Jewish or Jewish-American experience or identity. The gray areas of my personal experience as a Jew living at the turn of the millennium, whose father was born in Cuba; whose relatives speak a combination of English, Yiddish, and Spanish; who has recently become the father of a son who will eventually need to negotiate his own relationship to his heritage—this complex experience has informed my perspective throughout. My personal history, then, underlies and motivates the performance history which I present in the pages to follow.

Acknowledgments are a requisite part of the book-publication ritual for good reason. The simple fact of the matter is that without the generosity and wisdom of dozens of individuals this book could not have been completed. I gratefully wish to acknowledge the assistance of the staffs at the Hay Library of Brown University, the National Jewish Film Center at Brandeis University, the Theatre Collection of the Museum of the City of New York, the Billy Rose Collection of the New York Public Library (especially Annette Marotta), the Manuscript Collection of the Library of Congress, and all the collections of the University of Texas at Austin. I particularly want to thank Melissa Miller of the Theatre Collection of the Harry Ransom Humanities Research Center for her suggestions and support over the course of the past years.

When this book was but a dissertation-in-process, Oscar Brockett, John Brokaw, Ann Daly, Paul Gray, and Joni Jones all offered valuable input. Susan Glenn, Bruce McConachie, and Laurence Senelick have constructively responded to my work in a way that greatly strengthened it. Kim Marra has been kind enough to forward to me her own unpublished work. Portions of chapter 3 have appeared, in different form, in the *Journal of Ethnic History* 15 (Fall 1995) and *Theatre Annual* 47 (Fall 1994). My colleagues and students at the University of Massachusetts at Amherst have directly or indirectly provided me with support in the homestretch. It has been particularly inspiring to watch the excitement of Amy Levinson and Laura Tichler as they grappled with the challenges of adapting and producing Yiddish theater. Most recently, Martha Heller, Leslie Mitchner, and Marilyn Campbell at Rutgers University Press have been wonderful people with whom to work.

Friends and family have made a crucial difference during the five years it took to bring this work to fruition. Lisa Jo Epstein has been a key supporter from early on in my academic career. Roxanne Fisher, Bill Hudson, Sarah and Bob Scholle, Carol Cancro, and Tom Guttmacher all provided accommodations, food, and great company when I was a lonely researcher on a slim budget.

For their kindness, hospitality, and understanding during these past five years, I want to thank Joseph and Rosemary Erdman. My brother, Andrew Erdman, has been a source of great conversation, good humor, and sound advice; much of him is in these pages.

I save the most personal for last. My deepest love and thanks go to Sarita Hudson for her ongoing support, which has manifested itself in ways too numerous to list here. Finally, for the last fourteen weeks of my revisions, a newly arrived person has filled me with not only with joy but a persistent longing to get away from the computer as well. Jonah William Hudson-Erdman and I have enjoyed many good times together during this beautiful New England summer.

Staging the Jew

Introduction

"THE MEMORY OF THAT AGONY"

*T*he actor David Warfield used to tell a story about his professional debut as part of a second-rate West Coast company in the late 1880s. The play was Tom Taylor's Victorian melodrama *The Ticket-of-Leave Man*, a quarter-of-a-century-old English play that by then was an American stock repertory staple. The role was Melter "Aby" Moss, Jewish henchman and counterfeiter. When Warfield recounted the story to a journalist in 1926, after a long career that saw him celebrated first as the foremost Jewish "delineator" of the day and later as "the greatest living actor in English," he recalled the trepidation that accompanied the breakthrough of being cast in such a crucial role:

> I had no idea of the character of Morse [sic] but as he was a Jew, I supposed of course he must have an exaggerated nose. Now, I had no experience in mechanically simulating noses—no idea of the stuff of which such things were made. I should of course have used the regular make-up putty, but instead I obtained some of the stuff a glazier uses. With this I proceeded to build a pendant addition to my nose.
>
> I congratulated myself on the job. But . . . right after my entrance in the act my nose began to elongate, until it was like the trunk of a baby elephant—lengthy beyond my wildest dreams of what a Jew's nose should be. When I realized what was taking place, I became demoralized. Instead of calmly manipulating the thing into shape, as an accustomed actor would have done, I became panic-stricken. I roughly pushed my nose back and off, which gave it a bulbous, pear-shaped appearance. Thus it remained a few moments, then began to elongate again.

By this time the audience had caught on. It snickered. My panic increased. When I again grabbed the thing, which had now assumed the proportions of a banana, my fingers left deep ridges in it. Under pressure it began to flatten and spread. It changed its grotesque shape with every squeeze I gave it. It was at a serious moment in the play— a sensationally dramatic moment, that was supposed to create the tensest suspense. But the audience saw nothing but my ever-changing nose. Instead of howling with rage as becomes a well-trained audience at the melodrama, it guffawed. I was hustled off the stage abruptly, ignominiously.

I shall never forget the agony of humiliation I felt. The memory of that agony is with me still.[1]

This striking tale invites multiple readings, the obviously Freudian aside. First, there is Warfield, a Jewish actor, having to augment his appearance since his own markings of Jewish ethnicity apparently do not qualify as authentic enough to satisfy his audience's expectations. The chosen site of this augmentation? None other than that time-honored manifestation of Jewish difference, that badge of Semitic authenticity: the nose. Yet, in the process of performing this difference, which presumably the actor lacks but the character possesses, the inexperienced Warfield fails miserably, unable to embody somebody else's conception of himself.

That conception, and who authored it, becomes yet more complicated when one considers that Warfield, the son of immigrant parents, is performing for an American audience a part written by an Englishman for an English public, embodying traditional stock elements of English anti-Semitism as reflected in literary and dramatic images from Shylock to Fagin. However, Moss, unlike his Venetian-cum-Elizabethan forerunner who went cloaked in the gabardine of the Hebrews, does not have his Jewishness clearly inscribed in Taylor's written text. Nowhere in *The Ticket-of-Leave Man* does Moss call himself a Jew, nor does any other character refer to him as such, yet it remains understood throughout the script, by clues such as the character's name ("Moss" which suggests "Moses") and profession (counterfeiter, the traditional profession of the Victorian stage Jew) that Moss is nothing but a Jew and must be played as such in performance. The character's ethnicity, then, must express itself outwardly through other signs. It must be manifested through grotesque gestures, intonations, and appendages that can only be inscribed through performance. Hence the requisite putty nose.

And who exactly is this David Warfield? As his fame grew during the first decade of the twentieth century, the actor tended to elide issues of origin, to distance himself from the Jewish peddlers he made a fortune playing, to point out that "they" were not him. Magazine articles took pains to make visual points about Warfield the man—his sandy hair, blue eyes, modest nose—suggesting that he was not to be equated with the characters that he portrayed. When Warfield died in 1951, he was interred with Roman Catholic rites. In fact, a 1960s dissertation dealing with vaudeville comedy took for granted the irony that Warfield himself was not of Jewish heritage. The irony, however, points back the other way, since, as far as I have been able to ascertain, Warfield was born David Wohlfelt, the child of Orthodox Russian-Jewish immigrants.[2]

And to what extent do we accept the history of this performance as real? Warfield told many things to many journalists over the years, often contradicting himself from interview to interview. This story seems, like much melodrama itself, almost too perfectly constructed to be true. Consider the rising action of the dramatic elements: the neophyte's indecision, his nervous preparation, his initial entrance, the first sign of the *schnoz*'s melt, the mangling that takes the putty from bad to worse, the audience's mounting laughter, the exit in humiliation. If there is a grain of truth in the tale, it is difficult to sift it out from the storyteller's embellishment, aided as it is by the passing of more than thirty-five years of countless retellings. What's more, the tale carries its own curious footnote, a slip made by either Warfield or the journalist recording him, in that it misreports the name of the stage character in question. Moss is a name that may be Jewish. Morse, on the other hand, rarely is.

Where does authenticity reside in this story? To what extent is this fragment of history objectively real or merely a part of Warfield's public performance of himself? Is Wohlfelt the Jewish man more authentic a subject than Warfield the talented performer who played Jews but died Catholic? And is the performance itself to be seen as authentically English or authentically American, given the disjuncture between the origins of the text and the participants in this particular performance? How does a historian answer these questions to make sense of this story?

The authenticity of ethnic identity is ultimately not the issue, neither in this story nor in the pages to follow. The real Warfield/Wohlfelt is not going to stand up and I am not going to try to make him. Rather, this story provides me with a vortex where the issues I am concerned with converge and collide. My subject, after all, is how Jews and gentiles performed

Jewish characters on American stages in the last decades of the nineteenth century and the first decades of the twentieth. I am not concerned with the material circumstances of Jewish-American social history per se, but rather the fluctuating expectations gentiles have had of Jews and Jews have had of themselves, as represented by the performances of the commercial stage.

Most of these theatrical characterizations are not flattering. Many are specifically anti-Semitic. Perhaps as a result, Jewish representation from this long era, falling roughly between the Civil War and World War I, remains a topic many today would prefer to ignore, erase, or simply forget. "The memory of that agony," to cite Warfield, remains painful. However, I believe these performances merit historical excavation and critical examination. As Sander Gilman and Stephen Katz have argued, by accepting the central value system of a given culture, Jews prove the charges of the mainstream against them since they ultimately cannot stand apart from the performances expected of them. Therefore, "to understand Jewish identity in the Diaspora one must also understand the creation, generation and perpetuation of negative images of the Jew."[3] These negative images, in the tradition of Melter Moss, are the focus of Part One of this book.

However, my story cannot be told merely through a cataloging of Jewish stage characters who reflect gentile expectations of Jewish behavior. Men (and, to a far lesser extent, women) of Jewish heritage gradually became active agents in shaping these performances during this same era. As actors, directors, producers, playwrights, and patrons, they came to exercise influence and wield power in the popular performing arts. In this case, Warfield's example is once again instructive, for the actor went on to make his first fortune playing stage Jews who were not craven villains, but rather, endearing smalltime businessmen who transformed many of the ignominies associated with stage Jews into kinder qualities calculated to win an audience's sympathies. The point then, is not how Warfield failed at playing the Jewish villain but how he succeeded in reordering the elements of the popular image of the Jew, and in so doing, helped to renegotiate the terms by which Jewish males were to perform themselves as Jewish-American men.

Warfield, of course, did not manage this negotiation alone. As I show here, he was one figure in a complex network of performers, playwrights, producers, and theatergoers, both Jewish and gentile, who achieved positions of influence in the theater and transformed the nature of Jewish stage characters during this era. This transformation, like assimilation itself, came with compromise. The new performances had their own liabilities, which invoked new agonies and led to new ironies, even while they perpetuated many elements of the older negative images. These complex encounters are the focus of Part Two of this book.

By tracing the relationship between Jewish stage types and the artists fashioning and audiences receiving them from 1860 to 1920, I show how, in coming to power, Jews resisted, assimilated, or reordered images that a dominant culture constructed for them, and then emerged embodying new performances of themselves in ways that continue to impact Jewish-American culture today.

The tradition of Jewish characters in Western drama and literature before the twentieth century has been the subject of a number of important studies that have laid a solid foundation for my work here. The key seminal study, M. J. Landa's *The Jew in Drama* (1926), starts with the Hebrew origins of drama, then traces the genealogy of stage types in England from the Middle Ages into the twentieth century.[4] Edward Coleman's bibliography *The Jew in English Drama* (1943) remains the most comprehensive on the topic. Edgar Rosenberg's thoughtful and persuasive *From Shylock to Svengali* (1960) argues that "the image of the Jew in English literature has been a depressingly uniform and static phenomenon" in tracing the polarities of the Shylock and Shiva (evil and saintly) types.[5]

These studies have defined their fields through the boundaries of literature, whether dramatic or otherwise, and thus construct their histories through the examination of established and widely circulated texts. Recently, the fields of cultural and performance studies have pushed the limits of what constitutes legitimate subjects for historical inquiry. Louise Mayor's *Ambivalent Image* (1988), while not a work theoretically in line with cultural studies, defines its field more broadly to deal with the representation of the Jew in such diverse areas as drama, fiction, religious writing, and journalism.[6] More recently, Shearer West's "The Construction of Racial Type" (1993) and Frank Felsenstein's *Anti-Semitic Stereotypes* (1995) have provided excellent models for the incorporation of alternate discourses (from cartoons to popular sociology) into the history of England's representations of the Jews by constructing networks of associations between theater and other forms of representation. In a similar way, John Gross's creatively wrought *Shylock* (1993) is a history of responses to and receptions of Shylock, both on and off the stage.

Some of this scholarship has been enriched by the perspective that Jews themselves have had a hand in constructing these traditions. This framework is already evident in Edward Calisch's *The Jew in English Literature as Author and as Subject* (1909) and implicit in the way Louis Harap structures his useful *The Image of the Jew in American Literature* (1974). Above all, much of Sander Gilman's outstanding work has both influenced and reflected these recent trends in scholarship by examining the interrelationship of diverse discourses to create a sort of cultural history of how Jewishness has been constructed.

My particular approach to this material is shaped by critical theory of the past fifteen years, which has posited an anti-essentialist, anti-foundational notion of human identity. William Boelhower's *Through a Glass Darkly* (1984) views ethnicity as a "kinesis" which takes place in cultural encounters, a process of perceiving and being perceived that resides outside the context of the subject. For Boelhower, ethnicity is processual, an act of interpretation, a way of defining oneself in relation and opposition to others. Judith Butler's razor-sharp *Gender Trouble* (1990) posits gender as a process, arguing that reified categories such as "woman" and "man" represent terms in process, ever becoming and constructing themselves. Thus, "various acts of gender create the idea of gender, and without these acts, there would be no gender at all." Since gender attributes "are not expressive but performative," this flux becomes apparent in the ways in which people perform themselves—performances that, even for a given individual, vary depending upon time, place, and situation.[7] In different ways then, both Boelhower and Butler articulate the instability of identity and posit a subjectivity grounded in action rather than essence.

I should make clear that none of this anti-essentialism makes ethnicity unreal. Ethnicity, as shaped by history, as lived in the moment, is all too real most of the time. The power of culture, as expressed in both the beauty of difference and the injustice of oppression, asserts itself continually. In fact, anti-essentialism ultimately foregrounds the importance of ethnicity since it posits difference as the ongoing creation of complex dynamics which can never be reduced to a gene visible under a microscope; it is a process for which we all bear an active responsibility for perpetuating, in both its positive and negative aspects, as we perform as both actors and audience members in daily encounters. Anti-essentialism also opens the way for the critical cultural historian since it foregrounds history as a way of understanding culture today, under the assumption that performances shape as well as reflect material reality.

This type of history points me to the boundary between ethnicities, to those "borders [that] bleed as much as they contain," to cite the anthropologist Dwight Conquergood.[8] David Warfield walked in that borderland when he performed himself as Wohlfelt or Warfield, Jew or gentile, Victorian villain or lovable peddler. For me, that borderland is usefully represented by the theater, a site where playwrights, directors, performers, and audiences constantly impact each other, with no subject ever emerging from any given performance the same as he or she went into it. Performance then, is both my subject of study and operative metaphor.

If ethnicity is something that bleeds over boundaries, then much more so is that ethnicity known as Jewishness, the ambiguities and uncertainties of which have frequently characterized a culture through two thousand years of Diaspora. As many commentators have pointed out, "Jew" has rarely meant the same thing to two people. At times, the term has signified the member of a race; at times, it has designated the practitioner of a religion. At times, it has denoted the member of a nation; at others, it has indicated the member of a culture. In European tradition, Jews were vilified and segregated as the unapproachable Other, quintessential foreigners lurking both within and without. In modern America, on the other hand, Jews have largely been subsumed into the category of white, of European, on the privileged side of the gulf that separates "us" from "them." At times, Judaism has been constructed in arch opposition to Christianity; at other times, it has been accepted into a conceit known as the "Judeo-Christian" tradition. Revolutionaries have seen Jews as too capitalist, while capitalists have seen Jews as too revolutionary. Some have seen Jews as the purest of pure races, others as the most mongrel of all mongrels. For some, Jews have been too brash and noisy; for others, they have been too sly and secretive. For some, Jews have been acquisitive misers; for others, they have been gaudy spendthrifts. Albert Sonnenfeld has noted that "for each ideology . . . the Jew is the necessary adversary."[9]

These ambiguities affect not only the way others define Jews but also the way Jews have defined themselves. Is a Jew somebody born of a Jewish mother, as the state of Israel's policy of return suggests? Is a practicing convert who abides by the tenets of religious law less Jewish than the daughter of Jewish parents who has stopped identifying herself as Jewish? Or is anybody who chooses to identify his or herself as a Jew, a Jew? Moreover, how does the term "Jewish-American" fit into this equation? Does it refer to someone American by nationality and Jewish by religion? American by citizenship and Jewish by nationality? The ambiguities multiply.

My purpose is to explore rather than to answer these questions, assuming that, while a term like "Jewish-American" can never be absolutely defined, it does comprise a variety of ways of living that can be practiced, an array of roles that can be performed. Examining how Jews have historically been performed in America is a way of exploring the modalities of being Jewish-American without reducing the term to a limiting definition.

Critics and historians have attempted such a genealogical overview of Jewish representations in American performance before, but to date the focus of scholarship has been on images prevalent after 1910. Figures like Fanny Brice, Al Jolson, Sophie Tucker, and the Marx Brothers, whose work has been immortalized through the media of mass production, hover very much present in the memory, giving the impression that these individuals, along with figures like Irving Berlin and George Gershwin, were the fountainheads of Jewish-American mainstream cultural representation. However, these "early" artists seem like pioneers only in relation to where we situate ourselves, here at the end of the twentieth century, from which perspective vaudeville, silent movies, and early Broadway have become synonyms for the "good old days." In fact, these major figures represent the third and fourth generations of Jews active in American theater and show business. Their work, both in what it rejects and in what it assimilates, builds directly on earlier traditions, performed by Jews and gentiles alike, stretching back into the middle years of the nineteenth century. These neglected earlier traditions then, are what concern me here.[10]

In my research, I have discovered a blossoming of Jewish-American stage representation in the second half of the nineteenth century, particularly after 1860. I therefore take this year as a rough starting date for my work. After 1860, stage Jews of one type or another began to turn up on American stages, becoming widespread in the years right after the turn of the century. Increasingly after 1920, however, performing Jewishness in mass culture increasingly required varieties of masking. In deference to *Awake and Singing*, Ellen Schiff's recent fine anthology of "classic" American Jewish plays, which starts in 1920, I stake out this earlier era as one characterized by heightened Jewish visibility in popular culture, even if in literary quality the performances may qualify resoundingly as "pre-classic."

The broad boundaries of my research then, are 1860 and 1920, though most of the performances I document and analyze fall between 1875 and 1915. In setting these boundaries, I have largely excluded certain artists like Eddie Cantor, Al Jolson, and Sophie Tucker, who have been well examined elsewhere and whose work extends into the next era.

This same period roughly parallels the successive waves of Jewish immigration to the United States: the initial, modest wave of mostly German Jewish immigrants who arrived mostly between the 1830s and 1870s, and the much larger wave of Eastern European immigrants, mostly from Russia, who came by the millions between 1881 and 1917, before more restrictive immigration laws sharply curtailed their numbers.[11] It seems clear that the preponderance of Jewish stage representations between 1860 and 1920 reflects the growing visibility of the Jews in America, not to mention their growing presence in the theater world itself.

Given this outline, however, I want to refrain from invoking the theater as faithful mirror of society. If it seems to function at times like a mirror, it does so more like one at a funhouse, for Jewish stage representations of the time embodied curious amalgams of characteristics associated with both German and Eastern European cultures, with certain features and trends emerging in ways which did not directly coincide with immigration patterns. In some cases, as I show, society ended mirroring theater, rather than the reverse.

I am attracted to the theater not only because it both shapes and reflects cultural forces, but also because it conveniently offers me a concrete, defined site—a literal stage peopled with physical bodies—for analysis. I find it a fascinating laboratory of meanings and possibilities. In the period I am examining, however, the stage in America had a particular resonance which it no longer possesses today. As a phenomenon which catered to mass audiences from all walks of life, theater between the Civil War and World War I was peculiarly vital and self-sustaining; religious opposition to playgoing was largely a remnant of the past, and movies had not yet emerged as the nation's dominant mode of entertainment. Though from the purely aesthetic perspective one can bemoan its seemingly paltry artistic achievements, there is no question that the stage of this era, from saloon-style variety to grand opera, provided the main form of entertainment and recreation for an entire society. The performances I consider, then, are not coterie events but events that speak significantly and broadly to the types of socio-cultural issues with which I am most concerned.

In looking at theater, I cross a few boundaries, considering other forms which, while not to be conflated with the stage, bear enough connections to it to make their inclusion relevant. In a few instances, I consider early film which, while it was evolving its own codes and traditions, was a medium with many ties to the theatrical tradition. I also briefly consider the lyrics of Tin Pan Alley, whose work was directly connected to the stage, since songs were often published and marketed in conjunction with their interpolation into musical comedies, revues, and operettas.

I had originally envisioned a book with two easily distinguished, clearly divided sections. The first section was to consider how gentiles portrayed Jews for gentile audiences during this period. The second was to consider how Jews performed themselves for gentile audiences. Alas, in the course of my research, my borders began to bleed, my categories to come apart. True, the first section was simple enough to establish, if fuzzy around the edges; there clearly were "Jewish" performances in which Jews had little or no agency, whether as performers or audiences. These were the images and representations of a dominant culture considering a largely unknown Other. In the second category, however, I stumbled, precisely because perplexing figures like David Warfield seemed to fall betwixt and between classification. In this field where writers, directors, producers, comedians, and theatergoers all had hands in authorship, it became impossible to discern who exactly was performing what for whom. Polarities between Jew and gentile fell apart. So while for my first section I was able to fix certain forms where Jews were largely excluded, in my second section I was able to locate only transitional sites, a variety of performances and encounters in a borderland where Warfield, in his resplendent ambiguity, is a representative figure.

Some may wonder why I neglect to deal with the rich phenomenon of the American Yiddish-language theater, except in passing. After all, the era I am examining here corresponds closely to the peak years of New York City's Yiddish theater, which in both range and quality of productions, surely constitutes one of the outstanding ethnic moments in American cultural history. It would seem that the Yiddish stage bears a strong connection to the English-language performances analyzed here—a connection emphasized by the fact that figures like Jacob Adler performed the same role for both Yiddish- and English-language audiences, while others like Paul Muni actually crossed over from being Yiddish- to English-language stars. A number of significant directors and scenic artists also worked in both theaters, while many other notable Jewish-American performers were exposed to the Yiddish theater in their childhoods. Moreover, the audiences for these two theaters were never entirely mutually exclusive.

Ultimately, I believe that the arguments for excluding close examination of Yiddish theater are more persuasive than those for including it. First, from the purely logistical point of view, attempting to deal with the immense variety of stage types in the Yiddish theater looms as an enormous task that merits a book in itself, especially given that the Yiddish theater itself encompassed many of the same class, epochal, and generic distinctions as did the English-language theater.[12] More importantly, however, despite the network of informal connections tying the Yiddish-and English-language theaters in America, the strong case can be made for a disjuncture between these stages. In other words, twentieth-century Jewish performances in English represent a continuity with the nineteenth-century American theater not evident with the Yiddish stage of folk operettas, sentimental melodramas, and quasi-socialist problem plays. The break in language, in my view, reflects a break in tradition. What is most significant about Yiddish performances styles may be how relatively little of their *yiddishkeit* ever found its way into American theater. The Jewish producers of Broadway and early Hollywood, many of whom came from assimilated families that had immigrated before 1881, were all too ready to shunt aside the cultural politics of the Yiddish world.

Though my focus here is ethnicity, the issue of gender asserts itself throughout my analysis. While I had originally hoped to foreground gender issues in a way that offered a balanced treatment of Jewish female and male stage types during this period, such a balancing act proved difficult. The fact is, most of the performers portraying Jews during this time period were men, and the vast majority of the characters they played were male. Though the relative invisibility of the "Jewess" is discussed in these pages, such a discussion does not remedy the male-heavy historical imbalance, which remains reflected in these pages. In the course of my analysis, however, I try to make clear that I am often referring to males, not some hypothetical universal subject.

In earlier versions of this work, I had foregrounded class divisions among audiences, taking my cue from Lawrence Levine's notions of the "highbrow" and "lowbrow" forms which emerged during the nineteenth century. I had theorized, for example, clear distinctions between ways of staging Jews for working class and bourgeois audiences in the Victorian era. As I became more familiar with the material, though, I found it increasingly difficult to reduce the complexity of the late nineteenth-century performance scene, at least as it was reflected in these performances. The result is that, while I have tried to acknowledge class distinctions when relevant, they no longer serve as a point of orientation for my work. Suffice to say that Jewish presence in the theater was closely associated with those mass cultural forms possessing broad audience appeal that emerged near the turn of the century. I use the term "popular" to refer to these commercialized forms, which included vaudeville, Broadway musicals and comedies, the songwriting industry, and early film.

I should explain my use of other terms. By "Victorian," I am referring to a period of time roughly from the 1840s to the 1890s, which parallels the emergence of certain attitudes, classes, and cultural formations
which are generally understood.[13] "American" is more problematic, the
politics of its hemispheric implications aside.[14] In focusing on performances which took place in the United States, I have ended up including a
wide variety of plays and events, not all of which were American in the
strictest sense. In the international world of show business, where plays and
players frequently crossed the seas in search of new audiences, facile national distinctions tend to break down.[15] *The Ticket-of-Leave Man*, for example, is a play from England, yet for decades it held the American stage
as a stock-company standard, where it both influenced and was influenced
by American audiences. Sarah Bernhardt and Henry Irving are two other
continental figures who, due to the length and breadth of their repeated
tours, became influential players on the American cultural scene. If one extends the importance of a given performance beyond the sanctified realm
of author and performer to that of the audience, then national distinctions
begin to break down. I have taken the liberty, then, of including as American here any show that could be said to have had a significant impact on
audiences in the United States through repeated touring or performance.[16]

In appropriating the term American for my uses, I also acknowledge
being New York-centric in my focus, a perspective justified by the fact that
New York was the undisputed center of the national theater industry during
this period in a way that it was not before and has not been since. In keeping with this perspective, all years given for plays are for their New York
premieres, when known.

"Anti-Semitic" is another term which needs explanation. Historically,
use of the term dates to 1879, when it was coined to describe a newfound
racial antipathy toward the Jews, in contrast to earlier European prejudices,
based more upon religious difference.[17] In common usage today, the word
has two distinct though by no means mutually exclusive meanings. First, it
is often used to describe certain acts or attitudes of a specifically vicious or
hateful nature—the use of derogatory racial slurs, the painting of swastikas,
the perpetuation of hate crimes. However, many Jews also frequently invoke the term to describe institutionalized sets of attitudes and practices,
which while perhaps not consciously malevolent, reflect deeply ingrained
and no less invidious prejudicial perspectives. In these pages, I choose to
use the term anti-Semitic only when referring to the former specific actions
and attitudes; otherwise, almost every performance I discuss here would ar-

guably qualify as anti-Semitic and the term itself would lose its meaning. Even in this narrower context though, the word's usage here ultimately remains subjective for it corresponds to my own notion of what is specifically hateful.

Finally, throughout this study, in referring to Jewish stage characters, I try to use ethnically inflected words that might previously have been used to refer to the specific stage types, not to mention to Jewish-American women and men in general. Therefore female characters here are frequently "Jewesses" while villains are sometimes "sheenies." It goes without saying that my purpose is not to offend but to construct a context through which we can more clearly understand these performances, sometimes in all their ugliness.

It should also be noted that, in language, what is politically acceptable comes and goes, influenced by and influencing the aspirations and anxieties of a given moment. At earlier times in American history, "Hebrew" and "Israelite" were seen as more polite ways of designating a person of Jewish faith than the somewhat crass and blunt "Jew." In contrast, the shortened form "Hebe" could once be used without giving offense. Today, the word most American Jews prefer to use to describe themselves and have others describe them is "Jewish," a term which comfortingly suggests cultural and religious affiliations while eliding the stickier question of race and biology. In other words, it implies an ethnicity not innate and essential, but rather, an adjectival condition which modifies some more fundamental identity which remains elusive.

I do not divorce myself from this view. I accept the term's implications and use it as a way of reflecting my own understanding of what it means to be a Jew. This work ultimately reflects, I hope, the aspirations and anxieties of the moment, as we look to the next millennium to see what performing Jewishness in America can mean.

PART I

*The Burden of
the Dominant*

CHAPTER 1

Making the Jewish Villian Visible

AMERICAN APPROACHES TO SHYLOCKS AND SHEENIES

"Shylock is a bloody-minded monster, but you mustn't play him so, if you wish to succeed; you must get some sympathy with him."
—Henry Irving in a letter to William Winter[1]

An 1883 comic sketch by a long-forgotten company called the Larks features, in the nineteenth-century tradition of burlesquing well-known plays, a fanciful variety of Shakespearean characters intermingling at a fashionable health spa where they have come to take the waters. Hamlet is there, along with Macbeth, Portia, Romeo, and Juliet, not to mention the central figure in the play, Shylock himself. *The Shakespeare Water Cure*, as this satire is called, weaves references to contemporary events and parodies of then-fashionable Gilbert and Sullivan songs into a quasi-Shakespearean plot which has Shylock lusting after Portia's gold and bribing Lady Macbeth into inciting her husband to murder Bassanio. The scheme works, though Shylock, much to his chagrin, ends up having to foot the entire bill for his wedding to Portia. The burlesque ends happily ever after, with all the characters singing "Red, White, and Blue," while Othello, jabbering in the tradition of the minstrel-show "coon," strums merrily away on his banjo.

In its facile manipulation of character and incident, *Water Cure* manages to present virtually every major stage stereotype associated with the Jewish male during the era. First, it stars Shylock, the dominant Jewish figure bequeathed by the classic repertory to the nineteenth-century stage. This Shylock, however, is not so classical. He makes his initial entrance, for example, crying, "Old clo'es, old hats, here you are, very cheap!" thus embodying the prevalent stage type of the pushy yet comic Jew who sells secondhand clothes in lower Manhattan.[2] Moreover, as accomplice to the Macbeths in the murder of Bassanio, this Shylock steps into the role of Jew as comic henchman, the untrustworthy assistant who acts more out of a lust for gold than pure malevolence, a type performed repeatedly in popular melodrama. Note, too, that this Shylock, like many villainous Jews of melodrama, lacks the manliness and courage to effect a crime of violence; rather, he must bribe a surrogate—in this case, Lady Macbeth—to do the dirty deed for him. Not only does a lust for gold mark this burlesque Shylock as a traditional stage Jew but so does his lust for Portia, since the stage Jew traditionally preys upon gentile women, albeit often as a comically inept suitor (as in this case). The open-ended, topsy-turvy world of parody, where so much more is possible than within the closed portals of the legitimate drama, makes possible a character who is not only "the Jew that Shakespeare drew" but also song-and-dance man, old clo'es vendor, villainous miser, effeminate coward, and lecherous parasite.

I start with *Water Cure* here because its multivalent Shylock conveniently indexes this section. I examine the staging strategies that predominantly gentile performers and audiences used to make male Jewishness visible during the late nineteenth century, as English staging traditions were gradually adapted to and transformed in America. The tale these performances tell is not static; the era moved slowly toward a Shylock more rooted in pathos and a villain more rooted in comedy. Even as these performances gradually came to depict Jewish men as less intrinsically malevolent, however, they continued to portray them as oriental grotesques and effeminate lechers, always marked with clear signs of difference, including exotic dress, distended noses, halting accents, and peculiar gestures.[3] Collectively, then, the performances portray a dominant culture which, while increasingly willing to accord Jewish men a degree of sympathy, clearly made this sympathy contingent on these Jews performing themselves exotically and grotesquely.

Toward a Sympathetic Shylock

In the beginning, there was Shylock. Or, when it comes to the stage Jew, so it has always seemed.[4] The ghost of the Venetian usurer has not only hovered over every performance of a stage Jew but even jumped the walls of the theater as well, serving as a ready reference point for gentiles (particularly, it seems, those who have had little or no personal contact with Jews) when they are discussing the "Jewish question" in general.[5] The word itself has been an active part of everyday vocabulary; there are those who can remember when gentiles could openly refer to a Jew as a "Shylock."[6] For all these reasons, Shylock takes his place alongside Harriet Beecher Stowe's Uncle Tom as a fictional creation who has so shaped popular understanding of an ethnicity that he has become a ready reference point for debate and a lightning rod for criticism.

Despite Shylock's resonance and power in Western culture, however, there is little clarity about precisely for what he stands. In literary and dramaturgical debate, the same questions have been asked about him over and over again. Is he, for example, the central figure in *The Merchant of Venice*? What portion of an audience's sympathies does he deserve? Is he essentially a comic figure, a tragic one, or a villain? Does he merit pathos— that is, is he "pathetic"? Is he a character who happens to be Jewish, or is his Jewishness central to understanding his character? Readers, spectators, directors, and performers have answered these questions in a wide variety of ways.

I should briefly make my own position clear. As I see it, Shakespeare's Shylock represents an explicitly anti-Semitic characterization—an invidious creature whose malignancy is directly connected to his Jewishness. As many commentators have noted, both the folio and quarto versions of the play use the words "Jew" and "Shylock" in ready alternation when designating that character's dialogue, as though the two terms were equivalent. If one also considers that the other characters in the play routinely refer to Shylock as "the Jew," it becomes clearer that Elizabethans might have performed and perceived the character not merely as an individual but as a man who was somehow representative of his race, as emphasized by the fact that Shylock's unambiguous defects—his narrow sense of justice, his insistence on the lifeless letter of the law, his love of money, his thirst for revenge—are those same defects that European gentiles traditionally assigned to Jews. My own reading of *Merchant* then, is that a spade is ultimately a spade. Whatever redeeming qualities Shylock may possess, whatever case can be built in his defense, he remains but a humanized version of an anti-Semitic stereotype. He is not a man who happens to be Jewish, but in many ways, the archetypal staging of the Jew as Europeans have traditionally conceived him. If Shakespeare remains powerful today, it is not because he transcended popular prejudice, but rather, because he tapped into it so representatively and compellingly.[7]

As the foremost Jewish character in the canon of a man internationally heralded for two centuries now as "the world's greatest playwright," Shylock often emerges in the modern theater as too oppressive a burden for us in the twentieth century to bear. Staging him either comically (the oldest tradition) or malevolently (as has often been the tradition since Charles Macklin in 1741) presents difficulties, for such performances call attention to hateful attitudes in the script that threaten to alienate audience members, both Jewish and gentile, from a given production. The logical alternative for many modern directors and actors has been to call attention to details in the play that suggest a Shylock more sinned against than sinning—that is, if he acts viciously at times, it is only because he has been the victim of the injustice of gentiles.

From my perspective, this approach possesses its own dangers, since in defending Shylock, it tends to naturalize Shakespeare's portrait as a realistic depiction of how Jews act, rather than calling attention to the fact that the character itself emanates from gentile fantasy. When handled by talented actors, this strategy sometimes cloaks Shylock in a psychological realism that universalizes, rather than challenges, the rhetoric of Shakespeare's anti-Semitism.[8] Moreover, I suspect that sometimes these well-intended, vaguely sympathetic Shylocks have been performed less in defense of Shakespeare's usurer and more in defense of Shakespeare himself, as if to liberate the playwright from any suspicion that he might have seen the universe in a way distasteful to the modern mind.

The point is still the same. Whether you play him this way or that, or even if you don't play him at all, Shylock remains a formidable figure. If, as a popular maxim in Victorian England once put it, "each country possesses the Jews it deserves," then perhaps it can be also be said that each country possesses the Shylocks it deserves, as the staging of Shakespeare's Jew can be seen both as mirror and mold of a given society's conception of Jews in general. The recent "sympathetic" Shylocks of actors like Dustin Hoffman then, reflect and create contemporary American attitudes that manifest a liberal identification with Jews in particular and persecuted peoples in general.

This sympathetic Shylock, however, has his roots firmly in the nineteenth century. Since the heyday of the English actor William C. Macready in the 1830s, the dominant trend in staging the play has been to accord Shylock some degree of sympathy, even to make him the play's tragic hero.[9] My concern here is with the generations that followed Macready in the late nineteenth century. If Victorian America can be seen as a transitional period, a bridge between, then the Shylocks performed during these years (notably those of Edwin Booth and Henry Irving) also form a bridge leading toward a more modern—that is, sympathetic—conception of Shakespeare's Jew. Shylock becomes, in short, increasingly pathetic. In the process of undergoing this transformation, however, he dons much of the exotic paraphernalia with which well-meaning nineteenth-century gentiles tended to cloak Jewish culture as a way of making it visible. In order to perform himself attractively and sympathetically, Shylock ends up becoming a species of oriental grotesque.

Merchant, in various incarnations, has a long stage history in America. It was the featured presentation at the first performance by a professional theater company in the American colonies, in Williamsburg in 1752.[10] The play continued to hold the stage through the nineteenth and into the twentieth centuries, though often in radically mutilated versions. My own survey of major New York productions of Shakespeare plays reveals that between 1870 and 1919, only *Hamlet* was done more often, while only a handful of scripts—*As You Like It*, *Macbeth*, *Othello*, and *Romeo and Juliet*—were staged with comparable frequency. In other words, *Merchant* was a more common attraction in late nineteenth-century New York than such standards as *Julius Caesar*, *King Lear*, *A Midsummer Night's Dream*, *Richard III*, *The Taming of the Shrew*, *The Tempest*, and *Twelfth Night*. Virtually every major actor in the country played Shylock at some time during his career.[11]

Why the popularity of the play during this time? It would be unwise to assume that hordes of anti-Semitic producers and playgoers were eager to take part in performances that promoted a vision of a conniving, vengeful Jew. Still, it seems that part of the interest in the play did stem from audiences' general fascination with what loosely could be called "the Jewish question" in America. New York productions of the play became more frequent, for example, during peak periods of Jewish immigration, reaching an apex during roughly the same years (1881–1889, 1898–1907) that public interest in this new group of immigrants was at its highest, as reflected in journalism, painting, photography, and literature. Interest in Shylock, therefore, cannot be separated from turn-of-the-century interest in this rapidly growing and increasingly visible population. For the comfortable bourgeois audiences who were attending Shakespearean productions during this era, watching Shylock on stage may have served as a vicarious way of experiencing the cultures of these immigrants whose presence was so conspicuous in the daily newspapers, and less so in the places where this class of people lived and played.

There are other reasons for the play's popularity during this time. Albert Sonnenfeld has described, for example, how the romantic imagination, searching for a foil to idealized beauty, occasionally settled upon the Jew as a fitting symbol of the grotesque.[12] Indeed, *Merchant*'s stage history in England supports the notion that Shylock emerged in the nineteenth century as such a romantic tragic figure, a man struggling between base desires and higher yearnings, not quite human, yet more than beast. Until the performances of Macklin in the mid 1700s, for example, Shylock had routinely been played (when played at all) as a subservient buffoon in romantic comedy. From Macklin on, though, both the play and Shylock's perceived position within it grew in stature until, in the Romantic era, he became *Merchant*'s unquestioned lead, with actor-managers radically restructuring Shakespeare's text to highlight Shylock's tragedy at the expense of Portia and Bassanio (not to mention Antonio, the play's title character). The foremost representatives of English Romanticism, Junius Brutus Booth and Edmund Kean, embodied Shylocks who were by turn, pompous, terrifying, noble, and malicious—but always the commanding figures in their productions. Both these actors' successes in the role might have contributed to the perception that they themselves had Jewish blood.[13]

With the waning of Romanticism and the emergence of a new generation of performers like Macready and Charles Kean (son of Edmund), the Jew of Venice gradually became, if less Mosaic in his wrath, more sympathetic and human in his personality, even "noble and winning."[14] In 1857, Adah Isaacs Menken, a convert to Judaism who was soon to become America's most sensational actress, reflected this growing trend when she published an article pleading for a more sympathetic delineation of the character, even if, she admitted, such a performance seemed to contradict Shakespeare's own predisposition toward the Jew.[15]

The ensuing decades saw a long line of Shylocks parade across New York stages, most of them falling somewhere between the majestic tragic villain of blood-and-thunder Romanticism and the humanized-yet-loathsome father figure of late nineteenth-century realism. The most prominent of these were the internationally renowned Shakespeareans Edwin Booth and Henry Irving. Booth, son of Junius Brutus and brother of John Wilkes, was the foremost American actor-manager of his day specializing in the classic repertory. He played Shylock in New York nine different times. Irving, the first English actor to be knighted, played Shylock eleven times in New York, featuring it prominently in his repertory during each of his many American tours.[16]

The stage history of Booth (1833–1893) as Shylock dates to 1861 in London, where the actor garnered mild praise for an understated performance.[17] His New York debut in the role took place in February of 1867. From then on, Shylock remained a consistent part of his repertory until illness forced him to quit the stage in 1891.

It is important to understand that, through most of these years, Booth's playing version of *Merchant* was a severely truncated text, edited and reconfigured in various ways over the years to highlight his starring role and to facilitate manipulation of the productions' elaborate scenic effects. The arrangement Booth used in 1878, for example, gave Shylock the final word at the trial, thus weakening the victory for Portia.[18] In addition, Booth generally dispensed entirely with Act Five, the section that brings the three pairs of lovers to their requisite happy endings. His version of the play, then, was typical of his century in that it highlighted Shylock's quasi-tragedy at the expense of the play's romantic comedy. The resulting script was often billed as *Shylock*, as part of a double bill with another abbreviated cut-and-paste production, *Katherine and Petruchio*. The pairing of such abridgments suggests an intriguing evening of high comedy at the theater, each piece featuring the taming of a wild and unsavory creature, one a shrew and the other a Jew.

To understand Booth's performance of Shylock and how it related to American conceptions of Jews of the time, one has to start where Booth himself often started in conceiving of a play—the scenic decor. The stripped-down neo-Elizabethan decor which modern audiences have come to expect from Shakespearean stagings was, at the time of Booth, more than half a century away from common practice. In Booth's time, in contrast, the "artistic" quality of a production was frequently judged by the sumptuousness of the pictorial spectacle proffered to the eye of the discriminating viewer. Booth's *Shylock*, in accordance with these principles, provided just this sort of spectacle. Booth rearranged Shakespeare's text partially to accommodate spectacle, which evolved and changed with the production over the years but generally featured magnificent sets of old Venice, replete with elaborately painted vistas extending beyond alleys and archways to distant canals and palaces.[19] As conceived and implemented by the actor-manager, the sets were thus evocative invitations into the shadows and splendors of a glimmering, romantic world, both medieval and vaguely oriental.[20]

FIGURE 1. Edwin Booth as Shylock, 1870. *Harry Ransom Humanities Research Center, The University of Texas at Austin.*

This visual exoticism also manifested itself in the way in which Booth costumed himself as Shylock. The attire was suggested by a figure in a painting by Jean-Léon Gérôme, the nineteenth-century French master noted for his excursions into the exotica and erotica of North Africa and the Middle East.[21] The costume, evident in an engraving of Booth from the 1870 production (fig. 1), included a long green gown, billowy scarf, flowing sleeves, tassels and fringes, pointed red leather shoes, earrings, finger rings, fool's cap, and a gnarled staff. In describing this costume years later, Booth's friend, the eminent drama critic and theater historian William Winter, noted how it was "strikingly expressive of Oriental character."[22] However Shylock may have been embodied in the past, from red-haired clown to wrathful prophet, certainly he had never been seen before to mingle local color and alien wonder in such a way as to connote the mysterious land that started on the far edges of the Mediterranean and spread out to the most distant shores of Asia.

By performing the Jew as a species of oriental exotic, Booth was both creating and reflecting one of the dominant ways in which Jewish immigrants, particularly Eastern Europeans, were written about in the late nineteenth century. Journalists were attracted by the alien and eastern culture of this new American group and by the "strange and peculiar fascination" that their customs exerted.[23] In an 1892 visit to New York's Lower East Side ghetto, for example, a correspondent for *Century* magazine remarked upon "striking bits of Semitism translated from dreamy Orient to dreary Occident," and asserted boldly that Jewish orthodox worship "is substantially what it was in the days of Christ and his disciples."[24] The housing reformer Jacob Riis, who, as Keith Leland Gandal has demonstrated, was wont to transform the human subjects of his journalistic crusades into objects whose culture and lifestyle could be examined vicariously by sympathetic bourgeois readers, wrote in the 1890s that "a visit to a Jewish house of mourning is like bridging the gap of two thousand years."[25] The sociologist Robert Mitchell observed in 1903, that the Jews' "mental processes were not of the western order, but, after all, the Hebrew is only a more or less modified oriental still."[26] William Dean Howells, in recounting a 1890s ramble through the Lower East Side, wrote how

> everywhere I saw splendid types of that Hebrew world which had the sense if not the knowledge of God when all the rest of us lay sunk in heathen darkness. There were women with oval faces and olive tints, and clear, dark eyes, relucent as evening pools, and men with long beards of jetty black or silvery white, and the noble profiles of their race. I said to myself that it was among such throngs that Christ walked, it was from such people that he chose his Disciples as his friends.[27]

The immigrants, then, were often constructed as exotic Others, foreigners living in the modern industrial West yet somehow not of it.

It is significant that much of this discourse, like Booth's staging of

Shylock, was oriented toward visual descriptions of these Jews and their customs. Numerous photographs and illustrations accompanied many of the magazine and newspaper pieces, and the prose itself relied heavily on minute descriptions of Jewish dress, dwellings, synagogues, rites, customs, and religious paraphernalia. These descriptions, moreover, were ocularly oriented; they appealed to the eye and represented a travelogue exoticism, designed to make the invisible visible, the unknown knowable, the interior exterior. Though much of the discourse is admiring, it all tends to be based on what Edward Said, in analyzing Orientalism, has termed exteriority, a discursive system based not on hidden meanings but on outward signs. Though many dominant cultures throughout history have sought to mark differences by making the Other visible through such clear signs, the late nineteenth century reveled in this exteriority on both the grandiose and intimate scales.

While Booth did not by himself create this late nineteenth-century flirtation with the Jew as oriental exotic, he was already shaping this fascination by the way in which he staged *Shylock*. His theater, after all, was a theater for the eye, a theater of exteriority, designed as an ocular feast for spectators who, in the darkness and silence of his auditorium (both recent developments in theater technology and decorum), could absorb the light and color of his meticulously created sets and costumes. His Shylock, then, from the glittering rings on his ears through the glimmering bridges of his Venice, was a figure who embodied and inhabited this Orientalist exteriority.

Booth's performance fell betwixt and between the evil Shylock tradition, already on the wane, and the pathetic Shylock tradition, then ascendant. Kirk Mallory Reynolds has argued, for example, that Booth took Shylock a step back in the direction of the malignant villain Macklin made famous in the eighteenth century.[28] Winter, who saw the performance many times, implied something similar when he noted that Booth's Shylock "blended burning passion with Oriental dignity," embodying the smoldering resentment of a vindictive, hateful man.[29] Whatever the case, it seems that Booth had problems with the role throughout his career; his biographer, Eleanor Ruggles, called it "one of his least effective performances," despite the fact that it remained a cornerstone of his repertory for twenty-five years.[30]

Part of Booth's problem may have stemmed from the difficulties he had in identifying with the role. In an 1885 letter to Horace Furnace, he wrote, "Somehow I can feel no sort of inspiration or spirituality in the atmosphere of that play. *Shylock* seems so earthy that the little gleams of light that I have perceived while acting other parts are absent, and I can see no more than what is clear to the 'naked eye.' " In another letter that same year, he noted, "I can't mount the animal—for such I consider Shylock to be."[31] To Winter, in 1884, he expressed similar sentiments: "I have searched in vain for the slightest hint of anything resembling dignity or worthiness in the part."[32] The role, it seems, was a lifelong struggle.

There are a variety of possible explanations for Booth's difficulties with Shylock. They may reside partially in Shakespeare's script and would therefore confront any actor who attempts to make Shylock into a tragic, central figure in the face of an original text arguably designed for a malevolent buffoon who shares the spotlight with three other major characters, all of whom much more readily earn an audience's sympathies. However, the specific terms of Booth's struggles are instructive, I think, because they are similar to the terms that have marked gentile characterization of Jews over the centuries. First, note that Booth chided Shylock for being too "earthy," for lacking spirituality, a common prejudice expressed against Jews, whom Christians have often chided for what appears to be materialism, as most often constructed in the love of money. Moreover, Booth's language suggests that he saw Shylock as less than human, whether as the "animal" he cannot mount, or in other contexts, where he recommended playing Shylock as a "calculating animal," using a hand "as a claw," and noted that certain lines should be "growled."[33] By likening Shylock to a variety of animals, Booth reflected the traditional gentile image of the Jews as a dirty, debased, animalistic race.

My point is not that Booth was being anti-Semitic when he wrote about and attempted to perform Shylock. Rather, I am trying to understand why Booth had trouble with the role. In this context, it is instructive to note that Booth said that he depended upon a characterization clear even to the "naked eye." In other words, lacking some sort of internal understanding for what motivates Shylock, he resorted to a characterization grounded in exteriority. In this sense, the oriental garb and the exotic setting constituted the all-important visual characterization but also located the Jew as something Other than oneself, something Eastern in contrast to one's Westernness, something animal in contrast to one's humanity. In other words, they fashioned a performance which made any type of identification with the object of wonder difficult.

There are two interesting footnotes to Booth's struggles with Shylock. First, it seems that, in the end, he finally did mount the animal. In 1887, he recorded the following inspiration which occurred to him while on tour: "Hold on! The Jew came to me last evening, just as I was leaving Pittsburg [sic], and stayed with me all night, on the sleeping-car, whence sleep was banished, and I think I've got him by the beard, or nose, I know not which; but I'll hang on to him a while and see what he'll do for me. I'll have his pound of flesh if I can just get it off his old bones."[34] Out of this violent, quasi-sexual encounter with this centuries-old icon of racial antipathy, there seemed to come to Booth a new and more sympathetic conception of how to perform the Jew. The exact nature of this new conception is not clear, but those who saw Booth perform the role in the final years of his career suggested that the actor's embodiment of the role was evolving into something more sympathetic than what it had been before.[35]

Booth's progress with the part, then, can be seen as symbolizing the age's progress with the part: a tentative but discernible movement in the direction of the Venetian Jew as a vessel for pathos. It also symbolizes America's progress with the Jews as a whole, who gradually became not exotic objects to admire or loath at a distance, but rather, potential neighbors, associates, friends, and lovers, with all the attendant affections and anxieties which proximity inspires.

The final footnote is that in struggling to find a way to make the Jew visible, Booth was most likely aware of the fact that he himself probably had at least a hint of Jewish ancestry, stretching back to a Sephardic forebear in early eighteenth-century London. The irony is telling: no matter how hard one tries to locate the Other as something outside oneself, the anxieties it represents ultimately assert themselves as something that can be located within oneself.[36]

The performances of the actor-manager Henry Irving (Henry Brodribb, 1838–1905) serve as interesting points of comparison to Booth's Shylock, both in where they parallel and in where they depart from Booth. Though Irving was of the same generation as Booth, he premiered the role in New York in 1883, a full sixteen years after Booth first played the role there. Over the course of many subsequent tours, however, Irving not only probably exceeded Booth in the number of times he performed the part for American audiences but continued to mount the play in the United States for more than a decade after Booth's death. Moreover, Irving used a version far closer to Shakespeare's original text than Booth's abridgment, thereby providing a more suitable showcase for the talents of his celebrated leading lady, Ellen Terry. In any case, Irving's Shylock became the definitive English-language performance of the role for well over a generation.[37]

If orientalist fancy provided indirect inspiration for Booth, it proved a very specific stimulus for Irving during an excursion through the Mediterranean in 1879. Irving recalled the impetus this way: "I never contemplated doing the piece [*Merchant*] which did not ever appeal to me very much until when we were down in Morocco and the Levant. . . . When I saw the Jew in what seemed to be his own land and in his own dress, Shylock became a different creature."[38] According to Irving's grandson and biographer, Laurence Irving, it was in fact this "figure of the Levantine Jew, whose romantic appearance and patriarchal dignity against the background of his native landscape" that inspired a Shylock both exotically oriental and solemnly pathetic.[39] Note the telling irony of the inspiration. For models of dignified Jewish patriarchs, Irving had no further to go than his own London (the very city, after all, that gave birth to the play), yet to find a Shylock whom he could embody with such patriarchal dignity, he had to first encounter him in a distant land to the south and east.

For orientalist exotica, the visual aspects of Irving's production far exceeded those of Booth's. His Venice was a romantic, evocative place of shifting light and shadow, full of the chiaroscuro staging effects for which the actor-manager was famous. Moreover, Irving created stage business which specifically highlighted the Venetian locale. He had Jessica and Lorenzo, for example, elope in a gondola in act 2. As for costume, his Shylock wore brown gabardine, glittering earrings, flowing sashes, and a yellow-banded cap (fig. 2), which along with distended nose and protruding whiskers, resulted in a figure that was "distinctively Jewish and . . . Orientally pictorial," according to Winter, who documented Irving's performances with the same care he did Booth's. Irving also invented original stage business to call attention to the exotic costuming. In the scene in which Shylock prepares to go out feasting, for example, Irving wrapped his temple in the orange and tawny swaths of a turban-like headdress.[40] All these costuming touches led Henry James, upon seeing the play in London, to comment on its "grotesque horror," noting, "He looks the part to a charm, or rather, we should say, to a repulsion."[41]

It is interesting, however, that this orientalist costume cloaked a Shylock who was nobler and more sympathetic than he had ever been before. Consider, for example, Irving's own notes on the character: "I look on Shylock as the type of a persecuted race; almost the only gentleman in the play and the most ill-used. . . . Shylock was well-to-do—a Bible-read man . . . and there is nothing in his language, at any time, that indicates the snuffling usurer. . . . [He is] a representative of a race which generation after generation has been cruelly used, insulted, execrated."[42] To augment the

FIGURE 2. Henry Irving as Shylock, 1879. *Harry Ransom Humanities Research Center, The University of Texas at Austin.*

aura of pathos surrounding Shylock, Irving created novel stage business, notably a brief pantomime tableau inserted into act 2, in which Shylock, unaware that his daughter has eloped, returns home, knocks at the door of his house and waits patiently there for his beloved Jessica (who, the audience knew, would never answer) while the curtain slowly descends. In act 3, scene 1, where Shylock encounters Salerio and Solanio on the street, Irving, his dress disheveled and his gown rent in anger, played up the misery of a man broken by a daughter's betrayal. Later, at the end of the trial, Irving had his defeated Shylock collapse in agony, only to immediately gather himself together in order to take his final exit with his head proudly erect. Through all these touches, Irving was making a case for a pathetic Shylock who could stand among the great figures of tragedy.[43]

The evidence for such an elevation is equivocal, however. Irving's performance metamorphosed over the years, and according to Winter, who was most familiar with this evolution, the characterization gradually became more malicious. Winter noted that, particularly late in Irving's career, Shylock became a figure brimming with "sanguinary hatred" who at times had "the aspect of a lethal monster."[44] Partially, these sinister qualities may have stemmed from Irving's performance style, which tended toward grotesque bravura. However, it seems Irving himself possessed ambivalent feelings about the part, as suggested by this chapter's epigraph.

Like Booth's Shylock, Irving's performance represents a transitional performance in a transitional era, where the Jew's pathetic and grotesque accouterments served not only as bridges to a more sympathetic understanding of the Jew but also as fences which kept him at a distance.[45] It may be said then, that Irving approached Shakespeare's Jew the same way many of the more enlightened English and Americans of his day approached Jews in general—with a tolerance and good will clouded by fear of an eastern people guided by ancient rites and inscrutable customs. The Jews could be unjustly persecuted gentlemen but they also were potential monsters; one had to keep both possibilities in mind when performing or dealing with them, even if polite and educated gentiles were wise enough to foreground the former possibility at the expense of the latter.

Toward a Comic Sheeny

The Irish-born actor, playwright, and parodist John Brougham enjoyed the rare distinction of writing both a Shakespearean and a melodramatic Jew for the New York stage within a year of each other. His Shylock was a greedy, oyster-eating gambler, "a shamefully ill-used and persecuted old Hebrew gentleman" as Brougham ironically put it, who served as protagonist of the burlesque *Much Ado About a Merchant of Venice* (1869). His melodramatic villain was Mordie Solomons, rapacious counterfeiter and diabolic conspirator in *The Lottery of Life* (1868). While Brougham played Shylock himself, Solomons was played by Charles Fisher, the actor who had distinguished himself the previous year in the role of the Jewish henchman in *Flying Scud* by Dion Boucicault (another transplanted Irishman who occasionally featured Jewish villains in his melodramas).

I start with the example of Brougham because he represents a bridge between worlds. As a European-born performer who ended up spending the bulk of his career in the United States, Brougham bridged two continents in his work, as did so many nineteenth-century theatrical figures who were reared in the British Isles but transported to the United States. Through intermediaries like Brougham, traditional performances of English anti-Semitism were transplanted onto American soil. Moreover, Brougham bridged two eras. His heyday was before the Civil War; by the late 1860s, his vogue was already fading. Neither *Much Ado About a Merchant* nor *Lottery* enjoyed the success of his earlier pieces, such as the parody burlesque *Po-ca-hon-tas* (1855). Indeed, *Lottery* looks back to an earlier era in the way it takes its villain very seriously, virtually equating Solomons with the devil himself.

As I show here, American melodrama in the late nineteenth century traced an arc away from this sort of villainy, toward stage Jews who embodied deceit in more comic ways. If the Shylock tradition veered toward the pathetic, then the Jewish villain, often referred to by the derogatory term "sheeny," veered toward the comic.[46]

Thousands of melodramas of many genres, for many different types of audiences, were written and produced in the United States in the nineteenth century.[47] No more or less formulaic than many other dramatic forms which have flourished throughout history, nineteenth-century melodrama always needed at least one villain, and frequently at least one additional henchman, to attempt to thwart the aspirations of, and then ultimately be foiled by, its heroic protagonists. Depending upon the tastes of the audience, the villain could assume any one of a number of identities which connoted malevolence enough to bear the collected wrath of its audience. Villains ranged from rich bankers to exploitative landlords to vicious slave owners. At times, the villain's malevolence was linked to and produced by his ethnic difference, in comparison to the virtue of the usually native-born hero. Many immigrant or foreign villains, including Jews, served as heavies in these melodramas.

A number of frequently produced plays established the sheeny as one way of outfitting a villain in late nineteenth-century America. *Merchant* was one, since it provided an ongoing model of a Jew who was not only malicious but also used his advantageous economic position to exploit young gentile lovers, a standard plot device of melodrama. Another was Dickens's *Oliver Twist*, with its arch-villain, Fagin, first seen on the stage as early as 1838, shortly after the novel had begun to appear in serial form. Various adaptations of the play held the New York stage into the 1880s; every few years a major company attempted its own production of the play, with the role of Fagin attempted by many of the era's leading actors. Even Dickens himself, during his 1869 reading tour, performed Fagin in "The

Murder of Nancy" in a way that played up the character's sordid, greedy nature. A run as either of these stage Jews could train one for playing the other; a number of major actors played both Shylock and Fagin during their careers.[48]

In the wake of Fagin came other sheenies. By no means, of course, were most late nineteenth-century melodramatic villains Jewish, but when they were so, an audience expected certain characteristics of them. The sheeny's name, for example, was predictable. Playwrights were content to manipulate a handful of Jewish signifiers, notably variations on Solomon, Levi, Isaacs, and Moses. Sometimes these Jewish names could be used in various combinations both as first and last names. Thus, a Levi Solomon was just as much a possibility as a Solomon Levi. (Or both at the same time, such as in C. W. Hancock's 1891 *Down on the Farm*, where "Solomon Levi" in the cast of characters becomes "Levi Solomons" in the dialogue.) From Mordie Solomons to Solomon Isaacs, from Moses Bullheimer to Moses Simons, the name made the presence of a stage Jew transparent to everyone in the audience.

For a theatergoer, a character's physical aspect is even more visible than his name, and indeed, stage traditions dictated specific ways of costuming these sheenies. According to the opening notes to Forbes Heermans's *Down the Black Cañon* (1890), Goldstein should be "dressed in 'loud' clothes; a heavy black beard, much jewelry, false nose."[49] Solomon Isaacs in Charles Townsend's *The Jail Bird* (1893) similarly requires "loud and vulgar dress; checked trousers, short black velvet coat, flashy tie, profusion of diamonds." In his printed introduction, Townsend offers even more specific costuming directions: "Isaacs is a vulgar, brutal Jew of about forty-five. Use a dark shade of grease paint, shade the eyes and rouge the lips, so as to give them a thick, sensual look. . . . Isaacs is smooth-shaven, and a black Jew wig should be worn."[50] Though these many sheenies are far from identical to each other, a composite portrait nevertheless emerges of a swarthy, hairy, fat, middle-aged, hook-nosed man who trumpets his ethnicity through a grotesque and garish vulgarity immediately evident to the eye.

The ethnicity of these sheenies is evident to the ear, too. Their dialogue, as preserved in the printed record of the scripts, bears the clear imprint of pseudo-Germanic dialect. Though the nature of the dialect varies from play to play, and frequently transforms itself even within the course of an individual script, the general direction of the dialect is clear from the dialogue. Listen to Isaacs in *Jail Bird*, for example: "I vas too honest and respectable for de clothing business. I never have de nerve to sell a man shoddy. So I go into dis business, vere nobody asks any questions."[51] Additionally, this dialect involves some curious Judeo-Christian transpositions. When frustrated or excited, these stage Jews are wont to let fly oaths along the lines of "Oh Rebecca," "Father Abraham," and "Jumpin' Moses!" This logic is borrowed from Shakespeare, who has Shylock utter things like, "O father Abram."

These unambiguous markings of difference, performed through costume and dialect, reflect and perpetuate certain anxieties about Jews in general, since Jews, unlike some other ethnic groups, cannot be so readily categorized and labeled by distinctive, consistent sets of physical traits. The markings of Jewishness are ambiguous and multiple, so that even Jews cannot always identify each other as such. These villains therefore address gentile anxiety in much the same way as does Shylock's exotic paraphernalia. By making the male Jew so unambiguously visible, they allay the nervousness associated with his growing presence in America.

If names, costuming conventions, and speech patterns constitute clearly exterior ways of marking the Jew, then the activities he engages in constitute other ways of establishing his difference. The most time-honored of these activities involves the transaction of money. It has been, of course, through their traditional and sometimes legally prescribed roles as merchants, middlemen, and moneylenders that Jews have often been encountered by gentiles. In other words, the Jews who held these professions ended up with the greatest visibility in the gentile community, a tendency reinforced in nineteenth-century America by the prevalence of Jews in various aspects of the clothing and small-scale retail trades.

This reality played itself out ambivalently in nineteenth-century America, as Louise Mayor and others have noted. On one hand, Jews found themselves frequently and favorably compared to the canny Yankee, who was famed as a shrewd petty capitalist, celebrated in stage plays of the 1830s and 1840s. After all, Americans have often admitted at least a grudging admiration for shrewd small businessmen, allowing Jewish-American merchants to enjoy a certain measure of respect denied them in the more traditional economies of Europe.[52]

On the other hand, the Jews' visible connection to the exchange of money also led to a conception of them as dishonest, preying cheats, so much so that, by the 1840s, the verb "to Jew" was already a familiar part of American slang.[53] The fact that their businesses tended to be clustered in certain areas and in certain trades tended to give the Jews a high public profile despite their minute presence in the population of most American cities before the 1880s. David A. Gerber, for example, has written about public and private reaction to a cluster of Jewish clothing merchants in Buffalo in the 1840s. Although gentile financial leaders praised these merchants in public, Gerber demonstrates how these same leaders were suspicious of the Jews, privately investigating them for financial misdealings and often refusing to extend them credit. One such investigation of a Buffalo "Shylock," as the report called him, failed to turn up such evidence, yet concluded, "The more we know of this man, the less we think of him. But we don't know anything of him that will do us any good or him any harm."[54] The double bind is clear: the Jewish merchant, burdened by the legacy of Shylock, attracted suspicion because of the assumption that there must have been something duplicitous about him and his dealings.

Accordingly, the stage sheeny's villainy is often directly and explicitly linked to the dishonest use of money, even more so than other melodramatic villains, all of whom generally seek unscrupulous financial gain. In Brougham's *Lottery*, Solomons makes his initial entrance begging for money on a New York City street. The beggar persona, however, turns out to be a facade; the sheeny is duplicitously pretending to be needy in order to satisfy his greed. Duplicity and greed are linked in the scene which follows, where the audience sees Solomons in a secret den, located in the back of his old clo'es shop, thereby revealing that the Jew's very business is but a facade for hidden purposes. Appropriately enough, as the scene opens on Solomons in his shadowy hideaway, the Jew is busy counting his money. The connection to cash is not only palpable but deceitful as well, for it turns out that Solomons is a counterfeiter who passes off falsified currency onto the play's callow romantic lead, Robert Mordaunt, fresh out of jail for a robbery of which he has been unjustly accused. Even in his materialism, the Jew proves false in his transactions, since the very currency with which he trades is a lie.

Brougham's Solomons is not alone in his profession. Isaacs, in *Jail Bird,* is another counterfeiter and crook. His first stage transaction, in the sleazy concert hall that he owns, is to rook a patron by overcharging him for whisky and a cheap cigar. Moments later, he passes off counterfeit currency on Matthew Morgan who, like Mordaunt, also is an unjustly framed, "native" American youth trying to shake his reputation as a "jail bird" and win back his honor. Foiled in his counterfeiting scheme, Isaacs later plans a bank robbery; when he proves too cowardly to consummate the crime himself, however, he returns to his basic trade of pushing counterfeit on unsuspecting victims. Simons, the big-city Jew who comes to rural Tennessee in *Little Boss*, talks obsessively of money. His partner in crime, Lydecker, tells him, "I never saw you when you didn't want money," to which the Jew can only reply, "Who, me? Vat a scandal on the name of Simons."[55] In addition to drooling with excitement every time the possibility of touching hard cash presents itself, Simons, it turns out, is yet another "damned sheeny" counterfeiter, although incompetent at passing a forgery.

A specific class dynamic informs the economic relationships in these plays. Both *Lottery* and *Jail Bird* descend from the English *The Ticket-of-Leave Man*, that tale of a lad of modest means who, unjustly accused and imprisoned, waits patiently for his good deeds to win back his good name. In much the same manner, these American retellings of *Ticket* recount the same essential fable of working-class or rural heroes of Anglo stock struggling under difficult circumstances. These young men possess inward honesty and nobility but find themselves thwarted by a financial world of scheming crooks, of which these shady Jews are the most visible representatives. In this way, the plays thrive on a class-based resentment which draws its power from audiences in difficult circumstances who, cognizant of glaring inequalities between rich and poor in Victorian America, scapegoated the petty middlemen of foreign extraction who seemed to be benefiting from the expanding, restructuring economy. Of course, these plays' resolutions betray their own contradictions which displace the drive for social and political change; in the best of dramatic traditions, they routinely conclude with their heroes discovering that they are heirs to substantial fortunes, whether through marriage or rediscovered blood connections. The contrast is clear. On the one hand, the native hero gets rich through the bravery of his deeds, not through direct contact with corrupting cash. The Jew, on the other hand, fails to get rich even though he caresses the counterfeit most directly.

In addition to being economically deceitful, the sheeny often proves to be effeminate or sexually abnormal. This image of feminized, perverse Jewish masculinity has a long European tradition. Seventeenth-century folk belief held, for example, that Jewish men menstruated, a conceit later tied to the accusations of blood libel so frequently made against the Jews during times of persecution. In the nineteenth century, the European Jew was often seen as a prostitute, his reputed avarice an example of an unhealthy, debased, and sexualized relationship to capital.[56] By the turn of the century, Viennese social theorist Otto Weininger would write that Judaism "is saturated with femininity," that "the true conception of the state is foreign to the Jew because he, like the woman, is wanting in personality."[57]

Though this extreme view of Jewish male effeminacy did not become dominant in the United States, these European ways of performing the Jew nevertheless inflected the nineteenth-century American stage Jew. As a result, the sheeny's desire for money is routinely linked to unnatural lust, which is routinely thwarted either by own his cowardice or by the heroism of more "manly" gentile characters. Whether through cowardice, weakness, or effeminacy, these sheenies prove themselves incapable of living up to their society's expectations of how one must perform oneself as a man.

This effeminacy manifests itself, first of all, in the way these villains speak on the stage. Fagin often addresses other characters effeminately as "my dear" and this Faginism shows up in melodrama, from Solomons in *Lottery*, who is fond of using the phrase "my dear" when addressing other men, to Mo Davis in *Flying Scud*. In this context, one should recall that both were played by the same actor, Fisher.

The sheeny also displays his effeminacy in physical confrontations, at which he almost always fails miserably, whether through moral cowardice or physical weakness, where each implies the other. In the climax to act 3 of *Lottery*, a cockney boxer named Bob picks up Solomons and flings him out the door of a hotel. Act 1 of *Jail Bird* ends up with Morgan virtually choking the life out of Isaacs, threatening to "drive your nose through the back of your head" if he ever lays his filthy eyes on the play's female romantic lead. In neither of these two cases does the cowardly Jew even try to fight back. Later in *Jail Bird*, Isaacs gets too scared to go with his accomplice on a robbery and even abandons him when a barroom brawl breaks out, telling the audience, "I hates to leave him, but business ish business."[58] In the masculine stage world of melodrama, full of daring acts and physical confrontations, the stage Jew comes up short.

Little Boss's Simons epitomizes the feminized sheeny villain. A big-city speculator, he shows up in Tennessee with Lydecker (his "Jackie tear") for the purpose of bilking innocent country folk. As heavies, the native Lydecker and Jewish-American Simons make a curious kind of affectionate couple. Lydecker undertakes the play's physical villainy, doing most of the seizing, binding, stabbing, and killing, while Simons handles the money and does much of the brain work. Simons, though, turns out to be an incompetent villain. When he gets nervous, he loses control of his emotions. His thoughtless errors, such as leaving behind a pocketbook full of counterfeit money, continually foil Lydecker's plans. Though Simons concocts the plot to do away with Alice Wentworth (the play's romantic lead), when he and Lydecker discuss in detail the consummation of the act, Simons breaks out into tears. Later, when it comes to subduing her, Lydecker does the seizing, the gagging, and the fumbling with the dress, while Simons is left with only the job of putting the chloroform over her face. Later, in a moment of crisis, when Lydecker kills a female assistant, Simons cries, "Oh, Jackie, Jackie, ton't leaf me."[59] In the end, the villains end up foiled by the heroic tomboy Chippy. At curtain, they are handcuffed together, to form a final stage picture opposite the play's other couple, the clean-cut leads of Wentworth and Harry Woodson. The symbolism suggested by this final stage tableau seems evident: the latter pair represents the genuinely happy American couple, while the former suggests the grotesque parody of such a couple, with the Jew in the role of tearful bride.

Partially, these performances may reflect gentile misunderstandings of certain characteristics of Jewish culture that posited different sets of behaviors as masculine norms. In other words, the ways in which visible Jewish merchants and shopkeepers performed themselves in public may have conflicted with the ways American men were expected to perform themselves. On the other hand, these performances may also represent a strategy for neutralizing the threatening presence and the abstract threat to white gentile manhood posed by these immigrants by associating and conflating the Jew with other categories deemed inferior, such as women and homosexuals.

The sheeny was not a static figure during this period. One can start, for example with Solomons in *Lottery* in 1868. In the tradition of Fagin, he is the unchallenged villain in the piece and accrues both a diabolism and a peculiar dignity as a result. Unlike the stage Jews to follow him, he is perfectly capable of physical acts of infamy, even if they ultimately end in failure. In the play's final act, he disguises himself as a sailor, and with "an insatiate vengeance [which] fills me with a sense of devilish joy," drunkenly manages to set afire a ship carrying the rest of the play's characters, a sort of floating church which serves as chapel for the happy-ever-after wedding of the romantic leads.[60] Of course, Solomons's plans are foiled, and dying, he gets dragged to shore. There, even as he expires, he summons the energy to spring up in bitter fury at his would-be victims, a final imprecation hissing from his lips. It is an almost metaphysical vision of the diabolic Jew—a quasi-medieval villain who ultimately tries to win the day not through deceit but through fire, and who must be killed to be defeated.

Brougham's Solomons, however, is perhaps the last such Jew-devil to strut his hour upon the American stage. Goldstein in *Cañon* turns out to be no more than a comic facade, a disguise for the play's day-saving hero, the sheriff Jim Mosier. Isaacs in *Jail Bird* is primarily a comic character who pales before the deviltry of the play's chief villain, the chameleonlike master of disguise, Bill Jenkins. In Frank Eugene Chase's *In the Trenches* (1898), Moses Bullheimer, for all his cunning, is there primarily for comic relief. Along with his cohort, the Irishman Patrick Green, they provide the audience with zany shtick. In the end, Bullheimer even ends up redeeming himself and avoiding arrest by betraying his Irish partner. Simons and Lydecker in *Little Boss* also comprise a veritable comic stage duo, a strange incarnation of a vaudeville team, with the Jew providing the effeminate, low comedy and the gentile serving as "straight."[61]

This movement toward a comic sheeny is the result of the transplantation of the European stage Jew, in the tradition of Fagin, to America. The sheeny performs himself with the same greed and effeminacy that marks his European cousins in this genealogy of the Jewish male, but the same humor that humiliates him and renders him unmanly also makes him less of a threat, more a figure to be laughed at than a fiend to be exterminated.

As I show in Chapter Three, when Jews began performing themselves for American audiences, it was this comedy that they seized upon, appropriately enough, as both a mask and a method of defense. The sheeny's comedy thus continued to shadow Jewish-American performers into the twentieth century.

CHAPTER 2

Taming the Exotic Jewess

THE RISE AND FALL OF
THE "BELLE JUIVE"

"Later—she learns to smile."
—title card in D. W. Griffith's *Child of the Ghetto* (1910)

*W*hile traveling in England, Nathaniel Hawthorne paid a visit to a Jewish couple, whom he wrote about in his *English Notebooks* (1856). His description in many ways exemplifies the split perspective of the nineteenth-century gentile man regarding Jews of both genders. The husband, despite his "perfect manners," was "ugly and disagreeable" to Hawthorne, who "rejoiced exceedingly in this Shylock, this Iscariot; for the sight of him justified me in the repugnance I have always felt towards his race." The wife, on the other hand, entranced the writer who, despite the longing that he felt when he gazes at her, could not bring himself to imagine himself even touching her. "I felt a sort of repugnance, simultaneously with my perception that she was an admirable creature."[1] The contradiction of the "Jewess," as female Jews were often referred to then, emerges in this passage. She is admirable yet repulsive, alluring yet untouchable.

Hawthorne's description brings into focus a number of important elements concerning the "belle juive," a recurring figure of nineteenth-century literature and theater. First, she stands clearly apart from her male coreligionist. Whether as Shylock or sheeny, the male Jew serves as the grotesque object of gentile derision and almost inevitably ends up playing the villain in the piece. The Jewess, on the other hand, becomes the object of gentile male longing, an exotic and sometimes dangerous creature whose end is pathos and whose effect is frustrated desire. Hawthorne's conflicting feelings about her can be said both to create and reflect the terms of her status as tragic figure, since the gentile's repulsion is the force preventing any consummation of the relationship. It is fitting, moreover, that Hawthorne had to go to England to encounter this woman, since the belle juive was not a figure one could find at home, but rather, a woman associated with distant lands. In this chapter, I trace the staging of the belle juive and other female Jewish characters from the nineteenth and early twentieth centuries in order to understand how predominantly gentile playwrights, directors, and performers staged the Jewess. Though she frequently appears like Shylock, as an exotic, oriental figure, associated with ancient sufferings and alien customs, she almost always ends up implicated as an object of male fantasy, a reputation furthered by the examples of a number of famous actresses who played her.[2] If through most of the nineteenth century the Jewess seems incapable of being tamed by these men, by the early films of D. W. Griffith she begins to emerge as a more domesticated figure, retaining an air of tragedy and mystery, but now situated in the United States, where she is capable of being sexually conquered and religiously converted. Outside the passionate intensity of the belle juive, the only other performance commonly allowed Jewish women on stage during this period was that of a masculinized hag.

The Belle Juive as Actress and Role

A stage history of the belle juive snakes its way back to Jessica, Shylock's daughter, the only Jewess in Shakespeare's canon. The object of Lorenzo's love interest in *Merchant*, Jessica makes a fitting comparison with her father. Shylock is aging. She is young and voluptuous. Shylock lusts after money and flesh. Her money and flesh are lusted after by others. He defies the gentile world. She sides with it, against her father.

It seems fitting that Jessica and Lorenzo's love scene in the final act of *Merchant* was deleted from Booth's staging of the play, for a happy ending was not part of the nineteenth century's understanding of how a Jewess should be performed. Shakespeare's terms seem clear: Shylock is dismissed in humiliation and defeat by gentiles, while Jessica is conquered and converted by a gentile. This contrast is predicated by a world where Jewish difference is not conceived of racially, thus rendering Jessica's conversion non-problematic. The repulsion expressed for the threatening father is not applied to the alluring daughter, a secondary character whose ethnic difference is readily performed out of the script. By acquiescing to Lorenzo's courtship, she also becomes, the audience assumes, a Christian.

In contrast, the nineteenth-century prototype for a more unconquerable Jewess—what I refer to here as the belle juive—was the character of Rebecca, the noble and beautiful Jewess of Walter Scott's frequently dramatized tale of medieval England, *Ivanhoe* (1819). Like Jessica, Rebecca is the daughter of a perfidious Jewish wheeler-and-dealer, Sir Isaac of York. Unlike her Elizabethan predecessor, however, she not only steals the story's spotlight from her father but ultimately refuses to marry her gentile suitor.[3] In other words, as she resists the gentile's courtship, the belle juive inches toward center stage.

Another influential belle juive was Rachel Mendizabel in the French opera *La Juive* (1835), whose libretto was by Eugène Scribe, the most successful playwright of the day. (The score was by the Jewish composer, Jacques Fromenthal Halévy.) Set in the fifteenth century, the story centers on Prince Leopold who, in order to woo Rachel, poses as a Jew. Complications eventually result in Leopold, Rachel, and her father all being condemned to death. In the end, however, Rachel concocts a story to win a reprieve for Leopold and perishes without realizing that she is actually the true daughter of the same cardinal who has condemned her.

The opera has predictable dynamics. Rachel's father is old, unforgiving, and spiteful, while the Jewess is youthful, forgiving, and ultimately unattainable, even if in death her memory is sanctified by the fact that she was really of Christian extraction after all. Despite its surface-level philo-Semitism, the opera thus implicitly posits Rachel's hidden Christianity as the key factor that separates her from the vengeful legacy of her bitter father. It is a deft dramatic strategy for bridging the gap between the old Jewess (e.g., Jessica) and the newer belle juive (e.g., Rebecca), thereby accommodating gentile desire in a century when Jewish difference was increasingly being constructed in racial rather than religious terms.

Both *Ivanhoe* and *La Juive* were frequently staged in the United States, particularly before the 1860s. Scott's novel was frequently adapted, its first American production occurring within a year of its publication and its last major New York production taking place in 1874.[4] *La Juive* was first produced in New York in 1836 and for the next four decades made occasional appearances in that city, sometimes billed as a "grand drama" by the name of *The Jewess*. By the 1880s, the piece had almost entirely slipped from view in that city.

Together, these two products of European Romanticism shaped the century's performance of the Jewess. She is a beautiful woman with an unhappy destiny who lives in a rural area of premodern Europe. A brave and noble gentile loves and pursues her in spite of the sordid heritage represented by her avaricious father. Their relationship is never consummated. In many of these ways, she bleeds over into other nineteenth-century fantasies, from femme fatale to noble savage to tragic mulatto.

A different European play about an unattainable Jewess ultimately became a grand war-horse of the Victorian American stage and defined the performance of the belle juive more firmly than had its predecessors, while carrying the tradition into the twentieth century. *Leah the Forsaken* (1863) was the work of the masterful manipulator, entrepreneur, and appropriator, Augustin Daly (1838–1899), who adapted his script (in an age of copyright we would say "stole") from Salomon Hermann von Mosenthal's *Deborah*, which had scored a major success in Vienna in 1849. Changing the protagonist's name from Deborah to Leah subtly reinscribed the play in the grand tradition of stage Jews by invoking the name of Shylock's unseen wife.

Daly's production played to packed houses night after night and quickly spawned not only imitations but also that surer sign of success, the parody burlesque, such as *Leah the Forsook*, which featured the comedian Dan Setchell as "a Shrewish maiden."[5] In various incarnations and imitations, the play was thereafter produced dozens of times in New York, both by local companies and by touring stars from abroad. A line of leading actresses included the play in their repertories. The play became a standard "test piece" for amateurs wanting to make an impressive debut. Its flowery orations were extracted and published as exercises for students of declamation and elocution. From the 1860s through the 1890s, Leah was the quintessential American stage Jewess.

On surface level, Daly's *Leah* is philo-Semitic. In an idyllic central European village, young Rudolf prepares to wed Madalena, his betrothed. Meanwhile, Leah, a wandering Jewess camped in the forest nearby, narrowly escapes the violence of an anti-Jewish rabble incited by Father Nathan, the village schoolmaster, who, the audience discovers, is secretly concealing his own Jewish origins. Rudolf falls in love with Leah and meets her at midnight in the forest for a romantic tryst. Nathan spies on the couple and makes the affair public. Rudolf, under pressure from his family, forsakes Leah to wed Madalena. Cursing her lover and vowing revenge, Leah retreats into the woods, only to return with a band of wandering Jews five years later, when she encounters Rudolf and Madalena with their young daughter, whom they have named for the Jewess. Touched by the sight of her namesake, Leah takes back her curse, unmasks Nathan, and dying, departs feebly with her people.

Though the script depicts Leah as a commanding, nobly self-sacrificing tragic figure, it also presents her as a wild object of male desire barely in control of her own passions. In the play's first account of Leah, Madalena describes her as appearing out of the forests, "tall and strangely clad, her brown hair flowing over her naked shoulders," a baring of flesh which in Victorian America generally represented an open enticement to the male spectator. The rest of the script offers ample opportunity for the actress playing this "wild, uncouth woman" dressed in revealing rags, to throw out her arms and beat her breast, presumably revealing arms, shoulders, and throat in the process.

A tour-de-force scene for which the play became famous provides an example of such an opportunity. The scene takes place on the night of Rudolf's wedding to Madalena and features Leah showing up in the village churchyard with "her hair streaming over her shoulders." When she peers into the chapel windows and sees the ceremony taking place, she realizes Rudolf has betrayed her. After a tempestuous monologue, she screams "Revenge!" and "throws oft her mantle, disclosing white robe beneath—bares her arm, and rushes to the door." Confused, distraught, baring flesh and blazing fury, this is the Jewess at the peak of her untamed passion, when there is no telling what desperate act of vengeance she may commit.

It is precisely this wild, lawless passion, however, that makes Leah so appealing to the handsome young gentile hero. Rudolf is an upstanding young man in the village, son of the village magistrate and fiancé to the respectable, virginal Madalena. The wandering Jewess who dwells in the forest embodies for him an attraction to a type of passion outside the bounds of what is acceptable and proper. As Rudolf himself confesses: "Something seems to draw me toward the forest. First I went there trembling, as one about to sin; and when the church bell tolled the solemn benediction, it seemed to call me back to a holier faith. Yet I hurried on. She came to meet me—so wildly beautiful, so full of feeling, that only then I understood what is infinity." The wild darkness of the Jewess's forest is where the gentile goes to sin. It is an exotic and dangerous locale outside the bounds of chaste, Christian love, as represented by Madalena.

Rather than dwelling misogynistically on the dangers of a transgressive temptress, *Leah* turns out to be, instead, a play that hinges on issues of religious conquest and conversion. Leah, the play makes clear, has been weaned on a Jewish legacy of vengeance and hate. She carries in her blood the ancient tradition that demands, as she puts it, "An eye for an eye, a tooth for a tooth, a heart for a heart!" However, as she makes clear to

Rudolf during a tender love scene, her love for a gentile has made her wrestle with this inherited code: "For thee I have forgotten all else, even our people's deeply cherished hate. . . . You may burn our huts, drive our children into the wilderness, rob us of all else; but you cannot take from us that song of vengeance. But you—you dearest, you have robbed me of this last treasure. This hatred of the Christians. I asked you your creed, you answered—'Heaven is love!' I loved thee, and was converted."

In this moment of trembling passion, the play reveals its central dramatic questions. Will the Jewess be converted from the law of vengeance to the law of love by the charisma of the gentile hero? Will Rudolf lift Leah up "from these festering depths, where [her] girlish heart seemed fast falling to decay," or will she fall back to being "that hideous blot upon the face of nature, a Jewish outcast," as she calls herself? Even as the play strongly condemns injustice, exposing Christian persecution of the Jews as the product of ignorant superstition, it implicitly reinscribes Judaism as a religion of vengeance, since it posits the loving forgiveness of the Christian faith as its tender antithesis. The body and soul of the Jewess, then, become the staging ground for this conversion of the vengeful old law into the loving new one.

This semi-concealed thematic concern becomes even more apparent if one takes the play's other major Jewish character, the crypto-Jew Nathan, as a foil to Leah. In matters of religious duty, Nathan is such an unbending inquisitor that Father Herman, the kindly village priest, chides him, "You cling so closely to the laws. I fear you forget the spirit of Christian precept." Thus, even when posing as a Christian, Nathan marks himself as a Jew by his stubborn adherence to the dead letter of the law—the same perverse legalism that makes Shylock not only insist on his pound of flesh but bow before the cold logic of Portia's argument as well. Throughout *Leah*, moreover, Nathan proves himself an unreconstructed sheeny villain, who readily resorts to blackmail, demagoguery, and murder as a way of stoking the flames of hate in his heart. Like all villains in melodrama, Nathan gets his due in the final scene, when the other villagers, now aware of his Jewish origins, pounce upon him viciously, as if his sin were partially his refusal to be visibly Jewish to them.[6]

By juxtaposing noble Jewess and evil Jew, the dramatic finale brings to the surface the issues of Jewish conversion raised throughout the play. Through both the "outing" of Nathan and the lifting of Leah's curse, the Hebraic cloud of hate gets lifted from the village and the ancient law of vengeance, which the play explicitly associates with Judaism, evaporates in the face of the new love of love, which the play explicitly associates with Christianity. Nathan, the evil Jew, is conquered in the flesh as he is captured, while Leah, the tragic Jewess, is conquered in the soul as she expires. Though she remains physically unattained by the gentile, Leah has had her heart won over by Christian love. As a product of male fantasy, Leah thus negotiates the simultaneous attraction and repulsion she evokes in such a way that must have been satisfying for audiences, given the play's many years of success.

In performance, *Leah* was designed as an actress's vehicle, and its productions almost always were actress's projects. The play was originally created and produced by Daly specifically for Kate Bateman (1842–1917), a celebrated child star who needed a vehicle to prove her talents as a serious actress. As suggested by surviving photos and illustrations (fig. 3), Bateman came across as a fierce, intense, unsmiling Jewess with a touch of the lawless exotic; the self-conscious seriousness of the characterization reflected the seriousness of the actress's mission to prove herself in a new type of role. Reviewers indeed described her Jewess as an aloof and untouchable creature, unrelentingly intense, who brimmed with pathos and passions.[7]

Of the many actresses who shortly followed Bateman in the role, the most notable was Fanny Janauschek (Francesca Romana Magdalena Janauschek, 1830–1904), the actress from Bohemia known for regal grandeur and majestic passion. Janauschek showcased Mosenthal's original *Deborah* in German in her 1867 tour of the United States. In 1873, she performed the part in English under the management of Daly himself.

Bateman and Janauschek to a large extent exemplified what has been called the emotionalist school of acting, prominent through the middle part of the nineteenth century, which was characterized by grandiose emotional pyrotechnics and represented largely by the work of female performers. Through the work of Bateman and Janauschek, Leah became an exemplar of a style at its zenith in the 1860s. The belle juive thus became a way of achieving a style of acting expressly linked to the female body, even while that same style allowed the belle juive to be taken to new emotional extremes. These performances reflected and shaped the female body on the nineteenth-century stage as transgressive, both in terms of actress and role: a figure outside the confines of normal behavior and for this reason simultaneously fascinating and dangerous to the male spectator.

Associations between the seductive, emotional figure of the belle juive and the seductive, emotional figure of the actress were emphasized by

FIGURE 3. Kate Bateman as Leah, c. 1870. *Harvard Theatre Collection, The Houghton Library.*

the fact that a number of renowned actresses with scandalous or tragic personal lives had well-publicized links to the Jewish tradition. The religion of the French actress Éliza Félix Rachel was always openly part of her international identity, as underscored by her simpler stage name, Rachel, which coincided neatly with the character from the contemporary opera even while it emphasized her religious background. The American actress Clara Morris (another high emotionalist performer who worked with Daly) recalled Rachel as "the mightiest Jewess since the times of Miriam and Deborah," while also noting that she stood out against "the black cloud of her ever sordid family."[8] Morris's observation reflected the ongoing gentile expectation of the Jewess as somebody able to transcend her family's ignominy, to triumph and garner acclaim in spite of her heritage of materialism and greed.

The most celebrated and scandalous actress in America at the time *Leah* debuted was also known to be a practicing Jewess. Adah Isaacs Menken (1839?–1868) claimed to be from a Jewish family, but it seems more likely that her first exposure to the religion came after her marriage to Alexander Isaacs Menken in 1856. They resided in Cincinnati, then a center for German-Jewish immigration, where she studied Hebrew, published articles on Jewish affairs (including the aforementioned tract on Shylock), wrote biblically inspired poetry, and added the "h" to "Ada" to make it sound more Jewish. She also played Rebecca in a local production of *Ivanhoe*. As her fame grew, stemming mostly from her simulated bareback ride in *Mazeppa* (1861), her Jewishness continued to be part of her complex performance of self. The exoticism, intensity, and brilliance of the *belle juive* were thus part of the transgressive persona that the "belle Menken" (as she was called in Paris) cultivated for herself.[9]

If Rachel and Menken established links between Judaism and the lives of troubled, dangerous actresses, Sarah Bernhardt (1844–1923) strongly reinforced them.[10] Arguably, Bernhardt was for decades the most famous "Jewish" woman in the world. It was an ethnic and religious identity, as performed by herself and perceived by her public, which always occupied that borderland between the Jewish and the gentile. Though her mother was of Jewish origin, Bernhardt herself, born Sarah Henriette Rosine, was baptized as an infant, reared Catholic, and schooled for a number of years in a convent—perhaps to remove any taint of Judaism from the daughter of a socially ambitious mother in a Paris noted for rampant anti-Semitism.[11] In her autobiography, Bernhardt repressed any mention of her Jewish background.

In spite of this fact, Bernhardt's Jewish origins ended up an integral part of her public persona. Throughout her career, these roots were no secret, and journalists made frequent reference to her "Hebraic blood."[12] The context could frequently be admiring. An 1879 description of her in the *New York Dramatic Mirror* mentioned how "she combines with the semi-masculine energy of the children of the North the Bohemian instincts and the vagabond humor of the Semitic race," specifically noting in this context her "hooked nose."[13] Bernhardt often contributed actively to this image. When reporters mobbed her during her first tour of America, for example, demanding that she acknowledge her racial background, she announced, "I'm a Roman Catholic, and a member of the great Jewish race."[14]

(Menken had once responded to similar clamoring from the press by announcing that she was really Dolores de Ricardo Los Fiertes from New Orleans, daughter of a Spanish Jew and a French Creole.) Though Bernhardt could either trumpet or downplay her "Jewess-ness" as circumstances warranted, the identification succeeded in attracting persecution as well as adoration; the actress became the frequent target of anti-Semites, such as the bigots who stoned her carriage during her 1881 tour of Russia.[15]

The personas of the Jewess finally fully came together as both actress and character for American audiences when Bernhardt featured her version of *Leah* during her 1891–1892 tour, at a moment when the actress's celebrity was near its zenith. In contrast to the severe emotionalism of Bateman, Bernhardt inserted a seductive sexuality more openly into the performance of the character. The *New York Times* reviewer wrote of the "fiery" nature of Bernhardt's performance, of the "childish glee" and unchecked emotion which distinguished itself from the "chaste and formal" pathos which marked Bateman's interpretation.[16] Reading between the lines of this review, one can discern that part of the fire and glee in the Bernhardt performance derives from the seductive display of the Jewess's sexuality, suggested in the bare-shouldered Jewess of the script who was waiting there for Bernhardt to exploit. This display appears clearly in a standard publicity illustration that Bernhardt and her agents widely circulated (fig. 4) where Bernhardt-as-Leah, with flowing hair and bare shoulders, confronts the male viewer's gaze with an inviting glance.

Bernhardt's performance foregrounds the belle juive as object of male desire, a connection made more readily possible by Bernhardt's own Jewessness than by a "chaste" gentile American performer like Bateman. It should be noted that Bernhardt's own Jewish mother had enjoyed a successful, prosperous career as a courtesan in a Paris "where every self-respecting bordello offered at least one Jewish girl and one black girl for connoisseurs of exotica."[17] Bernhardt herself, in fact, probably practiced this profession briefly before becoming a star. The wraith-like eroticism and aura of decadent sexuality that separated Bernhardt from a more traditional "chaste" actress like Bateman can be said to be performed partially through her ethnicity, since both Bernhardt in specific and Jewesses in general had associations that marked them as objects of desire.[18]

As exemplified by Leah, the fiercely independent yet dangerously emotional belle juive loomed seductively just beyond the perimeter of proper gentile society. The late nineteenth-century actress was also suspect according to conceptions of proper Victorian gentile womanhood, since her

The Theatre Magazine Co.,
26 W. 33d Street, New York.   Mme. SARAH BERNHARDT

FIGURE 4. Sarah Bernhardt as Leah, 1892. *Harry Ransom Humanities Research Center, The University of Texas at Austin.*

profession made possible her economic independence, and her performances required her sometimes to stage dangerous emotions and uncon-
trollable desires. By uniting these two bodies, an actress who was also
Jewish was doubly exotic. When a Jewess/actress like Bernhardt chose to
perform the preeminent stage Jewess of the era, she highlighted for American audiences the dangerous sexuality of this figure. The belle juive could
go no further.

The Decline of the Belle Juive

The California-born actress Nance O'Neil (Gertrude Lamson, 1875–1965), lauded by some as the "American Bernhardt," was one of the last American actresses to work in the "grand passion" tradition of the emotionalist school, at a historical moment when more naturalized styles were coming to the fore. It seems appropriate, then, that the work of O'Neil intersected with a variety of different gentile ways of performing the quintessentially nineteenth-century belle juive just when the new century was beginning. First, in 1897, she toured the country in a version of *Leah* entitled *The Jewess*, making her the last major American actress to play the role. Second, she played the majestic, vengeance-seeking Jewess in *Judith of Bethulia* (1904), reflecting the nation's growing interest in Biblical drama. Finally, a member of O'Neil's company named David Wark Griffith fashioned a tamer performance of the Jewess when he started his career as a filmmaker. Appropriately, his first full-length feature, *Judith of Bethulia* (1913), was inspired by his connection with the actress.

I start with O'Neil here because these three different Jewesses index what the Jewess had become in America by the first decade of this century. The romanticism of the European-associated belle juive, as reflected by *Leah*, was disappearing. In her place, the Jewess on one hand was becoming more Biblicized and remote, as represented by *Judith of Bethulia*. On the other hand, the Jewess was becoming tamer, a fit object for a gentile's wife despite her tragic history. Both these strategies represent American ways of domesticating the belle juive—changing her contexts so as to downplay her danger.

The growing material presence of Jews in American society made difficult the tenure of the sympathetic belle juive. New theories of racialism, rooted in nineteenth-century science, became more pronounced in sociology around the turn of the century (as I document in Chapter Five). "Debased" immigrants from southern and eastern Europe were increasingly seen as representing a threat to Anglo-Saxon America's cultural order and racial composition. At the same time, the philo-Semitic high romanticism of *Leah* increasingly seemed outdated, because of both its outmoded style and its tragic, gloomy performance of the Jewess. As early as 1886, for example, six years before Bernhardt brought her Leah to the United States, the play was being lamented as "sombre and tedious."[19] Throughout the 1890s it continued to lose its luster, and after 1900, reviewers used terms like "almost unbearable" to label it, lamenting that it was burdened by "an almost unrelieved hue of sombreness."[20] By 1907, O'Neil's production of *The Jewess* had to be reduced to a ten-minute version for vaudeville.[21]

It seems appropriate, in this era of growing racialism, that O'Neil recast her Jewess as non-Semitic. A tall, fair-skinned woman described variously as "Viking," "Celtic" or of "unmixed Saxon blood," O'Neil played the Jewess in her natural golden-blond hair. At least one critic expressed attraction for this "beautiful blonde Jewess, a rare but perfect type."[22] The performance thus distanced the character from the immigrants who were far more visible in America in 1900 than in 1863, when Daly's play first opened.

If this "Anglo-Saxoning" of Leah was one way the belle juive became more Americanized, then the biblical epic was another. The nation's interest in these epics became clear with Lew Wallace's *Ben Hur* (1880), the best-selling American novel of the nineteenth century, which spawned a number of imitations and stage adaptations.[23] In terms of theater, the Old Testament angle to this trend peaked in the early 1900s, with short-lived biblical epic stage plays, including not only *Judith of Bethulia* but *The Shepherd King* (1905) and *Mizpah* (1906), the last two structured around the stories of King David and Queen Esther, respectively.

A number of things are clear about these elaborate biblical plays. First, while they all feature famous Jewish characters, their Biblical setting takes precedence over any but the most universal (that is, pre-Diaspora) connections to Jewish ethnicity or culture. Second, they are written in a verse which today seems stale and pretentious; self-consciously "literary" and highbrow, they distance themselves from associations with mainstream commercial theater, despite the fact that they were commercially produced. Finally, they are plays that played only briefly and to bad reviews in New York but that enjoyed, in a number of cases, a modicum of success touring smaller cities around the country. In other words, these productions existed at the margins of the New York–centered, Broadway theater, where Jewish men were playing an increasing important role and where Jewish patrons were increasingly a part of auditoriums, as I show in Chapter Four. For all these reasons, I situate this theatrical tradition as one produced largely by and for gentiles—in this case, white Anglo-Saxon Protestants. They are therefore part of the dominant traditions that characterize the first section of this book, despite their chronological parallel to performances that I examine in Part Two.

Thomas Bailey Aldrich's *Judith of Bethulia* provides an interesting example of how the belle juive fared when transplanted into this biblical environment.[24] The play was written especially for O'Neil, who had already toured the country in a turgid, badly translated version of Paolo Giacommetti's old Italian play *Judith*, once a touring vehicle for Adelaide Ristori. Aldrich's play is streamlined and classically concise. Judith, a young widow in the besieged city of Bethulia, is accepted by her Hebrew country-people as a prophetess, especially when a portentous dream fills her with "wild and dangerous intent." Inspired by this visionary dream, Judith determines that she must save her city by impersonating a courtesan and seducing Holofernes, commander of the Assyrian army besieging Bethulia. In a deadly game of mutual seduction in Holofernes's tent, Judith manages to drug his cup of wine, but only after resisting her own fierce attraction to the vital young man. After a moment of indecisive torment, Judith finds the courage to cut off Holofernes's head and save her city. While Bethulia celebrates the victory, Judith clads herself in mourning. Beatific and subdued, she withdraws into "mine house, where laughter may not come" as the curtain falls.[25]

Judith looms as one of those female idols of perversity, as Bram Dijkstra has called them, who turn up so frequently in fin-de-siècle beaux arts. As Dijkstra demonstrates, painters and sculptors returned repeatedly to Judith and figures like her, these lofty figures on pedestals, angels who stoop to whores, goddesses of vengeance who sever the heads of the men who love them.[26] Moreover, the biblical trappings of Aldrich's play, with its gyrating "cooch" dancers in Holofernes's tent, tie the piece to the then-current obsession with oriental exotica, as most notably reflected in Salome, another decapitating siren of the old Middle East with Jewish connections, who was then the rage on stages across Europe and America.[27]

More so than Salome, however, Judith is tied to the belle juive tradition by her haughty grandeur, her thirst for vengeance, her wild desire for the forbidden gentile man (and his wild desire for her), her willingness to sacrifice her own happiness for the happiness of others, and her utter gravity as she disappears unsmiling at the curtain's fall. While Judith is not to be conflated with Leah, it is no coincidence that O'Neil kept both characters in her repertory at the same time.

In many ways, however, Judith also departs from earlier belle juives. Rachel and Leah, one should remember, were tragic figures who, in various ways, nobly gave up their own lives for the men they loved. Their lovers, in turn, were permitted to survive, to return to their lives among the gentile; Rudolf even manages a happy ending, redeeming himself by petitioning the Emperor for tolerance, and in turn getting redeemed when Leah withdraws her curse on his daughter. Holofernes, in contrast, manages no such happy ending: he loses his head because he has allowed himself to be seduced by the beautiful figure. Thus, while *Judith* can be performed as a feminist play which dramatizes the resourcefulness and courage of a commanding woman, it also can be seen as a cautionary tale of what can happen to a noble young warrior-athlete when he lets himself be seduced by an exotic Jewess.

However one reads the play, *Judith* represents perhaps the final step in the stage history of the belle juive. Biblicized, the belle juive was stripped of any association to contemporary reality. A commanding, heroic, larger-than-life woman could not be specified as a Jewess. The quasi-Biblical context effectively downplayed the Jewess's connection to her ethnicity, universalizing her within a landscape ruled unambiguously by a Judeo-Christian God.

This "de-ethnicization," if you will, of the Jewess was taking place on other stages as well. C.M.S. McLellan's *Leah Kleschna* (1904), for example, was a Broadway success the same year that O'Neil's *Judith* toured the country. The play, which starred the celebrated actress Minnie Maddern Fiske, dramatizes the story of a young Austrian woman trained by her sordid family to burgle houses. Caught in a Paris burglary by the noble Paul Sylvaine, Leah ends up not only in love with him but converted to his honest way of life, the point being that innate goodness, with the help of Christian charity, can triumph over corrupt rearing.[28]

The classic elements of the Jewess fable are here: the evil father, the daughter (named Leah!) trying to distance herself from her upbringing, the high-minded gentile suitor. What's missing, however, is a Jewess. As far as I can determine, nothing in the script or in Fiske's performance of the part specified the ethnicity of this seemingly Jewish family. One reviewer did note that the play "hints of Austrian Salvonic, or more likely Jewish traits" but it seems that these hints were as far as the performance took the issue.[29] Though her shadow is clear, the belle juive in *Leah Kleschna* is ultimately neither dangerous, tragic, nor Jewish; in the end, she is destined to live happily ever after with her lover. On Broadway, this was the new answer to the European somberness of the old story. The fierce, unsmiling Jewess was melting in the light of the new century.

D. W. Griffith similarly worked to domesticate the Jewess. A journeyman actor who joined O'Neil's company in 1905, he eventually abandoned a stage career to try out his hand as a filmmaker. By 1908, he was directing his own short films for the Biograph Company. In his shorts *Romance of a*

Jewess (1908) and *Child of the Ghetto*, (1910) and his feature *Judith of Bethulia* (1913), Griffith rendered the belle juive more attainable, even marriageable.[30]

The nascent motion picture industry was not yet characterized by the presence of many Jews the way it has been since (or the way the theater world already was), though these early movies may have been partially aimed at Jewish audiences, who were frequent patrons of nickelodeons.[31] Whatever the case, Jewish material was both nationally of interest to gentile audiences and locally accessible to filmmakers as well. The movie industry, Biograph Studios included, was centered in New York, where the nation's burgeoning Eastern European immigrant community was most concentrated and visible; the Lower East Side ghetto in particular provided easy "documentary" footage of this immigrant culture, which the rest of the country had recourse to read about but rarely the opportunity to observe. Short films like *Romance* and *Child* incorporated footage of the ghetto's teeming street life as "realistic" local-color background for the fables of Jewesses they tell. The industry liked to play up these documentary qualities; the *Biograph Bulletin*, for example, in touting *Romance*'s release, mentioned that "several of the scenes are decidedly interesting in the fact that they were actually taken in the thickly settled Hebrew quarters of New York City."[32] Through the medium of the motion picture, then, the local became exotic and the exotic, local. The belle juive now had a domesticated background for her travails, in contrast to the villages of central Europe and the ramparts of Bethulia.

The earliest of these three films, *Romance*, is filled with the severe tragedy and intense pathos which traditionally surrounds the Jewess. Florence Lawrence plays the swarthy, long-haired immigrant named Ruth, who in the deathbed scene that opens the movie, receives a locket as a keepsake from her dying mother. From there the film moves abruptly to the pawnshop where Ruth assists her father. She rejects the marriage her father has arranged for her to a wealthy young Jew named Rubinstein, marked conspicuously by his bushy black beard and hawk nose. Instead, she elopes with a clean-shaven man with a smaller nose, a poor but American-looking Jew who runs a bookshop. Her father, as a consequence, disowns her. A few years later, the young husband falls from a ladder to an untimely death, leaving Ruth destitute and in ill health with their young daughter. Now on her own deathbed, Ruth sends her daughter to pawn the locket. The pawnshop that the daughter chooses, of course, turns out to be that of Ruth's father. Ruth's father recognizes the locket and embraces his granddaughter.

Finally, the three generations unite for a brief moment of reconciliation before Ruth passes away, the third tragic death in the film's ten minutes.

Romance both defies and reinscribes many of the ways in which gentiles had traditionally portrayed Jews. In contrast to many earlier performances, it depicts loving Jewish family relations, positive older Jews, and the possibility of a genuine Jewish-Jewish love affair. Lawrence's Ruth, though, appears as a curiously passive figure. She does little to forward the action of the film, and in fact, barely even moves in the film's frame, contenting herself mostly to react to the actions of the men around her. Compared to the active, commanding figures of Leah and Judith, Ruth appears strangely neutralized, devoid of personality, though she still embodies the unrelenting gloom and doom of her older cousins. In other words, though she is still a figure implicated in tragedy, this tragedy is more the result of bad circumstances than of her own personality.

This gloom and doom carries over into yet another long-haired, swarthy Jewess, the protagonist of *Child*, technically a far more sophisticated film than *Romance*. Once again, Griffith's young immigrant protagonist is named Ruth (Dorothy West); once again, the film opens with the Jewess losing her mother in a tearful deathbed scene. Unlike her namesake in *Romance*, however, this Ruth is left an utter orphan and "Must Fight Life's Battle Alone" in the big city. She tries to make a living as a Lower East Side seamstress, where she must deal with the rude, bearded Jews who run the business. Worse, like the struggling young protagonists of many a melodrama, she ends up falsely accused of a crime and must flee the police, ending up in pastoral countryside far outside the city limits. There, a young country boy in a cowboy hat (Henry Walthall) finds her on the verge of nervous collapse and takes her home to mother to nurse her back to mental health. Later, on a holiday fishing outing in the country, the policeman who earlier pursued Ruth in the city recognizes her as his suspect and threatens to arrest her. When he sees her kissing her beau, he decides to leave the young couple to idyllic happiness.

Child is fascinating for the way Griffith invokes and then repudiates the ways the Jewess has traditionally been performed. Ruth, like her forbears, moves in mists of somber gloom. Draped in black mourning at the beginning of the film, she cuts a severe figure under dark flowing hair, seemingly incapable of the slightest smile. She is prone, too, to wild bursts of emotion, breaking out into fits of tears and hysteria whenever she is confronted by difficulties. Unjustly victimized by others, she seems destined to wander alone like Leah. However, this dire Jewess turns out to be neither tragic nor destined for loneliness. Far from the corrupting ways of the city and its greedy Jewish men, she finds the gentle love of a gentile suitor. His great accomplishment in retraining her is reflected in a title card cited in this chapter's epigraph. Indeed, the film at this moment has a shot of her cavorting in the country with gentile children and breaking into happy laughter, as if she has undergone a sort of spiritual conversion. When the policeman encounters her by a rural well, he laughs and leaves her alone, despite the fact that he still believes her guilty of the crime. After all, she is no longer an Other, an outlaw, a wild woman, but the property of this all-American country lad. The gentile man and the Jewish girl embrace and kiss and live happily ever after.

In the brief ten minutes of this film then, Griffith succeeds in conquering, and in a sense, converting the belle juive. Through a sexual encounter with an uncorrupted rural lad, she finds a new rural Americana life, leaving behind her tragic heritage, which is connected to distant worlds, corrupt cities, dirty Jews, and insurmountable fates. In its own way then, *Child* represents Griffith's fable for ethnic assimilation in America. With it, Rachel and Leah and Judith, with all their grand triumphs and tragedies, reconfigure themselves in a domesticated body, tamed by a gentile man.

Griffith also changed the terms of the Biblicized Jewess when he filmed his *Judith* in 1913. As performed by Blanche Sweet, the Jewess reveals herself as a more domestic creature than was O'Neil's assertive siren. Sweet's Judith wears her hair up in many shots, giving her at times the look of a pert bobbed-hair soubrette. Whereas O'Neil's Judith, per Aldrich's script, was a public figure of epic dimensions, often shown discoursing with her people, Sweet's Judith, per Griffith's direction, spends much of her film time alone in her household, pondering her people's fate, leaving Griffith's battle scenes to convey the epic scope of the play's vision. Though still a grand figure, this Judith comes across as a courageous young housewife-turned-seductress, a domesticated figure, the determined New Woman ready to leave behind her household and subdue Holofernes (Henry Walthall again) if it serves the collective good.

In the performances of the new century, independent and assertive women marked as Jewish had little or no place. The more that gentiles could see Jewish women around them, the less frequently could they find commanding examples of them on the stage.

Domineering Hags

Jacob A. Riis's seminal work of social reform, *How the Other Half Lives* (1890), included a description of the inhabitants of New York's Jewtown: "Men with queer skull-caps, venerable beard, and the outlandish long-skirted Kaftan of the Russian Jew, elbow the ugliest and the handsomest women in the land. The contrast is startling. The old women are hags; the young, houris."[33] Though one may account for this "startling" contrast by referring to ethnic customs objectively rooted in the immigrants' culture, the fact that these polarized categories of "hag" and "houri" also show up consistently in representations of the time suggests a perspective rooted in the eye of the beholding male. It is a perspective certainly not unique to the Jewess, since it has affected female performers for centuries, right up to present-day Hollywood, which continues to offer limited roles to women. The nineteenth-century Jewess provided one type of body for playing out this subjectivity. In other words, if she were not young and unmarried, and therefore not the potential object of a gentile's advances, she could be only old and ugly. If she were not a belle juive, virtually the only other alternative was a masculinized hag.

This type of Jewish woman shows up in melodrama and in early films. *In the Trenches* (1898), for example, features the "fair, fat and forty" Rebecca, wife of Moses Bullheimer. In addition to these three qualities, Rebecca is also fearsome, aggressively bribing servants, brashly threatening men with violence, and relentlessly pursuing her wayward spouse into the middle of the battlefield. As such a grotesque monster, she takes on many of the masculine qualities which her effeminate spouse, like so many other stage Jews, lacks. The over-sized Jewesses in the early silent film *Cohen's Fire Sale* (1907) resemble or exceed the grotesque Cohen in ugliness and pulchritude. If the sheenies are effeminate, then these "fat and forty" Jewesses are masculinized. Their domineering natures prove their husbands' effeminate cowardice, and vice versa, thereby grotesquely inverting expectations of proper marriage roles.[34]

The case of Fanny Janauschek is instructive. As her youth faded, this commanding actress, once celebrated as "a woman of genius,"[35] fell to playing grotesque character roles in low melodrama, including her last major role, Frau Rosenbaum, the villain in Edward Alfriend and A. C. Wheeler's *The Great Diamond Robbery* (1895).[36] The plot of this play centers around yet another falsely accused young hero, Frank Kennet, framed for a murder he has not committed, and the efforts of his beloved girl, Mary Lavelot. In league with the play's evil conspirators is Rosenbaum, a fence for stolen goods, inspired by the real-life example of New York's "Mother Mandlebaum," whose similar racket was well-known to all who read the city's newspapers. Rosenbaum's position in the play then, centers on the grotesque oddity of an elderly Jewish woman turned vicious criminal. A character describes her this way: "There's only one woman in New York that's likely to be mixed up in this, and she's a desperate character protected by the politicians rolling in ill-gotten wealth. She has never hesitated at murder when it served her ends, for she goes to the senator there for protection. There stands the senator and there's the old hag's man talking to him."

It is interesting that Janauschek's hag Jewess, as reflected in the script, is both more masculine and more vicious than any male Jewish villain on the American stage since Brougham's Mordie Solomons. Though she deals in stolen jewels, for example, Rosenbaum refuses to wear them for adornment, unlike the play's other villainess, the distinctly feminine Latin temptress, Maria Marino. For Rosenbaum, in contrast, jewels mean business and business only, mere tokens in a cash transaction. Moreover, though Rosenbaum does have a henchman called Sheeny Ike, she uses him largely as a gofer, reserving for herself most of the nasty and violent business and undertaking it with vicious zeal. She speaks with "hissing intensity" and with almost loving care threatens Mary at knife point. "I put some ointment on my beauty's head, and I want to see her," she tells the audience before roughing up the heroine. After "viciously" doing "business with knife," she tells young Mary, "You shall play the maid for me. . . . You shall dress my hair. . . . No, I will dress your beautiful hair." All this business suggests the hag Jewess's unnatural sexuality through her homoerotic attraction to the play's heroine. If the sheeny performs his unnatural lust through his effeminacy, Rosenbaum, in contrast, performs hers through her masculinity.[37]

Janauschek, then, started her American career playing a belle juive and finished it playing an ugly hag. Obviously, Janauschek was not confined to playing Jewesses—the vast majority of the roles she played were not such characters—but it is significant that, when she did play the Jewess, only two polarized types of roles were available to her: one a beautiful young woman desired by a young gentile man, the other a grotesque old woman who desires a young gentile woman.

The polarities of belle juive and domineering hag have shadowed performances to the present day. In them, one sees the outlines of two dominant ways Jewish women have frequently been written about, represented, and performed in America: the Jewish American Princess (the haughty "bitch" unwilling to grant sexual favors to her husband) and the Jewish mother (the domineering woman who threatens to emasculate her son). The burden of the dominant persists to this day for Jewish-American women in mainstream popular performance, which has been shaped by many a Jewish son.

PART II

Emerging Encounters

CHAPTER 3

Becoming a Jolly Good Fellow

THE FIRST WAVE OF JEWISH COMEDIANS

"He's a good-natured Haybrew when he do be here; and though it's agin me Catholically spakin' to loike him—I have to do it."
—Mike the Irishman in *Sam'l of Posen,* as *The Drummer on the Road,*
also known as *Spot Cash* (1885)

*P*opular melodrama of the late nineteenth century always had room for a song and dance. Rarely did a play of revenge and redemption go by without an opportunity for a performer to insert his or her "specialty" routine or at least a rousing good lyric suggested by the playwright. One such rousing number which turns up occasionally in these scripts is the good old male barroom classic, "For He's a Jolly Good Fellow." During *In the Trenches* (1898), for example, the nefarious conspirators Moses Bullheimer and Patrick Green sing a mock version of it together. When the curtain goes up on *Jail Bird* (1893), the song's lyrics are wafting out of a lowlife concert saloon where the dregs of New York society gather. Who runs this saloon where the song of fellowship rings out? The scurrilous sheeny, Solomon Isaacs, who has left the clothing business to try his hand in the entertainment industry. The controlling presence of the Jew counterfeiter in this hall of masculine camaraderie and entertainment portends nothing but trouble for the gentile clientele. Indeed, in the play, nothing but trouble results.

These stage Jews who involve themselves in singing "For He's a Jolly Good Fellow" foreground the historical and cultural issues I explore in this chapter. When Bullheimer and Green, Irishman and Jew, sing a jolly good song of fellowship together, they invoke the day's conflict and companionship between Irishman and Jew, "mick" and "sheeny," who lived in close quarters in the immigrant wards of America's major cities. Their interactions, both on and off the stage, could result in camaraderie or erupt into violence, as both Irishman and Jew played out possibilities of mutual respect and resentment. Such is the case with Bullheimer and Green, strange bedfellows in crime, each full of suspicion and ethnic antipathy, but both of them buddies when it comes to song, dance, and shtick. At the end of the play, however, their Irish-Jewish partnership does not hold. Bullheimer betrays his partner to go free while Green gets arrested. Fellowship is thwarted.

Then there is the case of Isaacs's concert hall. In one sense, it seems a humorous anomaly that a Jew would dare serve as proprietor of such a den; stage sheenies, after all, more typically worked in secondhand clothing shops, even if these businesses sometimes turned out to be fronts for counterfeiting operations. However, Isaacs's profession in *Jail Bird* indeed reflects a contemporary reality—namely, the growing presence of Jews in many levels of the entertainment industry, not only as theatergoers but also as managers and producers. Storefront theaters and saloons, after all, were small businesses like so many others, and the new entertainment industry that was emerging in the wake of the declining nineteenth-century stock system possessed few of the social taboos of America's more established pillars of commerce from which Jews were both formally and informally excluded. "Show business" was a growing field which permitted petty entrepreneurs (many of whom were Jewish immigrants) not only easy access but the opportunity to amass small fortunes by the turn of the century.[1]

Isaacs, however, like other sheeny villains, is a malicious buffoon, constructed to elicit an audience's scorn rather than sympathy. In contrast, the comic stage Jews I examine here frequently occupy a sympathetic center stage with their madcap antics and tales of tribulation. They perform a low comedy which presents the possibility of an audience laughing with them, although the boomerang of their biting humor always threatens to arc back on itself and make these stage Jews the objects of the same laughter that they seek to elicit. This is the performance tightrope on which stage Jews had to balance in their transition from the margins to the mainstream of commercial popular entertainment.

"For He's a Jolly Good Fellow" usefully serves me a symbolic cultural test that Jewish men—that is, Jewish male characters—had to pass as they tried to perform themselves as Americans in this moment of transition.

Consider the label word by word. To be "jolly" means to be jovial, merry, high-spirited—traits far from the gloom, doom, and revenge with which gentiles performed Jewish men. Nineteenth-century Shylocks, whether pusillanimous or pathetic, were anything but jolly. Though the sheeny villain did trace a course toward the comic, never was his comedy high-spirited or lovable. Performing a Jewish character as jolly then, invites the repudiation of this tradition.

"Good" was another quality alien to the traditional sheeny villain. For their part, nineteenth-century Shylocks never merited the label either, even when they were performed as the victims of gentile injustice. Performing the Jewish man as good then, means disavowing a performance history of greed, lust, and hidden motives.

Finally there is the final term the song invokes: "fellow." The word carries implications of both class and gender. *Webster's Universal Dictionary* acknowledges the roots of the word as designating "an equal; a person of the same class or rank: peer." Indeed, Jewish stage characters from Shylock on down, while they might have possessed the financial resources to pose temporarily as gentlemen, were traditionally distinguished from their gentile counterparts as being of a lower social class, whether by dint of internal or external signs of such nobility (both readily conflated in melodrama). Moreover, this noun of identity has always been problematic for Jewish men, often seen by gentiles as effeminate. The term is gendered. A woman can never be a fellow, although like Portia, she may at times temporarily succeed in performing herself as such.

In the 1870s and 1880s, many gentile Americans for the first time were forced to encounter Jewish men as potential neighbors, acquaintances, associates, and friends, both in the professional theater world and in other walks of life. As performed by comic stage Jews in the late 1870s and early 1880s, the emphatic statement, "For He's a Jolly Good Fellow," could be said to have been cast as the cautious interrogative, "Is He a Jolly Good Fellow?" Different performances addressed the question in different ways, as Jewish men themselves became more empowered in creating their own performances, even if these performances continued to be shadowed by the bodies of Shylock and the sheeny.

After first considering the general meaning of fellowship for Jews and Americans in the 1870s, I consider how this question was answered through three performances which put Jewish "jolly good fellows" on the American stage: Milton Nobles's Moses Solomons, Frank Bush's variety act Jews, and M. B. Curtis's Sam'l Plastrick. Taken collectively, these three case studies represent the beginning of a transition toward a new American stage Jew who was sometimes jolly, sometimes good, sometimes a fellow, and occasionally all these qualities at the same time.

Fellowship in the 1870s

Until the arrival of the German Jews in the middle decades of the nineteenth century, America was, with the notable exception of some of its native population, almost monolithically a Christian country. Moreover, until the Civil War, these newly arriving Jews were few enough in number and negligible enough in cultural power for their presence to pose a concern to most Americans, particularly the leisured classes with whom they had little contact. This reality showed up on the stage. Louis Harap has reported that not a single American Jewish character, in an American setting, appears in any play from the first half of the nineteenth century.[2] The Jew and Jewess, when they did take the stage, were continental imports like Shylock and Leah, creations of the European imagination, inhabitants of a European landscape.

In postbellum Victorian America, however, as social and professional interactions between Jews and gentiles of all classes became more common, fellowship of all sorts first posed itself as a distinct possibility. With this possibility, formal social ostracism of the Jews became a reality. In 1867, a number of major insurance companies denied Jewish businesses insurance based upon the rumor that Jews had a proclivity toward fraud through arson. In 1877, the German-Jewish banker Joseph Seligman was denied admittance to Judge Henry Hilton's Grand Hotel in Saratoga. In 1879, resort owner and railroad magnate Austin Corbin denied Jews admittance to the grounds of his resort at Manhattan Beach in New York City. By the 1880s, formal and informal regulations at private clubs and hotels made exclusion of the Jews widespread. By the 1890s, such ostracism in the country's finer watering holes was general practice. Jewish upward mobility and gentile anti-Semitism went hand in hand. Working-class neighborhoods, meanwhile, developed other forms of containment, such as the street gangs that specialized in unprovoked attacks on Jewish youth.[3]

The Manhattan Beach incident, widely reported on during the summer of 1879, sheds light on the cultural politics behind the denial of Jewish fellowship. While issuing the statement that his resort would turn away any and all Jewish patrons who sought admittance, Corbin rationalized his policy by stressing that his decision did not amount to a racial ban. The

New York Times quoted him: "Understand me, this is no race or creed prejudice. Personally my principles are ultra-democratic, and I am acquainted
with many Jews whom I would like to receive anywhere." The management, in fact, said it was "prepared to entertain any well-behaved, respectable
and clean persons of any sect or religion, irrespective of race." However,
Corbin added, "It so happens that the Jews as a class are extremely vulgar,
ill-bred, and offensive people. . . . They cannot be made to submit to rules
and regulations. . . . They swarm all over the hotel piazzas, occupying the
best seats. . . . They have no consideration for the comfort of others. They
are loud and vulgar in conversation and dress, and unclean and ill-bred in
their habits."[4] The result, according to Corbin, was that loud, cheap, parvenu Jews were driving the resort's bigger-spending, higher-class clientele
away.

The anti-Semitism explicit in Corbin's rationalizations becomes even
clearer when one realizes that the previous month, he had met with Hilton
and other business leaders in Saratoga, New York, to found the American
Society for the Suppression of the Jews. The society resolved to exclude all
Jews "from first class society" but did not stop there. The group also
agreed not to patronize Jewish businesses, read books by Jewish authors, or
attend theaters where Jewish composers or actors worked.[5] In this context,
the Manhattan Beach incident comes into focus as Corbin's first attempt to
put the ideology of this society into action.

The blatant anti-Semitism represented by Manhattan Beach is also
rooted in issues relating to fellowship and class. Manhattan Beach was traditionally a "respectable" haven for a genteel public. The resort's admission
fees, as well as Corbin's railway line that one had to take to get there, discouraged people of lower social classes from visiting. By the 1870s, however, it seems that some German Jewish immigrants found they had the
money which put them in the economic class of people who had access to
resorts like Manhattan Beach. If these Jews had the economic power to enjoy the benefits of Manhattan Beach, however, in the way they performed
themselves in public—their dress, their habits of body and voice—they resembled, to the genteel gentile management, the lower classes whom eco-
nomics normally excluded. The Jews, in other words, did not conduct
themselves according to the same rules as the Victorian elite. By arriving at
the resort in visible numbers, they were in effect challenging these unwritten codes of social class. They were, in a sense, asserting a different mode
of fellowship, a different standard for social interaction which Corbin and the
management who encountered them were unwilling to accept or assimilate.

My contention here is supported by the fact that certain Jews continued to be admitted to Manhattan Beach even after the exclusionary policy
went into effect. Apparently, those individuals deemed by the management
not to be vulgar, dirty, or noisy—that is, those who in look or behavior
could pass as Victorian gentlemen and ladies—were permitted entry. A
prominent case in point was the resort's major attraction, the celebrated
Jewish cornetist Julius Levi, whom the hotel hired to entertain summer
throngs. Levi even went so far as to give a backhanded defense of Corbin's
policy: "I don't care who he throws dirty water upon," he told the *Times*,
"as long as he doesn't throw any upon me."[6] The conspicuous presence of a
famous Jew at the beach club, then, underscores the cultural, rather than
the purely racial, nature of the exclusion. A "jolly good fellow" like Levi
could be admitted and even displayed, especially since he brought income
to the resort, even if his presence specifically violated one of the resolutions of the society Corbin had helped to found. The fact that Levi was also
married to a gentile actress no doubt further eased his entrance.

New Yorkers spent most of the summer either applauding or lambast-
ing Corbin's policy, depending upon their point of view. The entire controversy was ripe for anti-Semitic humor, and some of the papers which most
forcefully criticized Corbin also took liberal pokes at the Jews and their behavior. The incident also ended up dramatized on the variety stage: only
two weeks after the story hit the papers, the sketch *Jew Trouble at Manhattan Beach* was seen at Tony Pastor's saloon, the top variety venue in the
city. The play included "Levi Mendathall, a Chatham Street Pawnbroker,"
"Corbin the in Jew-dicious," and "Mr. Levi, the celebrated Cornet Soloist"
in a large cast.[7]

Some commentators found comedy in a consideration of how exactly
Jews might pass their way into social fellowship at a place like Manhattan
Beach. Consider, for example, the cartoon spread which appeared in the
July 30, 1879 edition of the widely circulated humor magazine *Puck*. Entitled "Hints for the Jews—Several Ways of Getting to Manhattan Beach"
(fig. 5), the cartoon depicts grotesquely visible German Jews and Jewesses
lining up for admittance to the resort. The men are stout, hawk-nosed, and
hairy, replete with the sensual lips and garish dress that also mark the stage
sheenies. The women, in the tradition of the "fat, fair and forty" Jewess, are
often larger than the men they accompany. The absurdly cross-dressed
couple shown in the lower left only highlights the ridiculousness of this parade of sheenies who invert expectations of how gender should be performed.

However, the cartoon does suggest ways in which this vulgar multi-

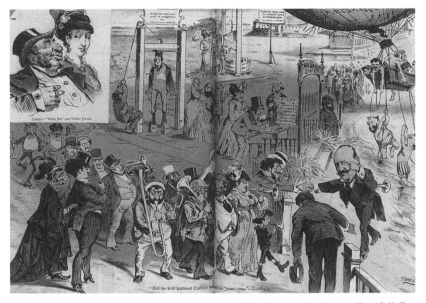

FIGURE 5. "Hints for the Jews—Several Ways of Getting to Manhattan Beach." Cartoon from *Puck*, July 30, 1879.

tude can gain entry to the beach. These Jews can, for example, modify their cultural habits by consenting to a bill of fare consisting entirely of pork. They can imitate other successful Jews by carrying cornets in the manner of Levi. Alternatively, they can modify their racial characteristics by trimming their "parabolic noses" and straightening their "kinky hair." To a degree, the cartoon mocks the inconsistencies of Corbin's policy and the absurdities that would result from their strict enforcement.

The savageness of the parody, however, comes mostly at the expense of the Jews, for the cartoonist's position seems to be that, due to their demeanor and appearance, there is no way these Jews can ever hope to pass as respectable gentiles. Their kinky hair cannot be straightened out, their "parabolic nose" can never be trimmed; these grotesque markings are racially inscribed. The inset at upper left makes this position clear. The "White Jew" and "Whiter Jewess" who fashion themselves Americanized enough to gain access to the club are both as culturally and racially outlandish as their peers, with rings as gaudy, hats as tasteless, lips as sensuous, and noses as parabolic.

Upon closer examination, the cartoon does seem to admit the possibility of such a White Jew, however. Welcoming Jews at the gate, cornet under arm, is a figure that I take to be Levi himself. With his svelte figure, clean-shaven chin, waxed moustache, and proper suit, he is the only figure who has succeeded in "whitening" himself into Victorian respectability and embodying everything the Jewish men in the cartoon fail at becoming. He is the "jolly good fellow" whom nobody can deny, who is able to play the part of the respectable American to perfection.

However, Levi's presence at the resort's gates threatens to ruin the entire establishment. After all, despite his pretense to having a discriminating eye, Levi is letting all his vulgar cousins pass onto the beach, where chaos now seems to be ensuing. The position of the "jolly good fellow" as intermediary between Jewish vulgarity and American respectability, as performer who stands at the gates between two cultures, seems to imperil the order of the whole. It is not the vulgarly visible Jews who pose the true danger but, rather, the invisible Jew who not only passes as gentile but also maneuvers himself into a position of cultural power.

It seems appropriate, in this context, that the American Society for the Suppression of the Jews specifically targeted Jewish performers. In fact, they were targeting what seems to have been a growing population. Anecdotal evidence suggests a significant and growing Jewish presence in show business throughout the nineteenth century. The trend may be rooted in Europe; as M. J. Landa and others have argued, Jewish artists were active in the European theater of the nineteenth century.[8] I have already discussed the examples of Rachel and Bernhardt, Halévy and Mosenthal. The image of the theater being a haven for Jews was further emphasized by the fact that both the elder Booth and Kean, as I have noted, were rumored (in Kean's case, without justification) to have Jewish blood.

In America, it is difficult to piece together a clear history of Jews in the theater before 1890, but strands of evidence come together to suggest such a presence. One of first celebrated American playwrights, Mordecai Manuel Noah, was also an outspoken leader of the nation's tiny Jewish community in the early part of the nineteenth century. On the stage, in addition to Menken, at least two Jews became famous actors: the versatile comedian and creator of the original Bowery Boy, Frank Chanfrau; and the emotionalist actress Rose Eytinge, who played opposite Edwin Booth for a time. Ironically, Eytinge became most famous in the role of Nancy in *Oliver Twist*.

Jews could also increasingly be encountered in the audiences of theaters. After an extended stay in Cincinnati in the early 1870s, Clara Morris called that city's "Hebrew citizens . . . enthusiastic and most generous patrons of the theatre." They did honor to Morris by affectionately dubbing her their "Rebecca." The actress in turn was "very proud, for better judges of matter theatrical it would be hard to find."[9] In 1881, as I show in this chapter, Jews packed Haverly's Theater in New York to see M. B. Curtis in *Sam'l of Posen*. By 1893, according to William Winter, the actor Richard Mansfield was consciously playing Shylock in a way "to win, particularly from a Hebrew audience, active sympathy with a despised, persecuted, injured man, pursuing a justifiable course to avenge the wrongs which had been heaped, not only upon himself, but upon his tribe."[10] All of these references except the latter predate the founding of Yiddish theater in America.

Given these strands of evidence, there is no reason to doubt that many Jewish Americans, from the earliest moment they acquired the means and the language skills, became regular patrons of the English language stage, given that the theater was as established a part of urban life then as television is today. The Yiddish-language theater in New York was thriving from the 1880s, but in the English-language stage Jews played a visible role on both sides of the footlights from at least that early a date.

In auditoriums and in the workplace, therefore, interaction between Jews and gentiles was increasingly a reality, even if the terms of this interaction were under contention. Appropriately, the stage of the day performed different ways of promoting and containing that fellowship.

Three Case Studies

Stealing the Show: **The Phoenix**

More than three decades after his popular melodrama *The Phoenix* (1876) opened in New York, the actor-playwright Milton Nobles (1847?–1924) reflected upon the piece's place in American culture, now that it had survived "the ridicule of the humorists and 'high art critics.'" Nobles acknowledged that the play's most obvious contribution to popular memory was a single line of dialogue: "And the villain still pursued her." The line appears in a novel that the character Carroll Graves is writing in the play, but *The Phoenix* has its own proper villain nevertheless, wherein lies the play's other contribution. The Jew in the play is neither villain nor accomplice. Nobles claimed this contribution as well: "I was the first to place on stage the modern young American Jew, a jolly, up-to-date man about town, and not a villain."[11]

My research confirms this assertion. It is fair to say that, with the character of Moses Solomons in *The Phoenix*, the jocular young Jew was first performed on an American stage. With it came the first possibility of a male Jew as a jolly good fellow rather than a villain or a Shylock.

Innovations often come from the least likely of figures. Nobles was an "inarticulate" actor who wrote and performed hackneyed melodramas in a crusty blood-and-thunder style that seemed dated even in its time.[12] Nevertheless, by 1875 he had ascended to the position of leading man in Wood's Museum Company in Philadelphia, perhaps partially due to his rugged good looks and charisma. For this second-rate company, Nobles premiered *The Phoenix* in 1875, playing the leading role of Graves, alias Jim Bludso, Detective. The production was successful, and in 1876, reached the stage of Woods Museum in New York. For a number of years thereafter, the play remained the centerpiece of Nobles' touring repertory. By 1880, he had already performed the piece 1,200 times.[13]

A variety of journeymen actors portrayed Solomons over these years. The old-school comedian William Davidge created the role, only to be quickly succeeded by an F. A. Tannehill. Next, Alonzo Schwartz, whom I take to be Jewish, held the role from the late 1870s until his premature death of apoplexy on New Year's Day, 1884. Though I have no idea what caused Schwartz's apoplectic attack, I cannot help but imagine that excess frivolity and jolliness the night before may have been a contributing factor. He was, after all, "very well known and universally liked," famous for his "rotund form and pleasant smile" according to one obituary.[14]

He was equally well liked on stage. Almost every review of *The Phoenix* in the 1880s that I have come across singles out his hilarious antics as Solomons, "the Jew that Nobles drew," as programs sometimes billed the part. Schwartz's Solomons, it seems, was *The Phoenix*'s show-stealer. Even when critics drubbed the tired play as something more appropriate "to the country theatre," they acknowledged Schwartz as "the one redeeming feature of the performance."[15] Both on and off stage then, Schwartz seems to have managed to perform himself as a jolly good fellow.

Indeed, based on *The Phoenix*'s script, "the Jew that Nobles drew" offers the actor playing him ample opportunities to come across as such a fellow. Though not the play's protagonist, Solomons is its comic whirlwind: raconteur, punster, master of high jinks, and man about town who is "always to be found ven dere's fun a going." Unlike the play's villain, the arsonist Leslie Blackburn, Solomons ends up allied on the side of good, including Graves-alias-Bludso the hero, Tom Fergus the detective, and Katy Moran the dancer. As the plot moves along, members of this jolly coterie gamble together at a fashionable keno house and go out drinking together on the glittering Bowery. Both episodes offer the actor playing Solomons ample room for show-stealing comic business. In the play's denouement, Solomons's skill as a manipulator foils Blackburn, just when it seems that the villain's scheming will succeed; wielding a pistol, the Jew manages to help subdue the villain. At curtain, Solomons takes his place in the final tableau of good guys. Over the course of the action, then, the Jew proves himself a good guy who not only entertains with his comedy (hence, jolly) but actually helps to save the day (hence, good). Fergus even makes clear how Solomons has proved his worth when, near the end of the play, he asserts, "Take a Jew out of his shop, and nine times out of ten he is a jolly good fellow."[16]

Is this stage Jew really such a jolly good fellow? Closer analysis of the script makes such an assertion problematic. Note, in the first place, that Solomons has a name which directly links him to nefarious stage sheenies. In his vulgar visibility he also performs himself as traditional sheeny. One old woodcut poster, for example, depicts the character as a bearded Fagin-esque Jew.[17] Additionally, the size of Solomon's nose is a source of humor in the play, such as when he gets it shut against the door panel to the gambling den. Moreover, Solomons speaks the German-Jewish dialect which was the standard discourse of stage Jews. When he curses in English, he is prone to those curious imprecations of the stage sheeny, along the lines of "Sainted Rebecca!" Lest the audience forget his ethnicity, Solomons repeatedly reminds them with the term he calls himself over and over again: "Jewsharp." In his every word and gesture, Solomons makes visible his ethnicity.

Solomons also partakes of the stage Jew's traditional connection to money. Moses Solomons is a "note-shaver" or forger who has "frequently found a forged signature more valuable to me than the genuine would have been." Throughout *The Phoenix*, Solomons has no hesitations about using his skill as a forger for the purposes of blackmail. He is also obsessed with getting rich. Playing keno, he whips himself up into frenzy after frenzy as he contemplates the possibility of a big payoff. During this same scene, he is ridiculously obsequious to a man who claims to be a wealthy railroad magnate—actually, the audience knows, Katy the dancer in disguise. Later, out on the town, Solomons entertains his friends with the tale of how his late brother "Schmule" requested in his will that his three thousand dollar fortune be buried with him rather than distributed to the needy. The punchline: Solomons honored Schmule's request by pocketing the three thousand dollars cash while placing "my sheck [sic] payable to his order" in the coffin.

In all these ways, Solomons is a materialistic fellow with a duplicitous relationship to financial transactions who redeems himself only by comically
putting this duplicity to the service of good.

Cowardice also marks this Jew's transactions. When he helps to save
the day at the play's end, for example, he does so with a ridiculous-looking
horse pistol which he can barely control; when it fires by itself, "he falls in
comic fright." Unlike the other characters, he cannot hold his liquor. In a
fight with a surly tavern owner who has sent him sprawling down a flight
of steps "like a spider," he resorts to sneaking up behind his foe and attack-
ing him with an umbrella. Most significantly, the closest he comes to true
fellowship with another character turns out to be a mock fellowship with
somebody who isn't a fellow at all but, as the audience knows, Katy in
male disguise. Arm in arm, the two "buddies" stroll together down the
Bowery, where they swear eternal friendship—"two souls with but a single
thought" says she, "two beats mit hearts like von" says he. Thus two bodies, one female and the other Jewish, both fail at a masquerade of what it
means to be a real man; neither qualifies as a genuine fellow but a travesty
of the concept. Katy, however, knows she is playing a game, while
Solomons believes his performance of jolly good gentile out on the town to
be convincing. The Jew emerges as the greater dupe; like Shylock before
Portia, he becomes, in a social encounter with a woman in male guise, the
lesser of the two fellows.[18]

Despite his show-stealing comedy, Moses Solomons emerges as a
jolly good fellow with a question mark. Through him, *The Phoenix* posits
equivocal terms for Jewish fellowship. In order to be liked, the Jew must
perform himself as a less-than-masculine money grubber who borders on
laughingstock. As such a marginalized laughingstock, the Jew can be accepted as a good guy in the melodramatic struggle against evil. Only
through a comic spiel which effaces dignity and self-respect, then, can the
stage Jew move into the spotlight as a sympathetic American subject.

It is relevant that elsewhere in his work Nobles reveals himself more
overtly as an anti-Semite. "The Isaacs-Crummels Boom," a prose satire in
his collection of theatrically oriented stories and sketches entitled *Shop
Talk* (1889), uses a series of mock newspaper clippings and press releases
to tell the story of how the theatrical manager Abe Isaacs procures the services of the actress Mamie Crummels for an engagement as Juliet in
Bilgeville, Iowa. Nobles's fictional clippings hint at sexual relations between the manager and his "prize" and make clear that Crummels's performance as Juliet (opposite Isaacs's Romeo) is a disaster, both financially

and artistically, which earns the scorn of the local community. In the wake of this failure, Isaacs resorts to selling hats in Bilgeville while Crummels goes off to New York where, unable to find a job, she is reduced to advertising her services as an instructor of elocution.

"The Isaacs-Crummels Boom," while parodying both the excesses of theatrical publicists and the vagaries of small-town combination companies, depends for its stinging satire upon a faintly concealed anti-Semitism, with most of its jokes revolving around Isaacs's and Crummels's ethnicity. Isaacs, "the epitome of monumental gall and superfluous idiocy," is a tasteless, untalented, cheapskate who obviously has no business in the theater; when he tries to make a speech on opening night, he is "appropriately squelched by the boys on the front bench." Before taking up theatrical management, he has worked as a clerk in Openheimer's clothing house in Bilgeville, and Nobles's parody suggests that this is where vulgar Jews like Isaacs belong. Nobles directs his most biting satire, however, at Crummels, yet another version of the aging hag. Though Isaacs touts her as a "young, gifted, beautiful southern belle, descended from an aristocratic Georgia family," Crummels turns out to be "dark, fat and forty, with a matronly and Hebraic cast of features."[19] As if there were any doubt as to her physical qualities, an illustration in *Shop Talk* clarifies her as a flabby-cheeked matron with a huge hooked nose.

Abe Isaacs and Mamie Crummels, Nobles's pair of Jewish grotesques, offer a fitting balance to his jolly good fellow, Moses Solomons. As Georgian belles and passionate lovers, the Jews are parodies of themselves. As Shakespearean thespians, they are doomed to failure. The point seems clear. Vulgar Jews like Isaacs and Crummels, one duplicitous and the other ugly, are not fit for the theatrical business and should stay in the clothing line where they belong. In this way, the sketch represents a reaction against the growing Jewish presence in the theater, rejecting Jews both as romantic leads and as theater artists.

Nobles's work then, establishes its own parameters for Jewish fellowship. As a lovable but sleazy low-comedy buffoon, the Jew is welcome, but he is denied the right to be a respectable Romeo or theatrical manager. Though he may steal the show temporarily, he cannot own it.

The Violence of Laughter: Frank Bush

The Phoenix had an immediate impact. Later in 1876, another variety-style melodrama, *Moses, a Dealer in Second-Hand Clothing*, played a short New York run. Before the 1870s came to a close, a minor "Jew comic" craze had caught on, with performers doing comedy Jew acts in concert saloons and variety theaters in a number of major cities.[20] According to Douglas Gilbert, for example, two Jews from Philadelphia named Bert and Leon flirted with fame around 1879 with a number called "The Widow Rosenbaum" before sinking back into oblivion.[21] The leading variety comedians of the day, Edward Harrigan and Tony Hart, incorporated a Jewish old-clothing merchant into their "Callahan the Detective" sketch.[22] While stage Jews were not as prevalent as sentimental Irishmen, dancing "coons," and foolish "Dutchmen" (Germans), they now at least enjoyed a presence where previously they had been absent.

Of this wave of variety Jews, Frank Bush (fig. 6) looms as the most outstanding figure. Little has been published about Bush (1856?–1927), but many vaudeville histories and memoirs acknowledge him in passing as a master entertainer and gifted mimic who could play a wide variety of types. My own research has him turning up in New York City playbills in 1876, although he was not doing stage Jews at this time. By the 1878–1879 season, however, according to Odell's *Annals*, he was a regular on that city's variety circuit, featuring such characters as "Luvinsky the Old Clothes Man" and "Abraham Mendel Cohn the Pawnbroker" in his one-man routine. A program from Tony Pastor's from March of 1878, for example, has Bush way down the bill as "the peculiar Delineator of Eccentric German Characters, singing genuine HEBREW Songs, Dances and funny scenes."[23] Between 1878 and 1880, a series of Frank Bush Songsters were published, featuring the lyrics to his most popular numbers. By 1880 then, with the Jew as his primary vehicle, Bush had established a niche for himself in the hectic world of New York's variety halls.

Bush rode the Jew routine to a modicum of success in spite of the fact that he himself was not Jewish, but rather, "a light-haired German" as Tin Pan Alley tunester Edward B. Marks recalled him, who "imitated an East Side Hebrew . . . to perfection." Marks later recorded how Bush went about creating his characterizations:

> It was a studied mimicry. On Grand Street, near Pitt, there was a pawn broker called Old Man Nelson. This was the character that Frank Bush studied. He watched him wait on customers day after day for years. As people came into the dingy hock shop to pawn their belongings, Bush absorbed every story, every jest, every bit of kindly and witty philosophy, and every mannerism of the Old Man. Bush hung around the shop hours on end. . . . Then he brought to the

FIGURE 6. Frank Bush in character, c. 1890. *Billy Rose Theatre Collection, The New York Public Library for the Performing Arts, Astor, Lenox and Tilden Foundations.*

variety stage the pulsating kaleidoscopic story of the East Side taken right from life, with a power of mimicry that was uncanny. With his perfect delineation of the humorous, kindly, philosophical old East Side Hebrew, he could stay on Pastor's stage half an hour, entertain any audience, and leave them applauding for more.[24]

These observations typify admiring theatrical criticism of the period, when a "realistic" representation of everyday life was the articulated goal of a wide variety of performances. The fallacy of such naturalism is clear from the liberties Bush took with his "studied mimicry." Who would have gone, for example, to see a stage Jew who billed himself as "Old Man Nelson"? In the case of the all- important signifying name, reality failed Bush. In its place, he chose the more markedly Jewish yet less real alternatives of Luvinsky, Levi, Solomons.

If Bush's mimicry foregrounds the limitations of realism, his act also emphasizes the problems of virtuosity in ethnic impersonation. By all accounts I have come across, Bush was a genuinely gifted character comedian, a virtuoso who not only could do Jews to perfection but also included imitations of Italians, Irishmen, and Germans in his repertory. In such virtuosity, a problem presents itself. How does a gentile play a Jew perfectly and yet, in an age when being Jewish meant being the object of ostracism, scorn, and violence, avoid any personal ethnic taint to one's character? If one is known as a "Jewish comedian" (as Bush was often called, following the standard way of naming ethnic acts in the day), how does one make it clear that one is not Jewish?

It seems that, in subtle ways, Bush did in fact take steps to distance himself from the characters he played, lest his audiences make the same assumption. Consider, for example, the cover illustration to his 1880 "Pesock the Pawnbroker Songster" (fig. 7), which depicts Bush, in character as a Jewish pawnbroker, tormented by two Bowery toughs, the taller one in the top hat and swell dress associated with working-class Irish lads. The upside-down portrait behind the counter displays Bush the actor, as he appears off-stage. It hangs there not only as a salute to Bush's authorship but as a defensive gesture as well, as if to emphasize the disjuncture between performer and character, for anyone who, due to Bush's virtuosity, might be led to think otherwise and to torment the actor in the same way in which the two youths are tormenting Pesock.

If Bush's act contains at least the possibility of objectifying its Jewish

FIGURE 7. Cover to Frank Bush's "Pesock the Pawnbroker Songster," c. 1880. *Brown University Library.*

characters, it also contains, in the dynamics of the solo act, the possibility of engaging sympathy for these same characters. The solo comedian, after all, shares the spotlight with nobody; he speaks directly to the audience, tells his own stories, and must command the stage on his own terms. In the body of a purely ignominious figure of ridicule, the variety comic risks losing the audience's attention. The performative context of the one-person routine demands a character who can at least lay claim to being sympathetic protagonist of the show, however briefly.

Bush's act, as described by a few vaudeville old-timers and surviving songsters, thus appears to be full of contradictions about how to play the Jew. Like most variety "turns," Bush's routines were structured around a song and dance. In his Jew make-up, Bush would make his entrance as a peddler, old clo'es man, or smalltime merchant, under such names as "Levy," "Solomon Cohen," "Solomon Bulerinsky," or in a deft reversal of Nobles's jolly good Jew, "Solomon Moses." Tall and thin, in a "tall, rusty plug hut, long black coat, shabby pants, long beard which ran to a point, and large spectacles," Bush's Jew used pseudo-Yiddish phrases, funny gestures, and lively songs to tell crazy stories of his trials and tribulations. The tunes themselves were often borrowed from other songs popular at the time, resulting in the anomaly of this Jew, played by a gentile, singing Irish folk tunes in a German accent, with verses like "hast du gesehen der kleiner kinder? / un der sox iss in der vinder" thrown in along the way. According to Douglas Gilbert, "his dance was no dance at all; it was more like a Hopi Indian ritual, except for his spectacles, as he shuffled around with his hands behind him and he peered at the audience over his glasses. For his exit after the second verse (of "Solomon Moses") he accomplished a kind of schottische movement, using his hands and arms more than feet."[25]

In the songsters, Bush's variety Jews are petty businessmen and peddlers who, though aggressive in their practices, rarely come across as downright duplicitous (see Appendix Ai). There is Pesock, for example, who says he is "honest" and "gives the best rates":

> My store's in the Bowery,
> One hundred and thirty-three,
> It's the best place on the street,
> And my prices can't be beat,
> I'm the squarest one you ever did yet see.[26]

The implication of this seminal "I-can-get-it-for-you-wholesale" shtick is equivocal. Are these peddlers really "good"? Interpretation may depend on the subtleties of performance, but the implication seems to be that, their claims to the contrary, these businessmen are shrewd merchants who indeed sell "shoddy" to take advantage of a customer. However, Bush's routine backs off from making this chicanery explicit, and in so doing, performs the Jews as canny petty capitalists who disarm their audiences with a quaint, lovable humor recalling the old stage Yankee. His act hints at ridicule then, without embracing it.

The lyrics to many of Bush's songs indeed, engage the dynamics of ridicule. There is, for example, the Jew who goes yachting at Coney Island with his family, only to hear a gang of young toughs yell:

> Oh! Moses, oh! Moses
> Look at them sheenies,
> Oh! ain't they got noses.[27]

Solomon Cohen contends with loafers who play practical jokes on him and break into his clothing store. Occasionally, this ridicule escalates into interethnic violence, often between the Jew and the Irish loafers who are his torment. The Jew at Coney Island, for example, gets hit with a "goose-egg" in the eye. Solomon Cohen gets threatened, abused, and ultimately chased from his shop. Levy gets poked in the eye with a billiard cue. Isaac Moses gets grabbed by the collar and tossed around by Pat McMann.

An 1879 Bush sketch for two actors, "The Hebrew Glazier," dramatizes this violence explicitly. It explores the comic possibilities of an encounter between Solomon Bulenrisky, "a member of the proscribed race," and Mike, "a sprig of the Emerald Isle." Bulenrisky, a glazier, describes himself this way: "Ah, it takes a sheeny to get the best of anyone when it's a case of cunning against cunning. He can bamboozle anyone from the common place Irisher up to the North American Indian. Oh, ain't I glad I was made a sheeny." In revenge for a duplicitous business transaction, Mike decides to "pounce on the putty-souled son of a sea-cook," and seizing the Jew by the neck, drags him around the stage, calling him a "thick-skinned, yellow-tanned, graisy, slippery, thaivin', botching glass puddiner." The Jew in revenge, bites Mike's leg, tearing off the seat of the Irishman's trousers in the process. The two calm down, and in a piece of "striking and ludicrous" business, Bulenrisky uses a piece of glass to cover the Irishman's derrière. They break out fighting again, grappling and tumbling amid crashing glass as the curtain rings down on the sketch.[28]

Though the early variety theater regularly reveled in this sort of brutal slapstick, what is one to make of the fact, for example, that in Bush's performances, the Jew is the butt of the violence, and the gentile (usually the Irish youth) the aggressor? Such a performance invokes the traditional effeminacy of the stage sheeny since it casts the Jew as puny weakling, unable to defend himself, so tiny and rarefied that, in the words of one Bush song, his own father can "use him for a walking-stick." This lack of manliness shows up throughout Bush's material. When Bulenrisky gets beaten up, for example, his response is to bite like a girl, after which follows the "ludicrous" business involving the Irishman's exposed ass, replete with its homoerotic comedy. Additionally, the ethnic inflection of the violence recalls the class conflict of working-class melodrama, with its idle urban youth, jobless and poor, resenting the modest successes of petty "foreign" businessmen for wrongs, real or imagined.[29]

It is possible to locate the joke in these songs and sketches—whether it is on or with the Jew—by positioning them in the context of their original audiences. In 1879, Jews would likely have had little presence in the audiences for working-class variety theater. The spectators who went to see these lowbrow shows more likely resembled and identified with the streetwise Irish youths who abuse Bush's Jews. The songsters support this

point, as they intersperse Bush's dialect spiels with Irish-American sentimental ballads, some associated with then-popular stage Irish like Harrigan
and Hart. In their ethnic politics then, Bush's performances, while they wa-
ver between sympathy for and ridicule of the Jewish characters, lean in the
direction of the latter. Their violence, rather than invoking pathos, reflects
the hostility of their original audiences.

Sometimes the cruelest violence results when the Jew dares to perform himself as something he is not. Consider the song "Levy's Night,"
which chronicles the plight of a Jewish performer who rents a hall so he
can star in a "seven act drama composed by himself." Though the play is a
tragedy in the Shakespearean mode, the audience breaks out smiling when
Levy comes out with his sword. From there, things only get worse. Bush-
as-Levy-as-tragedian sings:

> . . . here I am after twenty long years
> And the villain I tracked to this spot;
> He stole my chee-ild, my idol, my heart
> If I catch him, I'll make him feel hot.
> The villain came out, his name was Sam Cohen,
> And he yelled out, quite loud, Who are you;
> He says I'm king Henry, and the villain cried out
> You lie you're a Hester St. Jew.
> The poor Jew turned white and he looked like a ghost
> And he yelled out by heavens I'm beat;
> He went for the villain, but quickly fell down
> For someone hit him with a seat.
> The crowd all got up, and the gas it went out,
> The whole of the scenery was tore.
> The actors all gathered and got in a crowd
> And kicked Levy all round the floor.
> You ruined us now they all cried in one voice
> And they kicked him again in their rage
> And when they were searching the ruins the next day
> They found Levy under the stage.[30]

The Jew, according to the song, can attempt to be a jolly good fellow and
invite all his neighborhood friends to see him; they will probably even pay
money to see the spectacle. However, when he tries to play a serious role, a
dignified part, he reveals himself as ridiculous. Out of the audience's
laughter comes violence. Out of the violence comes laughter. The metaphor

of performance once again circumscribes the roles Jews will be allowed to play as they perform themselves as Americans.

The overall dynamics of Bush's act, circa 1880, come into focus. His Jews try to be jolly good fellows but often end up paying the consequences as victims of violence and objects of ridicule. So while Bush, like Nobles before him, empowers the stage Jew by taking him out of the body of the villain and into the body of comedian, he also fashions performances which implicitly set the limits for Jewish fellowship in America.

Bush went on to enjoy a long career in variety and vaudeville, where he influenced many other acts. For a while he had his own touring variety company and was a featured character comedian in such Broadway shows as *On the Bowery* (1894). However, the "turn" which made him famous, the Jew routine, eventually became too grotesque and offensive for a later generation, though it had been praised in its day as the epitome of naturalism. Though Bush toned down his act in the 1890s and 1900s, performing the Jew in tailcoat, he was perceived as an outdated figure, and never re-created his earlier successes.[31] The historical irony remains, though, that the shtick of this gentile virtuoso significantly impacted the way in which Jewish comedians of Jewish heritage performed themselves on stage in the next generation.

A Partner in Power: M. B. Curtis

On May 16, 1881, a comic melodrama called *Sam'l of Posen; or, The Commercial Drummer* premiered at Haverly's Fourteenth Street Theatre in New York. Featuring the heroic antics of a cocky young Polish-Jewish "drummer" or traveling salesman, it became a hit, increasing the vogue of the jolly stage Jew pioneered by Nobles and Bush. It spawned many imitations and made its leading comedian, a previously unknown young actor named M. B. Curtis, a figure of minor renown.

From the perspective of more than a century later, the *Sam'l* script does not have a lot to recommend it, though it certainly is no worse than hundreds of other melodramas which also enjoyed success during the era. As a performance however, *Sam'l* stands out as something special, as the star of the show was Jewish, as were many members of his audience. The Jewish presence on the American stage was now a fact that nobody could deny.

I have been unable to unearth much information about Curtis (1852–1921). Born Maurice Bertrand Strellinger in Detroit to a family of Jewish immigrants, he learned his craft playing in minor stock companies in the West, jettisoning his ethnic name for a stage name more suited to success in the field.[32] In 1880 or so, Curtis commissioned an Irish-American playwright named George H. Jessop to write a script, entitled *Isadore Plastrick*. With the possible assistance of the comedian Ed Marble, Curtis revised the play into *Sam'l*, which premiered in Curtis's native Detroit before reaching New York. Curtis created the role of the play's title character, Sam'l Plastrick; Marble, the minor character role of West Point; and Curtis's wife, known by her stage name Albina de Mer, that of the villainess Madame Celeste.

Sam'l is set in an unspecified American city and centers around characters associated with Mr. Winslow's jewelry store. Jack Cheviot, Winslow's nephew, is the thousandth in a line of melodrama's ne'er-do-well romantic leads. He is resolved to overcome his tendency toward gambling and dissipation but finds himself competing with the manipulative Frank Bronson for both a partnership in the firm and the affections of Ellen, Winslow's custodial daughter. Into this situation enters Sam'l, a fast-talking, aggressive, eager-to-please young immigrant peddler who, due to his generosity and cocky demeanor, gets hired almost immediately as a drummer for Winslow. Throughout the course of the play, Sam'l courts the store's young Jewess employee, Rebecca Heyman, foils Frank repeatedly in his plots to discredit Jack, and in the end, gets started in his own business with the help of Winslow himself.

Though as a drama *Sam'l* may be unimaginative, as a cultural performance it embodies a new conception of the male stage Jew, eschewing or modifying traditional markers of his visibility. The name "Sam'l Plastrick," for example, while still noticeably Jewish, departs from the codified practice of having stage Jews signified as "Solomon," "Levi," or "Moses." Sam'l's dialect, understated in the script, includes the occasional Yiddish phrase, distinguishing it from the butchered "vens" and "Mother Rebeccas!" that stood for Jewish speech on the tongues of other sheenies. The play's setting is telling too. While Jessop sets the original *Isadore Plastrick* in New York, Curtis's revised version detaches the peddler Jew from the lowlife shops of lower New York, placing him instead somewhere in the nameless heartland of America. Sam'l then, talks in different ways and walks in different places than other stage Jews.

In physical aspect, too, Curtis's Sam'l lacks the beard, make-up, and other expected grotesque accouterments of the stage Jew. His appearance is suggested by a poster, probably for the play's sequel, *Spot Cash* (1885) (fig. 8), which documents, in four poses, Sam'l's transition from ridiculous immigrant boy peddler into respectable American businessman. The poster

FIGURE 8. Poster for *Sam'l of Posen, as The Drummer on the Road (Spot Cash)*, c. 1885. *Billy Rose Theatre Collection, The New York Public Library for the Performing Arts, Astor, Lenox and Tilden Foundations.*

presents the development of one body as it traces a course toward imagined assimilation and success in America, as emphasized by the outline in the background of New York's Castle Garden, the country's chief reception point for immigrants before the opening of Ellis Island in 1892. By projecting the gradual effacement of ethnic difference as a solution to the problem of Jewish visibility, the poster thus constructs the assimilationist ideology a generation before it was the norm. Yet the poster suggests that the play it advertises and the historical moment it occupies still inhabit that liminal borderland between the ridiculous and the respectable represented by the space between the two handshakes where the Jews of past and present seem to be encountering themselves.

Sam'l reveals the stage Jew trying desperately hard to prove himself a jolly good fellow in this transitional borderland. His jolliness, certainly, cannot be questioned. From the moment he steps on stage, Sam'l is a fast-talking jokester, quick of tongue and full of witty retorts. Moreover, Sam'l complements his liveliness with a genuine goodness, helping out his gentile friends in times of need and offering small acts of charity. Ultimately, over the course of the play, the Jew usurps the role of character comic and becomes the central figure leading the fight for the side of good. His good nature earns him the following recommendation from Jack: "He is an honest and industrious young fellow, and I am proud of him as a friend."

Sam'l also shows himself thoroughly masculine by the standards of the day. He rarely hesitates, for example, to face danger in defense of his gentile friends. In the play's climax, he defends himself competently with that ultimate sign of masculine prowess, a gun. He is even permitted a romance; his courtship with Rebecca parallels the affair of the play's main romantic leads, Jack and Ellen, and distinguishes Sam'l from many other nineteenth-century stage Jews, who repudiated through their performances any connection to "healthy" heterosexuality. There are even hints that Sam'l lives up the drummer's reputation as womanizer and adulterer; in interactions with Rebecca, he hints cunningly at flirtations, inviting the audience's complicity in situations not fully understood by the naive Jewess. This new performance of the Jew as an assertively heterosexual man, then, comes at the expense of the Jewess, who by contrast is reduced to the position of harebrained and devoted bride. Gender roles, so frequently inverted in gentile versions of Jewish comedy, right themselves in ways that are comforting to the male order.

A fascinating comic vignette in the play's final act emphasizes this new performance of the Jew. The scene takes place in that traditional site of stage Jewishness, a pawnshop, owned by Rebecca's Uncle Goldstein, a stage Jew in the tradition of Frank Bush. With his long coat, beard, and hat, Goldstein is a kindly but cheap old man who bears the taunts of neighborhood boys who call him, "you old Sheeny." When Goldstein leaves the shop in Sam'l's hands, the drummer, in order to frustrate Frank's plan to pawn some stolen diamonds, dons a long coat, beard, and hat to impersonate the old Jew. The disguise works. Frank takes Sam'l for the old Jewish pawnbroker. Sam'l, throwing off his mask, subdues the scoundrel with a pair of oversized revolvers.

Through his performance as grotesque old sheeny then, the jolly young fellow foils the villain and validates himself as hero. In this way, through the simple act of performing his Uncle, Sam'l reveals the sheeny-style guise for the stage show it is. By putting on the old mask, he usurps its power and demonstrates his authority over it, as if to posit the old embodiment as stage-convention sham and the new embodiment as authentic truth (despite the fact that the new embodiment remains, of course, as much a performance as the old one).

In spite of these departures, Sam'l also assimilates elements of his sheeny stage cousins. He bears, for example, their obsessive, aggressive connection to money and commerce. In small matters, too, Sam'l proves himself occasionally duplicitous, overcharging his customers for worthless items (see Appendix Aii). His ambitions, moreover, pose a vague threat to those around him; after securing the job with Winslow, he tells the audience, "I'll own this business in a year!" If Sam'l sometimes performs himself as perhaps way too jolly, he does not necessarily always perform himself as all that good. In this juxtaposition, Sam'l foreshadows stage crypto-Jews of two generations later like Groucho Marx, whose ethnicity no longer performs itself through clear physical markings but rather, through the personality of an aggressive, wisecracking shyster who thrives on a relentless comedy which at times threatens the social order.[33]

Curtis had support in negotiating the terms of his performance, for the audiences who attended *Sam'l*'s New York debut were different from other sorts of audiences. The reviewer for the *Spirit of the Times* observed, "If Judge Hilton, and the managing director of Manhattan Beach, and the proprietors of seaside hotels, had occupied some of the boxes, instead of the theatrical managers who were there in force, they would have fainted away at the sight of the audience. We looked about in vain for a straight nose or a blonde beauty. In every direction the view was aquiline and brunette."[34] As if to underscore this point, the reviewer emphasized that these audiences laughed uproariously at Sam'l's "Hebrew" phrases, apparently catching "in-jokes" only accessible to Yiddish-speakers. The *Dramatic Mirror* was more specific: "It seemed as if all Jewdom was at Haverly's Fourteenth Street Theatre Monday night. . . . Probably two-thirds of the entire audience were Jews."[35]

It was a novel situation in America: Jews and gentiles in fellowship together in an audience, with the gentiles uneasily sensing themselves in the minority. Curtis seems to have specifically solicited this Jewish audience, since some of the original posters for the production featured Hebrew lettering (which caused a minor uproar among the religious when a careless printer misplaced a crucial vowel mark).[36] *Sam'l*, then, was the first American play produced in English for reception by a significantly Jewish audience.

It is appropriate then, that the play's first critics ended up in one way or another invoking the Jewishness of the character in larger ways. The *Dramatic Mirror*, for example, invoked all three terms of the jolly good fellow, noting that Sam'l "has an honest heart, a clear head, and the attributes of manliness. Nobody can object to Curtis's Jew. On the contrary, everybody would like to grasp him by the hand and hear him speak his strange conceits."[37] This reviewer extended the gentile hand of fellowship which the play so eagerly solicits, welcoming the nature of the performance itself into the community of fellows.

In contrast, reviewers from the *Times* and the highbrow *New York Daily Graphic* chafed at accepting this fellowship. The former derided the Sam'l character as "feeble and worthless," the play as "asinine" and "stupid."[38] The latter invoked Shylock in dismissing the performance:

> No Christian can leave the theatre after witnessing a true performance of *The Merchant of Venice* without feeling pity and sympathy for the Jew. . . . [But] when a man undertakes to present the type of a race he must expect to be measured by accepted standards. No Hebrew who has seen *Shylock* performed as Shakespeare presents him can feel ashamed of his race, but from "Sam'l of Posen, The Commercial Drummer," angels and ministers of grace defend us!

The review continued: the play is "vile" and Sam'l a "miserable type of Jewish humanity" who is "gross, coarse and vulgar throughout. Nothing can redeem this. He is offensive, and one sickens of him long before the piece is ended."[39] The critic, moreover, was offended by the strong laughter with which the "Jewish element" in the house reacted to what the critic took to be Sam'l's Yiddish vulgarisms. The threat of an encroaching power was registered in the *Graphic*'s review—a threat not unlike the parvenu Jewish multitudes that two years earlier had invaded Corbin's genteel haven. It is a threat which the reviewer warded off by invoking the power of Shylock and the dominant tradition he represented.

In the broadest sense, the threat perceived by the *Graphic* was real and involved the intersection of complex social, cultural, and economic factors. The genteel Victorian bourgeois elite to whom the *Graphic* appealed was indeed threatened by emerging cultural configurations. The *Graphic* itself was out of business by the end of the 1880s. In this context, *Sam'l* speaks for and to a new audience, which included but was by no means limited to immigrant Jews who identified with neither the old Protestant gentility nor the urban working classes. Structurally, for example, though the play can be characterized as a low melodrama, it departs from the formula in which the struggling, working class native boy redeems himself and regains a lost legacy. Sam'l neither needs redeeming nor has a lost legacy to regain. An immigrant social climber on his way up, he aggressively uses his wit and daring to achieve his ends and to become a bourgeois partner in power; Winslow at the end does not reinstate a lost birthright, but rather, sets Sam'l up in a new business. In this sense, the play performs a new myth for an emerging immigrant middle class. If the bastions of genteel elitism—clubs, hotels, and beaches—denied Jews fellowship, theaters and other commercial entertainment forms could not.

Following *Sam'l*, other important theatrical events in New York used Jewish subject matter in a way calculated to appeal at least in part to this emerging audience. The normally comic Harrigan tried pathos with his melodrama of an overbearing Jewish father, *Mordecai Lyons* (1882), partially inspired by Irving's Shylock. The play features the novelty of a Hebrew Glee Club drinking at a bar, smoking cigars, and singing a song of "mirth and jollity" in praise of Jewish-gentile "fraternal fellowship." (Harrigan himself lived that fellowship through a long-time friendship with his composer and father-in-law, David Braham, the son of an Orthodox Jew.) Harrigan's unwieldy play was a critical and box office failure, and he quickly returned to his accustomed comic stage Irish roles. The next time he included stage Jews in a play, they were the grotesque, song-and-dance old clo'es men of *The Leather Patch* (1886). For *Reilly and the Four Hundred* (1890), he considered using a Jewish protagonist again, only to decide against it. The result was perhaps the only play in American history about an *Irish* pawnbroker.[40]

Bartley Campbell's *Siberia* (1883) was another work with clear appeal to Jewish audiences, dealing with the very persecutions of Russian Jews which were beginning to result in large-scale immigration. Famous for its massacre scene, it played to boisterous audiences. Again, it seems appropriate that the play's initial run was at Haverly's, the same theater where *Sam'l* had enjoyed such a warm reception from "all Jewdom" less than two years before. The theater site, the play's enthusiastic reception, and the tone of contempt in the *Times* review (which described the audience as "the poorest class of playgoers" who would applaud even "flaming rubbish") suggest that Jews might have packed the house for this event as well.[41]

Other plays were more directly inspired by the Sam'l Plastrick novelty. Frank Dumont, the prolific craftsmen of minstrel variety sketches, created *My Hebrew Friend* for the comedian Dick Gorman in 1882.[42] Other *Sam'l*-inspired titles included *Moses Levy* (1882), *Morris Cohen, the Commercial Drummer* (1882), *Levy Cohn* (1883), and *Levy the Drummer; or, Life on the Road* (1885). The last of these featured the attraction of a peppy young Jewish go-getter adventuring in the Wild West, where he gets tricked into eating bacon by a gang of cowboys.

The master of the Sam'l spinoff, however, proved to be Curtis himself, who built a career out of the character. He toured *Sam'l* across the country, fashioning a publicity campaign that lured audiences to see the famous sensation of the "YOUNG AMERICAN HEBREW OF THE PERIOD, the recognized flower of Fashion, the buoyant, spirited Companion, the expert in Diamonds, and the Virtuoso in Finance."[43] With Marble's help, Curtis created a sequel, *Spot Cash, or The Drummer on the Road*, which he started touring in 1884. It was an even more forceful repudiation of the old stage Jew, with Sam'l on the road in upstate New York acting as comic whirlwind and asserting a vigorous white masculinity: flirting with an African-American servant, drinking with clients, taking the rap for a gentile friend, being falsely accused of forgery, solving a crime, and dispensing wisdom throughout.[44] Various Sam'l paraphernalia were marketed with *Spot Cash*, such as a souvenir card featuring a poem, mock-statistics on the lifestyle of "Der Drummer," and an illustrated booklet that recounted in verse the Sam'l legend from his roots in Poland through his success in America.[45] The marketing of the character paid off for Curtis in a big way: by the early 1890s, the role had reputedly earned him over half a million dollars.[46]

Unlike Bush, who seems to have foregrounded the disjuncture between his on- and off-stage personas, Curtis overtly played up the connections between himself and Sam'l. Photographs of Curtis suggest a man strikingly similar in self-presentation to the specific role with which he was always associated. One poster for *Spot Cash* featured Sam'l arriving at a hotel with a traveling trunk embossed with the monogram of the actor, M.B.C.[47] For their brief fling at fame then, Curtis was Sam'l and Sam'l was Curtis. After all, Curtis had a limited, specific talent: he was outstanding at performing variations of himself but could play little else. When the vogue for the jolly good fellow Jew faded, so did Curtis. His later vehicles, *Caught in a Corner* (1886) and *The Shatchen* (1890), proved failures. The novelty Curtis helped to create was no longer novel; by the late 1880s, the fad of the Jewish comedian had passed, at least for another decade.

Once validated as a jolly good fellow, the male stage Jew ceased to be a figure of interest. Those who would accept him as partner did so, whether by choice or not. Those who would ostracize him had already organized to exclude him. Incidents like the one at Manhattan Beach, which had caused so much outcry in the 1870s, no longer made the papers in the late 1880s. By then, it was an obvious matter of fact that, in some social settings, Jews were excluded from fellowship, while in others, they already constituted a presence that nobody would deny.

Curtis had a troubled life and reputation. By 1890, his star was already fading, though various investments, including real estate holdings in his namesake California development of "Posen" (another conflation of actor and role) had made him a wealthy man. In late 1891, he killed a San Francisco policeman during a late-night altercation, the details of which never became totally clear. The case dominated papers there for two years; three juries cleared Curtis of all charges but the actor eventually came forward to claim that authorities who had bribed juries on his behalf were now extorting further payment from him. The truth of the case may never be known, but it is clear that, from that moment, Curtis's situation took a more precipitous dive. His *Sam'l* closed after one day in London in 1895. As a theatrical manager in 1899, he stranded a group of black "Jubilee" singers in Australia. In 1904, he ended up under suit for bad debts. In 1907, he was apprehended in New York for grand larceny. In 1913, he was arrested in California for public intoxication.[48]

While he succeeded in renegotiating the performance of the stage Jew in a way that marked the transition from grotesque sheeny to jolly good fellow, Curtis was unable to effect the next transition Jewish men in the theater were to make, from occasional on-stage characters who were expert in comedy to behind-the-scenes producers who wielded considerable power. Curtis's failure as theatrical manager contrasted with the experiences of Jews of the following generation, who were to become powerful in the business of running the show.

CHAPTER 4

Managing Power

THE ENTRANCE OF JEWS INTO
THE SHOW BUSINESS MAINSTREAM

PINKLE (Hebrew would-be manager): I play de part
of an English lord. . . .
DINKLE (German would-be actor): Do you tink you vill look it vit
such a nose stuck on your face?
PINKLE: Never mind my nose. My nose belongs to me.
—"Dinkle and Pinkle," vaudeville sketch by Harry Lee Newton (1901)[1]

*I*n May of 1898, *Life* magazine, a journal noted for publishing pieces with anti-Semitic overtones, featured an editorial commenting on New York's theatrical scene. Lamenting the dearth of quality shows, the article criticized the men running the theater business in New York for "using their peculiar Jewish judgement to determine what is and what is not art." These men monopolized the nation's theaters, the article noted, keeping many theaters dark and reducing everything to a commercial bottom line. The only hope for the stage was the emergence of an art theater "outside of purely mercantile and Jewish control."[2]

The article was responding to a contemporary reality. Economic hardships of the 1890s had resulted in the failure of many theaters, making possible the emergence of the Theatrical Syndicate, the trust created by six prominent booking agents and producers, all of them Jewish. For a time, the Syndicate indeed manipulated and nearly monopolized theatrical production nationwide, wielding control over all levels of management and production and forging the twentieth-century concept of a centralized "show business" industry, which in turn became a model for the future motion picture industry.

While today the Syndicate symbolizes for many the overly commercialized state of the American stage in the era before O'Neill and the art theater, it also had its positive effects—opening the doors for African Americans to headline on Broadway, for example.[3] Nor was the Syndicate the first robber-baron-age business to exploit and monopolize burgeoning, unregulated industries and technologies. One does not have be a defender of the Syndicate, however, to see the anti-Semitism in *Life*'s perspective. It is not merely the monopolization of theater that the magazine decries but the specifically *Jewish* control of that monopoly, as the editorial almost obsessively makes clear in reference after reference.

The editorial's anti-Semitism is highlighted by an accompanying cartoon. Set in the wings of a Broadway house, "The Drama in New York" (fig. 9) depicts an obviously Jewish theater impresario, sucking a cigar, lasciviously eyeing an aspiring actress who stares wide-eyed back at the reader, as if either seeking to establish a bond or to find protection. She asks the manager: "I wish to go on the stage, and would like your opinion as to my chances of success." He replies: "Well, did you bring your tights?" The point of the cartoon, as underscored by the editorial, seems clear. Vulgar and lecherous Jews who are influencing or controlling cultural production threaten to debase both the art of the stage and gentile womanhood. The anxiety is that gentiles are now at the mercy of Jews.

The *Life* editorial and cartoon foreground issues that I discuss in this chapter. On one hand, they highlight the fact that by the turn of the century Jews had become prominent players in almost all aspects of the American theater, particularly behind the scenes as "managers" (producers). They also remind us that this coming to power was openly resented by many gentiles. Growing Jewish power directly correlated with growing anti-Semitism, reflected in the types of exclusions which gentiles were readily enforcing at vacation resorts and in "old money" business endeavors that were far more lucrative, powerful, and stable. Though gentiles were unable to keep Jews from wielding influence in the theater, they were in fact successful in limiting that influence elsewhere.

In this chapter I examine the contradictory ways in which Jews and others performed and managed this growing theatrical power around the turn of the century. First, I look at the phenomenon of Jews in the performing arts industries, both as cultural reality and as represented on stage. Next, I look at how this power was reflected in the veritable explosion of Jewish comedians who became nearly ubiquitous on Broadway and in vaudeville and burlesque in the early years of this century. Finally, I look at how the role of Shylock changed during this era, now that Jews were more active in fashioning and receiving these performances. The result was that

FIGURE 9. "The Drama in New York." Cartoon from *Life* magazine, May 12, 1898.

in an era of pronounced anti-Semitism, Jewish visibility in the performing arts had to be negotiated in ways that satisfied the expectations of gentile audiences without offending the sensibilities of Jewish ones. For those like David Warfield who used their power to negotiate new performances of self, an ethnic mobility became possible that played out the problems of Jewish-American assimilation.

Jewish Management in the Age of Svengali

The issue of Jewish presence in show business remains a sensitive one today. The perception has become entrenched that Jews "control" the

American entertainment industry, notably the movies and television. While such hegemonic control, let alone the conspiracy it implies, does not exist, it remains true that throughout the American show business industries, including theater, Jews have been and remain prominent in far disproportion to their numbers nationally, especially behind the scenes as producers, directors, writers, agents, and managers.

Such Jewish power, such a presence, is not insidious. Power of one kind or another has always existed and will always exist in every imaginable type of social, cultural, or economic organization. If it does lie not in the hands of certain individuals, then it will lie in the hands of others. To speak of such Jewish power as malignant, therefore, invokes the anti-Semitism of the speaker since it implies that Jews themselves are not worthy of wielding such power. To acknowledge, however, that such power is not depersonalized and disembodied but inflected by the ethnicity, gender, class, and other characteristics of specific persons whose imaginations are shaped by these social and cultural affiliations—that observation, it seems to me, is integral to the work I am doing here.

The businessmen who formed the Syndicate—Abe Hayman, Charles Frohman, Marc Klaw, Abe Erlanger, Sam Nixon, and J. F. Zimmerman—were not the only Jews active behind the scenes in the commercial theater. Overall, "the growing influence of Jews in theatrical matters," as the *Indianapolis News* put it in 1901, was recognized around the country.[4] Jewish entrepreneurs like the Shuberts and Marcus Loew emerged as key players in the show business industry, benefiting from what Irving Howe has called the "roughneck sort of egalitarianism" that gave Jews equal opportunity in a growing field at a time when many other doors remained closed to them.[5] Jews also figured prominently in the highly professional joke- and song-writing industries (the latter known as "Tin Pan Alley," a phrase reputedly coined by Monroe Rosenfeld, a Jew) which fed material to Broadway and vaudeville. It was a Jew, Henry J. Wehman, who published the first series of professional "gag" books in the 1870s.[6] Among composers, Irving Berlin (Israel Baline) and Jerome Kern are but the two most famous of the many Jews who had established themselves by 1910. Overall, this Jewish presence, while not easily quantifiable, is plainly evident in the names of the actors, managers, agents, songwriters, musicians, publicists, and journalists who were working vaudeville in the 1900s and 1910s, lending credence to Leonard Dinnerstein's recent estimate that by 1905, half the people working in the entertainment industry in New York were Jewish.[7]

Without echoing *Life*'s anti-Semitism, some historians have regretted the rise of this highly commercialized and centralized theater. As I see it, whether the old theatrical repertory system, controlled locally and personally by often tyrannical actor-managers, was better than the new system, subject to the often monopolistic dealings of producers and booking agents, is not the issue. The fact is that a modern theater industry, centered in the immigrant capital of New York, emerged relatively suddenly from the ruins of a relatively localized, guild-like system. The bare historical fact of its rise precludes any nostalgia for some more remote golden age. The point is, by the first decade of the twentieth century, Jews were prominent in most aspects of this new national industry, which became one of the most notable concentrations of Jewish business activity in the United States.

That Jewish presence was also increasingly obvious in theater auditoriums, at least in New York. Commentators throughout the 1890s and into the 1900s noted that Jews were becoming major patrons of theaters and concert halls.[8] In certain urban neighborhoods, where local vaudeville houses flourished as breeding grounds for talent, this Jewish presence in the auditorium could be dominant. When the vaudevillian Sammy Howard made his debut at a New York amateur competition in the early 1900s as a Jewish comic, he capped off his act by going down to the footlights and telling the audience, in a direct appeal for support, "Ich bin ein id." ("I am a Jew.") He won the competition by popular acclaim.[9]

The aesthetic effects of this Jewish presence have been the subject of extended scholarly discussion. Albert McLean has noted the Jewish influence on the incisive, hard-hitting "New Humor" of vaudeville, with its "impulse toward hysteria," in contrast to the more genteel and sentimental comedy which characterized the late Victorian age.[10] Howe points out the formative Jewish influence in the "long-suppressed vulgarity" of the urban street culture which helped to define new styles of music and comedy.[11] Neal Gabler sees the Hollywood Jews as overcompensators, so to speak, who constructed a fantasy Americana out of the suppression or rejection of their own heritages.[12] Stephen Whitfield has written, "In the unstable mixture of mass entertainment touched by high culture, the dynamics of a specific American Jewish expression are most likely to be located."[13] Out of this creative tension between the commercial and the high, Whitfield argues, Jews made their primary contributions to American entertainment.

Whatever the aesthetic implications, the practical implication of this Jewish presence, which fed gentile anxiety, was that Jews were now in a position to influence the way gentiles performed themselves on the stage.

The stage of the day provided examples of Jewish characters who served as such impresarios and shapers of gentile talent. The most resonant performance in this tradition was the character Svengali in the play *Trilby*, based on the enormously successful English novel (1894) by George Du Maurier. An adaptation by Paul Potter was a hit in New York the following year, featuring Wilton Lackaye as Svengali, a role he would revive in 1905 and 1915. In 1896, the English actor Herbert Beerbohm Tree (who also included both Fagin and Shylock in his repertory) brought his production of Potter's script to the United States. He would do so again in 1906. Through both the best-selling novel and these various productions, the *Trilby* story became famous, spawning theatrical parodies and journalistic commentary. As the *Times* noted of the original Lackaye production, " . . . the seats are all sold many days in advance—because it is the thing to know 'Trilby,' to talk 'Trilby,' to eat 'Trilby,' to dream 'Trilby.'"[14]

The title character of Du Maurier's novel is a young female model living in Paris's Latin Quarter, where she leads a Bohemian life, along with her friends, three British expatriate artists. Much to these artists' dismay, the unsuspecting Trilby falls under the influence of Svengali, a "tawdry and greasy" Eastern European of "Jewish aspect" who peppers his speech with German phrases. The "leering" Svengali is not only a captivating musician but also a mesmerist who uses hypnotic persuasion to bring Trilby under his power, molding her into both his wife and "La Svengali," the celebrated operatic singer, whom he conducts at venues for kings and emperors throughout Europe and the world. When Svengali dies of a heart attack, Trilby is left desolate and without talent. She passes away with the words "Svengali . . . Svengali . . . Svengali" on her lips.

Though there was little doubt as to Svengali's ethnicity in the novel (which included Du Maurier's own illustrations of a bearded, hawk-nosed Svengali), in performance the character's Jewishness came to the fore. This was partially the result of Potter's adaptation, which dispensed with the novel's many subplots and focused on the Trilby-Svengali part of the story. Tree in particular played up the character's Jewishness, making amendments to Potter's script, such as having Svengali intone a garbled Hebrew prayer in the heart attack scene.[15] As performed on stage, the evil Svengali became grotesquely and unmistakably Jewish.

Much has been written about Svengali and his role as a Jewish literary type. Elaine Showalter, in casting Trilby as less of a victim, reflects on the character as a fin-de-siècle expression of the power and genius of Jewish blood. Edgar Rosenberg ranks the character with Shylock as one of the defining negative gentile stereotypes of the Jewish man, a Wandering Jew who also invokes traditions of the Jew as black magician and degenerate artist.[16] I would add that fin-de-siècle fascination with Svengali can be related to the growing reputation of the Jew both as performing artist and theatrical manager. Though a talented musician, Svengali cannot find success in his own right but rather must ventriloquize his gift through the body of a young gentile woman, whom he manipulates at will, both on stage and off. By managing Trilby's career so as to leave her no voice of her own, he also lures her into falling for his repellent sexuality.

The *Trilby* fable then, speaks implicitly to the same anti-Semitic anxiety about Jewish men managing gentile women in show business that was expressed in the *Life* cartoon. Svengali's magical powers reflect gentile wonder at groups like the Syndicate that so quickly and effectively achieved an almost unholy power in the theater through methods that were transparent to those who knew the industry and yet presumably invisible to those sitting in auditoriums. While I am not arguing that this anxiety over Jewish show business power was either *Trilby*'s overt message or the chief way it was received, it nevertheless seems appropriate that the same years that the play was most popular in America (1895–1906) were the years in which Jewish presence in show business first became unmistakable and most remarked upon. *Trilby*'s performance of the Jew was consistent with the anxiety of the moment.

The work of Lew Fields and David Belasco, two Jews who became successful in both the artistic and business sides of theater, illustrates the ways in which Jews negotiated and managed their power in this age of Svengali. Fields (Lewis Maurice Shanfield, 1867–1941) became famous, with his partner Joe Weber, as half of the top burlesque-revue team in the country between 1896 and 1904, when their satirical musicals regularly packed houses at the Weber and Fields Music Hall. Although from poor Polish Jewish families, the team never played Jewish characters. Their forte was the "Dutch double" routine which, while influenced by the team's Yiddish-speaking background, featured the antics of two grotesque German immigrants. Armond and Marc Fields have noted the irony of Fields's Dutch comedy: "It is as if this pioneer of ethnic humor had to purge himself of his own ethnic identity to create the characters that would make him famous. Offstage, he made himself ethnically 'neutral,' a living *tabula rasa*." This quest for ethnic neutrality was also evident in Fields's stage name, which he chose early in his career specifically to avoid such associations.[17]

Weber and Fields learned how to use power both to combat and avoid the sting of anti-Semitism. The pair, for example, often included a "Hebrew comic" in their shows, as a way to highlight the distinction between their Dutch act and Jewish caricature. Called "Sheenys" in print by a Jewish columnist in the *New York Mercury* in 1897, they immediately sued for libel and won. When, in a famous sketch that same year, they parodied their bitter competitors, the Theatrical "Skindecat," the managers whom they played spoke in German rather than Jewish accents.[18]

Eventually, Fields decided to "cross over" from burlesque to Broadway—that is, from satirical revues to the legitimate stage—and from performing to managing. In 1904, he dissolved his decades-long partnership with Weber (the team had formed in grade school), gave up the Music Hall, and became a successful Broadway producer. Becoming invisible to audiences by going behind the scenes was both a solution to Jewish visibility and a way of legitimizing oneself. In Fields's case, becoming a theatrical manager and influencing the performances of others could be said to serve the same strategy of evading acknowledgment of one's own ethnicity in one's own act. "Crossing over" from the footlights to the wings also highlighted the myth of cultural and economic mobility that Weber and Fields represented. As their business associate Felix Isman recounted in 1924, their story was that of "two young American boys born in the ghetto, raised in the slums, with all the disadvantages of foreign parentage of that period, who by their lives and their living became shining examples of true American manhood."[19] If "true American manhood" was the neutrality Fields sought to embody in his life, then logical professional work for one aspiring to such manhood was to organize and finance the *tabula rasa* on which other artists would perform themselves.

The playwright and director David Belasco (1853–1931) was another Jew who sought legitimacy behind the scenes. Born in San Francisco to English Jews of Portuguese extraction, Belasco started out as an actor in regional stock companies where, like David Warfield, he found himself at times obliged to embody the invidious sheeny, such as Fagin in an 1870s dramatization of *Oliver Twist*. After launching his own New York company in 1882, he gradually established himself not only as a competent playwright, but more importantly, a master of scene design, lighting effects, and overall production, thus extending the old role of actor-manager into a prototype of the non-acting modern stage director. Belasco became a leading figure in the New York theater, wielding significant control over most aspects of his productions, launching technical innovations, and like Fields, struggling against the Syndicate.

Though a practicing Jew, Belasco's religion did not preclude him from performing himself in curious ways. Legend has it, for example, that a Catholic priest in Victoria, British Columbia, was a key inspiration for the youthful Belasco. In a 1879 production of *The Passion* in which Belasco showed obsessive interest, he created elaborate scenic decor which teemed with Christian iconography.[20] Even Belasco-the-playwright's one exemplary Jewish character, Israel Cohen in *Men and Women* (1890), owns a stained glass window depicting Mary Magdalen at the feet of Christ. When a character asks Cohen why he, a Jew, possesses such a picture, the banker replies, "Because of my admiration for the man. Whatever the Nazarene may have been, his treatment of mankind, His help to them, His hope for them, puts the breath of heaven into the words of his philosophy. What picture could I have in the house of a Jew more appropriate than this picture of a Jew?"[21] This attraction to Catholic forms was performed by Belasco himself. The director was given to wearing a clerical collar around New York, earning him the epithet, "The Bishop of Broadway."

The neutrality sought by Fields was paralleled by Belasco's curious flirtations with Catholic aesthetics. Their strategies made sense in an era when Jewishness was not only excluded from any construction of legitimate American manhood but was also the target of anxiety over who was calling the shots in the theater. They downplayed their own ethnic connections to "whiten" themselves, lest what was obvious to many become acutely visible to all. After all, there was no visibly Jewish way of performing oneself as a successful American; social and cultural mobility required flexibility and evasion in self-presentation.

By working behind the scenes, these Jews also were able to impact the way in which Jewish characters on the stage were portrayed, from vaudeville comedians to Shylocks. The ethnic mobility that Fields and Belasco sought for themselves in the theater could also be realized through the careers of others, especially at a time when Jewish characters had never been so prominent on the American stage.

Ethnic Mobility in the Heyday of Hebrew Comedy

If the comic stage Jews of the 1870s and early 1880s constituted a minor fad, the "Hebrew comics" (as they were sometimes called) who began to appear in musical revues, vaudeville, and burlesque around the turn of the century were far more widespread. Never before or since in the American theater had Jewish characters enjoyed such a visible presence.

Their growing importance thus paralleled the emergence of Jews in other aspects of theater.

I have been able to trace the emergence of these stage Hebrews through an examination of the acts at Tony Pastor's concert hall. Through most of the 1890s, Frank Bush seems to have been the only Jewish delineator to take the stage there. In July of 1899, however, Julian Rose turns up with an act entitled "Our Hebrew Friend," its title recalling the final lines of M. B. Curtis's *Sam'l of Posen*. The next month, Harry and Sadie Fields are featured there in a "Yiddisher Dance." In September, Jess Dandy takes the stage as a "Hebrew Dialect Parodist," and Howe and Scott present their "Dancing and Hebrew Cake Walk." By 1900, Joe Welch joins these names as a semi-regular attraction.[22]

Throughout the next decade, Hebrew comics were a regular feature in vaudeville and could often be found doing character comedy in Broadway musicals. Additionally, almost every major traveling burlesque show had a wisecracking Jewish comedian, often a bearded, unkempt figure who walked with a limp and stood in grotesque contrast to the alluring dancing girls who surrounded him. (The form by then was evolving away from its roots in musical parody into shows which more openly foregrounded the display of the female body.)[23] According to Paul Antonie Distler, these comedians who came into prominence around the 1900s can be broadly broken down into two types: the fast-talking, aggressive winner and the pathetic, world-weary loser.[24] Both can be seen as descending from performances evident in the earlier generation, the former in the tradition of Curtis's Sam'l Plastrick and the latter in the tradition of Bush's old clo'es men.

The fast-talkers included two men of Jewish heritage, Julian Rose and Ben Welch. Rose, who reputedly could utter up to two hundred words a minute, was by 1903 a national headliner on Martin Beck's western vaudeville circuit. He ultimately became famous for his standard monologue, "Levinsky at the Wedding," which at the peak of his career was earning him $850 a week (see Appendix Aiii).[25] Welch became lead comic in the *Parisian Widows' Show* burlesque revue, playing a witty Jew of "slouched shoulders, screwed-up face, gesticulating mannerisms, and singsong accent."[26] Vaudevillians later recalled him as the courageous comedian who continued to take the stage even after he went blind, masking his disability so effectively, legend had it, that his audiences were not aware of it.

Welch's brother Joe specialized, in contrast, in the world-weary loser who went around lamenting his poor luck (fig. 10). His act traditionally

Figure 10. Joe Welch in *Cohen's Luck*, 1904. *Billy Rose Theatre Collection, The New York Public Library for the Performing Arts, Astor, Lenox and Tilden Foundations.*

started with the key-line, "Mebbe you t'ink I'm a happy man?" and ended with the lament, "Und I vished dot I vas dead!" Welch starred in a number of Broadway vehicles in the early 1900s but ultimately enjoyed greatest success in vaudeville.[27]

All three of these performers dressed in strikingly similar stage costume, partially in direct imitation of David Warfield (whom I discuss later) but also recalling the sheenies of old melodrama who were always grotesquely and visibly marked as Jewish. The standard Hebrew getup included stringy beard, long nose, and black derby pulled down tightly over the ears. Frequently, too, these characters had terrible posture; they walked with limps below oversized coats that hung to the ankles. Their physical appearance was matched by their pseudo-Yiddish dialect, with its attendant comic butchering of the English language.[28]

A number of comedians deviated from this physical type, though. Jess Dandy played a stout, jolly, clean-shaven Jew. Dandy, perhaps the most prominent of all these comedians, was not himself Jewish; his delineations, as a contemporary newspaper put it, "were greatly applauded, no more enthusiastic admirers of his humorous creations being found than among the folk of the race that he so cleverly burlesqued."[29] Sam Bernard found success as the clean-shaven, cocky Jewish "bounder," Piggy Hoggenheimer. In two successful Broadway musicals, *The Girl from Kays* (1903) and *The Rich Mr. Hoggenheimer* (1906), Bernard played this "boastful yet cowardly Jew" with a "likeable personality" to financial success, before moving on to other roles.[30]

If there were comedians who specialized in playing Hebrews, so were there a handful of writers who specialized in scripting them. The prolific Hal Reid created *The Peddler* (1902, for Joe Welch), *Israel Isaacs; or, A Jew's Gratitude* (1904), and *The Money Lender* (1907), among other works featuring Jewish comic leads. Aaron Hoffman, Junie McCree, Harry Lee Newton, and Harry Shelland became adept at churning out vaudevillian vignettes that placed Jews in a wide variety of comic circumstances. Shelland's pun-laden *Two Wandering Jews* (1904), for example, plays on the conceit of two Hebrew types in conflict. Newton's *Second-Hand Man* (1903) pairs an unscrupulous Jew and an unsuspecting country rube. McCree's *Hebraic Types* (1915) features such curiosities as the absent-minded Hebrew who forgets his own wedding; the Hebrew baseball player who gets so roughed up that he swears, the next time there is a game, "you can bet your life I'm gonna stay home;" and the Hebrew janitor whose incompetence borders on negligence.[31]

Many of these performances clearly bordered on the anti-Semitic, despite the fact that Jews were active in writing and attending these shows. The polarities of aggressive and world-weary Jew evident throughout these sketches, even while they mirrored the work of Curtis and Bush, reflected the older gentile staging traditions of the aggressive/unscrupulous and effeminate/incompetent Jew. Shylock was the former; the sheeny villain was both. In helping to fashion these performances, in other words, Jews in the theater were actively collaborating with older staging traditions. To be visibly Jewish on stage meant invoking these older performances, whether directly or indirectly.

This heyday of Jewish comedy was equally marked by the Jewish types it neglected to perform. In contrast to the many two-person Irish and Dutch teams, the Hebrews tended to take the stage as "singles." When they did work with a partner, the second performer tended to play the non-ethnic straight in contrast to the Hebrew's comic grotesque. Female Hebrew comedians were also rarities. There were a handful of male-female stage teams, notably William Hines and Earle Remington, whose "Our Pawnshop" sketch dated to the 1890s.[32] However, this sort of comic interaction between slightly grotesque male and straight woman, a common vaudeville combination, was a possibility rarely embodied with a Hebrew, possibly because Jewish men were still construed as too unsavory to be paired with a woman on stage in any routine more intimate than the impersonal spectacle of the chorus line of the burlesque revue. The most prominent comic stage Jewess of the era was featured in the musical *Sally in Our Alley* (1902), which starred Marie Cahill as a Bowery girl. The character's ethnicity was strongly downplayed; Cahill, one of the most popular stars of the day, was "more redolent of Newport . . . than of anybody's alley."[33]

There were other "freak" variations on Jewish comedy. The team of Morris and Allen did Irish singing, dressed in Scotch kilts and Hebrew make-up. The Hakoah, a "championship Jewish soccer team," made at least one tour of the vaudeville circuit. Abe Reynolds played a Jewish sultan in the burlesque revue *Runaway Girls*. These oddities were exceptions which proved the rule of the Jew as solo comedian, often lonely and troubled, a vaudevillian version of the ancient Wandering Jew.[34]

This era of Jewish comedy had its limitations. First, as Distler notes, these stage Jews had trouble working the road outside of New York, a fact understandable given that the Eastern European Jewish community that provided the models and part of the audience for the humor were most visibly concentrated in that city. Moreover, it consigned these grotesquely typed performers to work in vaudeville, and more often, the less respectable form of burlesque. Joe Welch never made a career for himself in legitimate Broadway shows, despite repeated attempts. Rose's fast-talking, lowbrow Hebrew was seen as too vulgar for such an extended Broadway vehicle when he attempted a major role in a full-length show.[35] If some of these characters had the world-weariness of the Wandering Jew, the profession of the men performing them fittingly reinscribed the notion of the Jew as lonely wanderer, traveling from venue to venue, facing audiences hostile or indifferent.

In contrast, the two "cleaner" Hebrews, Dandy and Bernard, found more flexibility and upward mobility. Dandy, for example, developed an expert Dutch delineation that he used for Hans Wagner, the comic lead in the operetta *The Prince of Pilsen* (1902). The show was a smash hit and Dandy thereafter left the Jew behind, playing rotund Germans in musicals for many years.

To specialize in Hebrew comedy then, was to do work that was less than legitimate in both the general and theatrical senses of the word. The way to wider commercial and artistic success meant "whitening" oneself into bodies other than the Jew. One could make a career out of playing the bearded, splay-legged Jew but that very performance circumscribed the success one could normally enjoy. Ethnic visibility translated into limited cultural and economic mobility. If the Jewish body had finally transcended the sheeny villain, it remained mired in the low comedy which had been the vehicle of that transcendence.

This reality is underscored by the career of Warfield (1866–1951), the man who first popularized the turn-of-the-century Hebrew comic type and either directly influenced or strongly overshadowed all the other Jewish performances of the period. After his humiliating debut as Melter Moss in *The Ticket-of-Leave Man* (c. 1888), Warfield gained experience in the West Coast theater before breaking into the New York show business scene in 1891. He got his first major opportunity in 1893 when he secured a principal place in the burlesque company of John Russell's Comedians. In 1895, George W. Lederer took him on as a leading comic player in his Casino Company, a pioneer in the development of the Broadway revue and light musical comedy. With Casino, Warfield created such roles as "Madame Sans Gene" in *The Merry World* (1895), and the "Duke of Mulligatawny" and "Mrs. Maryland Ta Ta" in Hugh Morton's hit musical *In Gay New York* (1896).

According to Warfield, the actor had during this time been working on perfecting a Hebrew delineation, inspired both by Frank Bush as well as by his own personal observations of Russian immigrants on the Lower East Side.[36] However, when Warfield approached Lederer with the idea of using a stage Jew in a Casino show, the manager ridiculed and resisted the suggestion. The type, after all, was rarely seen; in 1896, the journeyman Bush was virtually the only comic of note doing Jewish comedy in New York. While the spieling old clo'es men of the Victorian era might once have been perceived as fit objects for comedy, the darker and far more impoverished Russian and Polish Jews who now crowded the immigrant wards of the city may have seemed more frightening than funny to Lederer.

Undeterred, Warfield used an off-stage performance to push his case. In an exhibition baseball game between the Casino Company and another burlesque troupe, he outfitted himself as a Hebrew peddler, replete with scraggly beard, baggy pants, and hat pulled down tightly over his ears. In this costume, he shambled around the field trying to sell souvenirs, so splay-legged that it looked as if he "were about to fall apart." This direct appeal to the crowd worked. The audience that had assembled to watch the exhibition loved Warfield's clowning. Lederer relented. The 1897 incarnation of *In Gay New York* included Warfield's comic peddler Solomon McCarthy. Subsequent Casino revues continued to include opportunities for Warfield's increasingly popular Jewish delineations.[37]

Through his work with Lederer, Warfield attracted the interest of Weber and Fields, who invited him to join their company. The situation is ironic: Weber and Fields, sons of poor New York Jews, famous as stage Germans, hiring Warfield to play New York Jews, despite the fact that Warfield himself was from San Francisco and had only first observed (so he claimed) Hebrew peddlers after moving to New York and taking a "slumming" tour of the ghetto there.[38] Through his work with Weber and Fields however, Warfield quickly became one of the chief comic stars in New York, creating Solomon Yankle in *Hurly Burly* (1898), Isidore Nosenstein in *Helter Skelter* (1899), and Shadrach Leschinski in *Fiddle-Dee-Dee* (1900). The latter was a Jewish huckster who impersonates a Turkish magician at a Paris fair and ends up having to imitate a life-size mechanical doll. Thus, while Weber and Fields became famous by finding ways to suppress their ethnicity, the "diminutive, blue-eyed" Warfield found success by finding ways to assert it, as his visible stage Jewishness diverted attention from their own.[39] Warfield also influenced others; the connection seems clear between Warfield's success at the Music Hall and the comedians who were shortly thereafter showing up at nearby Tony

Pastor's, many of whom were sporting the exact look and gait of Warfield's Jews.

The next Jewish impresario to impact Warfield's career was Belasco. After seeing Warfield perform with Weber and Fields, the director tried to convince the comedian to star in a play that he, Belasco, would produce for him. Warfield apparently thought Belasco was joking: Why would an "arty" director like Belasco be interested in a burlesque-company comedian like himself? Belasco persisted, finally persuading Warfield to leave Weber and Fields in order to star in *The Auctioneer* (1901), which the director, with the help of playwrights Lee Arthur (Arthur Lee Kahn) and Charles Klein, fashioned specifically for him. (Sam Bernard, later to play Piggy Hoggenheimer, replaced Warfield in the company.) The production became a Broadway hit, making Warfield one of the top actors in the country and stimulating yet more interest in Jewish comedy.[40]

Though the original script for *The Auctioneer* has not survived, a promptbook for its 1913 remounting, which also starred Warfield, follows the original script closely enough that it can serve as a guide to the original 1901 production. The plot is thin. Simon Levi, proprietor of a Baxter Street auction house, has finally made enough money that he and his wife Esther can "move up" to Lexington Avenue, the same fashionable neighborhood where his brother and sister-in-law, Isaac and Rose "Leavitt," have established their residence. Isaac is desperate for money and concerned that his brother's move will tip off his lowly Jewish roots to the neighbors; goaded on by his wife, he concocts a scheme to defraud his brother. As a result, Levi and Esther lose their new home. Nearly penniless, Levi resorts to peddling toy monkeys on the street for a few dollars (fig. 11). While aware of how he has been cheated, Levi nevertheless accepts his fate cheerfully, though he seethes with resentment toward his brother, whom he believes has died in South America. Isaac suddenly turns up in New York and begs his brother's forgiveness. The play ends up with Levi and Esther receiving Isaac and Rose into their home and pardoning them for their transgressions.[41]

Though *The Auctioneer* may sound like traditional melodrama, it actually represents a different, emerging genre of light comedy that would characterize Broadway for decades. Though the Leavitts' scheming drives the plot, it serves as mere background to Levi's extended character comedy, which allows the Jew room to dominate the show in a genial way. Though capable of being aggressive and manipulative, Levi shows himself repeatedly to have a heart of gold; the audience repeatedly sees, beneath the mask

FIGURE 11. David Warfield in *The Auctioneer*, 1901. *Harry Ransom Humanities Research Center, The University of Texas at Austin.*

of canny salesman, the loving family man sympathetically engaged with the plights of those around him (see Appendix Aiv). Moreover, Levi remains unflappably comfortable with himself, never denying his heritage, always faithful to his roots. Even when he moves uptown, it is with misgivings and the pledge that his rising social status will not alter his genuine sense of decency. Leavitt, in contrast, is a flashy social climber who changes his name, denies his heritage, and tries to perform himself as something he is not.

The Auctioneer therefore serves as an apt fable for this age of rising Jewish power. Ultimately, Levi's simplicity, honesty, and good humor help him successfully negotiate the transition into American bourgeois life without losing a sense of his "essential" self. For the many Jews in its audience, this must have been a comforting message which assured them of a conservative, consistent path through which immigrants could perform themselves as Americans and yet remain visibly marked as ethnic in name, speech, and dress. For the many gentiles, it reassured them as to the non-threatening nature of the Jew. In performing the Jewish-American businessman as lovable family man and pathetic hero, Warfield legitimized him as a figure that both Jews and gentiles could accept.

The irony remains that, unknown to these audiences, the actor playing this down-to-earth Jew had himself not only adapted an ethnically neutral stage name (becoming Warfield instead of Wohlfelt) but had also, in 1899, married a young Catholic on his way to becoming a practicing Christian. Later in Warfield's life, one interviewer even took note of the extensive Christian artwork on the walls of the actor's apartment, recalling the curious taste of Belasco's Israel Cohen in *Men and Women*.[42] By the terms of *The Auctioneer*, then, Warfield-the-actor resembled Isaac-the-fallen-brother far more than he did his own Levi, the character who made him famous.

The Auctioneer also poses problems in the way it performs its Jewesses. The wild and exotic stage Jewess, that figure of gentile romantic fantasy, has disappeared entirely, and in her place seem to lie three possibilities, as embodied by the play's three major Jewesses: Esther Levi, Minnie Leavitt, and Rose Leavitt. Esther is a seminal Jewish mother of the English-speaking American stage: warm, loving, gossipy, housebound, devoted, yet, like Rebecca in *Sam'l of Posen*, a figure half in shadow, marginalized in comparison to her commanding husband. Minnie, a gay young Jewess with ambitions of going on the stage, is a minor character at best. However, the central Jewess here, the one with the most stage time, is the villainess Rose Leavitt, the overbearing hag and nag who absorbs most of the responsibility for the evil perpetuated against Levi during the play. Through Rose, the domineering Jewish wife ends up shouldering the blame for the errors of Isaac, the Jewish husband. Jewish power, as performed in *The Auctioneer*, not only benefits men at the expense of women but specifically casts the woman as domineering bitch as a way of legitimizing the male Jew's claim to sympathy.

Through *The Auctioneer*, it seems clear that Belasco and Warfield were attempting the difficult task of taking the figure of the Hebrew comedian out of his variety-hall context and building him into a figure of pathos. Journalists writing about the play in 1901 perceived this intention; the 1901 article "How I Discovered Levi" noted, "David Belasco believes that the Hebrew can be made a character replete with human interest, one that must be taken seriously, one whose sorrows will attract sympathy." Apparently he did appeal to Jewish audiences; this same writer noted that Warfield did "nothing offensively, and unlike some other Hebrew actors, never offend(ing) a very lucrative percentage of the theater-going population . . . Warfield certainly came out admirably. He was so exceedingly subdued, and painted it all in such very dim colors that you knew once again that he was an actor and not a buffoon. He did artistically what others of his ilk do obstreperously." Accordingly, Belasco had Warfield's make-up of his Weber-and-Fields days naturalized and modified, in keeping with the actor's stated goal of playing the Jew as "vividly true" rather than exaggerated. It was a way of finding a new body for the Jewish comedian beyond the splay-legged, baggy-clothed clown that Warfield himself had helped develop and that others had slavishly imitated.

To raise the Hebrew comic out of the body of buffoon, Belasco and Warfield conducted a publicity campaign which emphasized that Levi was a real-life character from a real-life ghetto. In the same "How I Discovered Levi," Warfield discussed how he took an "expedition to the Ghetto in search of atmosphere." Upon "discovering" his subject and "studying life," Warfield learned how to perform him in a way that was faithful to reality, down to the splay-legged, shambling gait typical of the Eastern European race which, Warfield claimed, was easily observable in certain neighborhoods. Belasco, for his part, hoped in the article that the play would "take the place of a slumming expedition." Condescending reports like these must have generated some controversy in the Jewish community because, a month after the play opened, Warfield went on record fervently denying that he ever went to the slums to come up with such a portrait.[43]

The following year, however, Warfield negotiated this contradiction by coming up with a third story which authenticated the realism of Levi without positing him as something stolen from life. In this version of the story, Warfield reported that, having perfecting his character on his own, he then decided to take a bicycle ride through the ghetto, in full make-up and costume, to test it out. Based upon the responses of the ghetto Jews, who noticed nothing peculiar in the figure other than the curious fact that he was riding a bike, Warfield realized that his "'make-up' must be a success." However, acceptance by the ghetto Jews was not the crowning achievement of Warfield's bike ride, for, en route to the ghetto, his characterization received no derisive remarks from gentiles by whom he pedaled past. "This I thought was the highest compliment ever paid to my skill in making up," noted Warfield. Warfield conditioned his performance success then, on his ability to pass in both worlds—to be ethnically specific enough to be accepted among Jews as authentically Jewish and to be ethnically neutral enough to avoid being mocked by gentiles.[44]

To negotiate this narrow middle ground, Warfield often went to great lengths to distinguish himself from the roles he played. In the wake of *The Auctioneer* success, he asked a reporter, "Don't I resemble the Irish more than I do the Hebrew?"[45] One typical fan article, from September of 1901, amply displayed the "versatility" which Warfield marketed for himself, pointing out not only that the actor was able to play a wide variety of physical types with ease, but also that, in his "proper person," he cut a dignified, beardless, elegant figure, in stark contrast to the stage Hebrew, Levi. While there is nothing unusual in an actor's attempting to emphasize his versatility to avoid being categorized as a one-role wonder, this article belied the fact that, at the time, Warfield's major claim to fame was his Hebrew delineation.

In fact, much of the publicity surrounding *The Auctioneer* suggested the ambiguous nature of Warfield's relationship to his own ethnicity. From his tales of bicycle rides through the Lower East Side to his occasional speculations as to the racial bases of Russian Jewry, Warfield made clear to reporter after reporter that he was not one of "them"; he spoke of the Jews always as a "they." When asked by one writer, for example, if he thought his Levi was accurate, he replied: "So many Jewish people tell me it is just the thing that I presume it must be."[46] Articles stressed the way Warfield "discovered" Levi through purely external observation, not through any internal experience. In fact, it is easy to peruse these materials and come to the simple conclusion, as Distler did in the 1960s, that Warfield himself was not Jewish.

One can read many things into these articles. On one hand, they seem to describe a self-hating Jew, a man who has so internalized the image of a Melter Moss that he is desperately using the stage to run away from himself. From another position, they can be read as the defensive reaction of a man trying to maintain dignity in an age of intense anti-Semitism, when Jewishness was readily associated with the effeminate and the grotesque; he was no more evading his ethnicity than were Weber and Fields or other

Jews active in show business. I prefer a third perspective: to read them as acts of ambition, as attempts to use the power of the stage and its attendant publicity to circumvent the narrow professional and social limits associated with turn-of-the-century Hebrew typing. By distancing himself from the brand of comedy he created, by "discovering" Levi in some neighborhood outside his own neighborhood, by locating him in some body outside his own, Warfield sought to establish control over the performance of his own self. In doing so, he attempted a cultural mobility denied to actors who, by dint of talent or choice, became inextricably identified with the ethnicities they portrayed.

Belasco and Warfield were successful with *The Auctioneer*. Levi provided the American stage with its most sympathetic, engaging Jewish male character to date, and Warfield managed to use the role to get taken seriously as an artist, earning the label "actor" as opposed to "comedian." Levi, however, turned out to be but a stepping stone to a stage world where Warfield could perform himself as a gentile and be taken seriously. He trumped *The Auctioneer* with even greater national success in a variety of non-Jewish roles on the legitimate stage, notably Anton von Barwig in *The Music Master*, Wes Bigelow in *The Grand Army Man* (1907), and the title character in *The Return of Peter Grimm* (1911). All were Belasco productions. By the time Warfield and Belasco revived *The Auctioneer* in 1913, Warfield had established himself as one of the most famous actors of the day, a man called "the greatest living actor in English" by some. While Rose and the Welch brothers were struggling in vaudeville and burlesque, Warfield achieved a life of comfort and fame. Under the guidance of Belasco, he first transformed the performance of the stage Jew and later evaded it, while constructing a life to parallel his art.

From poor immigrant to rich American, from Jewish son to Christian father, from Melter Moss to Peter Grimm, Warfield pushed the limits of American economic, social, and cultural mobility. With Lederer, he first demanded that the Jew be accepted into the company of lovable comedians, establishing him as a jolly good fellow. With *The Auctioneer*, he demanded that the Jew be treated sympathetically as naturalized protagonist of his own show in the legitimate theater, not just as grotesque and lovable buffoon in variety-style comedy. With his later work, he demanded that a Jew not have to play a Jew at all. Only a gifted performer could have pulled off all three acts in one career, using performance as a strategy for ethnic mobility.

The Jew as Shylock

Shylock posed a complex problem for Jews involved in theatrical production. On one hand, the character was clearly linked to a long history of stage anti-Semitism; the performance invoked, directly or indirectly, the most negative gentile traditions of staging the Jew. On the other hand, Shylock was clearly the most famous Jewish character in the dramatic canon, the one most consistently legitimized by audiences, and the one who possessed the greatest power to legitimize the actor playing him. More than any other Jewish role, Shylock guarded the portals between Art and mere entertainment. The ultimate challenge for some Jews in the theater then, was to find ways to positively inscribe the character's Jewishness in performance, as though by redeeming Shylock they could also redeem Jews from the scourge of anti-Semitism that was the product of the same European history. By making Shylock "really Jewish," they could thereby extend the tradition of sympathetic pathos already well established by Irving.

The ethnic reinscription of Shylock was clear as early as 1893, when Richard Mansfield played the role (to a partially Jewish audience, as I have noted) with a cadence suggesting a contemporary Jewish-American accent.[47] The trend accelerated when the foremost actor of New York's Yiddish Theater, Jacob Adler (1855–1926), "crossed over" to play Shylock on Broadway in 1903 in his native Yiddish opposite an English-speaking ensemble. Adler articulated his approach to the role this way:

> I am not a historian; far from it, but my understanding of the Jew in history is as follows: He is a patriarch, a higher being. A certain grandeur, the triumph of long patience, intellect and character has been imparted to him by the sufferings and traditions that have been his teachers. Not only can he go through life; he is rooted in life and has grown strong in it. And so he has much joy, much reality, much blood in him. All this must be seen in his bearing, his figure, his appearance. Weighty and proud his walk, calm and conclusive his speech, a man of richest personal and national experience, a man who sees life through the glasses of eternity. So I played him. So I had joy in him. And so I portrayed him as Shylock.[48]

Adler's comments conflated Shakespeare's character with his own personal conception of the "universal Jew," reversing the process by which many gentiles had extrapolated their experience of Shylock into their own ideas of the Jew. The pathos of Irving had to be converted to ethnic pride, given the "authenticity" the audience surely would have expected in the work of so "authentically" a Jewish actor, particularly one who would be speaking the role in the "authentic" Jewish language.

The stumbling block to this proud and regal Shylock, however, was *Merchant* itself. Adler plied the difficult script by adding a number of touches in the tradition of Irving. In the famous scene where Shylock discovers that Jessica has fled, for example, Adler had the curtain come down on the sound of Shylock rending his clothes. Adler's courtroom scene included Gratiano assaulting Shylock, highlighting the theme of the persecution of the Jews. For his final exit, Adler's Shylock picked himself up, dusted himself off, and made a proud exit, emphasizing the conception of the Jew as one who suffers hardship with dignity.[49]

Critical reaction to Adler's performance was mixed. While some Yiddish theater historians have since praised it as one of the summit roles of his career, initial reviews of the 1903 production and its 1905 revival (in which Adler spoke English) were not all enthusiastic. Some felt that Adler's characterization was too colloquial, lacking in dignity. The *Times*, in fact, in a largely negative write-up, labeled the performance "almost grotesque."[50] The grotesqueness might have resulted from the seeming incongruity that resulted when Adler's own colloquial Jewish body intersected with the imagined Jewish body of Shakespeare's usurer. Perhaps Adler was cognizant of this fact: after 1905, he never returned again to the English-language stage, which had allowed the great actor access only through one of the most ignominious stage Jews in history.

The other memorable "Jewish" production of *Merchant* in New York during this broad period requires me to jump forward a few decades in time to 1922, when Warfield himself attempted Shylock in a production directed by none other than Belasco. The history of this performance is full of Warfield's usual storytelling contradictions. As early as 1902, he was on record as having the ambition to play the part. In later interviews, however, particularly those accompanying the production itself, he denied ever having had any interest in the role. In any case, it was a widely publicized production, seen as a tour de force for two of the American theater's most prominent Jewish figures, both nearing the end of their careers, yet still near the peak of their powers. Moreover, the promising actress Julia Adler, daughter of the Yiddish star, was to play Jessica. The leading players in this production then, both in front of and behind the curtain, were figures whom the audience either knew as Jews or associated with Jewish roles.

Warfield seems to have taken the same approach to Shylock that he did to Jewish comedy more than twenty years earlier in *The Auctioneer*. Amid Belasco's elaborate decor, Warfield played Shylock with understated realism lightened by a touch of sentimentality: an average man struggling with extraordinary circumstances. Belasco heightened the realism by adding Jewish effects, such as having Shylock's initial opening scene introduced by a cantor intoning in Hebrew. If Adler sought to make Shylock into the proud and majestic Jew of universal history, then Warfield and Belasco naturalized him into the everyday Jew of contemporary America, less in the tradition of Elizabethan England and more in the tradition of the world-weary, lovable Hebrew which Warfield had played years before.

Though from the commercial point of view the production was a modest success, critical reaction was mixed. Some observers, like Stanislavski, who caught the show during a visit to the United States, were impressed. However, John Corbin, the *Times* reviewer, complained that Warfield's "subtle and delicate artistry" was not up to the "physical vitality" demanded by Shylock's "volcanic outbursts."[51] Corbin and other reviewers also ridiculed Belasco's overwrought stage settings and bombastic directing style which left the naturalistic Warfield a tiny voice "pathetically crying in a producer's weird wilderness of understanding."[52] Generally, from an artistic standpoint, the production fell far short of the expectations it had generated.[53]

Merchant brought the ambitions of Warfield and Belasco to a height and also helped to bring their careers to a end. It was the last classic Belasco attempted to stage. Warfield retired after its run and never once returned to the stage, though he lived nearly thirty more years. Moreover, the two men became estranged during the tour of the show, thus ending a twenty-one-year partnership in which each had so effectively served the other's interests.

Warfield's retirement after *Merchant* makes sense from a variety of perspectives. Having attempted Shylock, there was little left for him to prove. He had started with the lowest stage Jew there was, the sheeny Melter Moss, before moving into the body of the Hebrew comedian, raising him from burlesque buffoon into the naturalized body of Simon Levi. Next, he left stage Jews behind to fashion a career playing lovable gentiles. Finally, in Shylock, he returned to the one stage Jew with unchallenged credentials in the world of dramatic literature and theatrical art. Throughout most of these performances, Belasco had been present behind the scenes, using his power to help Warfield formulate and surmount these challenges.

However, Warfield also possessed another type of power which enabled him to leave the stage early, a luxury not available to most other actors, even the most celebrated ones. By the time he retired, he was no longer hailed merely as "the greatest living actor in English," but according to some, "the world's richest actor."[54] Though some of this fortune had been made through his two decades of work with Belasco, much of it came from his investments off the stage. Like others, Warfield had invested early and wisely in the field of theatrical management. Many years before, he had entered into partnership with his friend Marcus Loew, the Jewish entrepreneur who owned a string of smalltime vaudeville houses. Loew eventually expanded his business into a veritable show business empire that later became the parent company of Hollywood's most celebrated film studio, MGM. Warfield's partnership with Loew made him wealthy, permitting him to live in great comfort during his long retirement.[55]

The ultimate stage in Warfield's social mobility then, both resulted from and reflected his decision to take a position in the business side of the show. He had ascended steadily from sheeny to Jewish comic to gentile lead to Shylock, but his greatest security both financially and ethnically occurred when the Jewish "Wohlfelt" body with which he was born no longer was an object for audiences to examine. Despite "the memory of the agony" of his stage debut, he left the ignominious form of Melter Moss behind and died a Roman Catholic in an age in which Jewish writers and producers were shaping television and Hollywood, but an openly Jewish comedian was rarely seen beyond the Catskill Mountains. He had effectively used his power to manage his way into invisibility.

CHAPTER 5

Breeding New Generations

RACE, SEXUALITY, AND INTERMARRIAGE
IN PROGRESSIVE ERA PERFORMANCES

*"Down there, in dark alleys and filthy holes,
the future of America is teeming."*
—Tony Wayne in *Husband* (1910) by John Corbin,
drama critic for the *New York Times*[1]

*W*hat's in a cover? The jacket to the
published version of Harry Lee Newton and Aaron Hoffman's vaudeville
sketch *Glickman the Glazier* (1904) depicts a potbellied stage Hebrew comedian encountering an attractive gentile young woman in high heels, styl-
ish skirt, and fashionable coiffure (fig. 12). Cane in hand, the Jew gestures
toward her. The young woman listens with apparently avid interest, though
the crease in her lips suggests a touch of bemusement, while the riding
whip in her hand indicates dangers that he may face if he attempts to press
his intentions further. These intentions, moreover, seem less than honor-
able. While the two bodies, Jew and gentile, stand a safe distance away
from one another, their heads hover uncomfortably close together in what
seems an encroachment upon each other's personal space. This mismatched
pair thus stands perched at the point of a grotesque kiss, an image emphasized by the looming shadows in which the figures of aging Jew and young
woman entangle.

Reading beyond the cover, one finds that *Glickman* indeed turns out
to be about a quasi-sexual encounter between a Jewish glazier named Jacob
Glickman and an aspiring gentile actress named Charlotte Russe. In the
sketch, the actress flirts with the Jew, finds him "cute and clever," calls him
her "sweetheart," and caresses his beard. Glickman, in response, grabs the

118

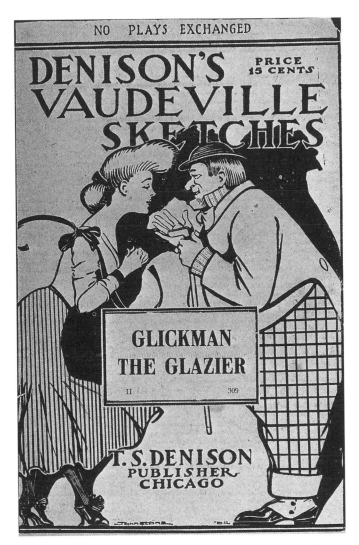

FIGURE 12. Cover to Harry Lee Newton and Aaron Hoffman's *Glickman the Glazier*, 1904. *Harry Ransom Humanities Research Center, The University of Texas at Austin.*

actress by the waist. In the end, Glickman gets horsewhipped for his advances, in a performance that is as much a sexist presentation of the overbearing young "bitch" who uses her sexuality to achieve her ends, as it as an anti-Semitic profile of the grotesque and lecherous Jew. The whorish showgirl and vulgar Jew deserve each other, though in the tradition of classic vaudeville, the piece ends without any resolution, the two performers abruptly launching into their specialty songs once all the comic possibilities of the encounter have been exploited.

Though *Glickman* is a forgotten moment in the history of the popular stage, sometimes the most significant cultural concerns play themselves out in the most seemingly insignificant venues. My reading of dozens of Progressive Era plays, sketches, and songs involving Jewish characters reveals that sexual encounters between Jew and gentile become strikingly characteristic of performances, particularly after 1905. The dynamics of these encounters vary from performance to performance and by no means always resemble *Glickman*. They can engage an audience's sympathies, presenting, in a recasting of the Romeo and Juliet fable, young lovers struggling to come together despite the disapproval of parents and the weight of tradition. They can arouse an audience's revulsion, depicting lecherous Jews lusting after wealthy old widows or randy young showgirls. In all cases, the stakes of these performances derive from the dramatic potential inherent in romantic relationships between Jews and gentiles.

I am not suggesting that earlier performances did not play out the possibilities of such encounters. The belle juive, for example, frequently found herself the object of a handsome young gentile's advances. From her high pedestal though, she generally managed to resist these advances, even if she underwent a sort of spiritual conversion in the tortuous process of resisting. The sheeny villain also frequently found himself in situations with erotic overtones. The sexual nature of these encounters, however, normally remained veiled or implicit; in his impotence, the sheeny rarely posed the threat of consummating a relationship with the gentiles upon whom he preyed. A more contemporary performance like *The Auctioneer* featured, in a subplot, a budding inter-ethnic romance between Levi's daughter Helga and Dick Eagen, an Irish neighbor. To the comfort of its audiences, this coupling elided the racial implications of intermarriage since Helga is actually an Irish orphan whom the Levis have adopted as their own. The occasional plays which dealt directly and openly with intermarriage, like *The Ghetto* (1899), by the Jewish-Dutch playwright Herman Heijermans, were European imports in the tradition of the realistic problem play which had limited commercial viability in the United States.

After 1905 though, an interest in the ramifications of Jewish-gentile romance emerges as a near-obsessive concern in performances with Jewish characters. Why this new obsession? Despite the occasional celebrated case, like the wedding of millionaire James Graham Phelps Stokes and settlement worker Rose Harriet Pastor in 1905, statistics do not suggest any great increase in intermarriage. A study done as late as 1920, for example, revealed that only 1.17 percent of American Jews were intermarrying. In other words, during the era in question, Jews were marrying Jews and gentiles marrying gentiles, despite the fact that a new generation of more assimilated immigrant children lived in close enough proximity to result in many a passing flirtation.[2]

The recurrence of the intermarriage theme in performances indicates, therefore, a broader cultural preoccupation not so much with realities as with possibilities. Children, after all, come only out of sexual encounters. In the bodies of these children, the ethnic make-up of coming generations inscribes itself. In these coming generations, the future of a nation inscribes itself as well. These performances' repeated concerns with interethnic romantic encounter represent, therefore, the era's broader concern with the future ethnic make-up of America, in the wake of massive immigration that was challenging the racial hegemony of a country that until recently had consisted largely of a Western and Northern European population served by a segregated class of African Americans. Rapid industrialization though, depended upon large-scale immigration, and immigration in turn challenged this rigid stratification, provoking an anxiety which laws could not so readily contain. Performances responded by playing out possible responses to this challenge, by embodying this anxiety in varying ways.

The Progressive Era's response to this challenge was contradictory. On one hand, the period saw the ascendance of racialist theories, which asserted the superiority of certain races and the inferiority of others, while arguing for the maintenance of racial purity. This response was segregationist and Anglo-supremacist but also potentially multicultural since it encouraged the preservation of ethnic and cultural difference in each of America's "races."[3] On the other hand, this era saw the ascendance of the ideology of the melting pot, which implicitly assumed racial blending—that is, intermarriages which would "melt" ethnicity out of individuals, leaving behind only the pure essence of the American. This response was egalitarian but also, in a sense, monocultural since it sought to eliminate rather than tolerate difference. Though the distinctions between racialism and the melting pot seem clear, both paradigms thrived together at the same time and the same place, sustained in a dialectic founded on the same interests and anxieties, the same drive to establish purity, and the same assumption that race lay at the heart of culture and was therefore the key to America's future.

To talk about ethnicity in Progressive Era America, then, was to talk about race. To talk about the future of America was to talk about the confluence of race and sexuality. In this chapter I examine this discourse through a variety of roughly contemporaneous plays and performances to show that when stage Jews performed themselves in this era, they often invoked these issues, even while continuing to display characteristics of the major Jewish-American performances of past generations, including lecherous sheenies, haughty Jewesses, jolly good fellows, and luckless comedians.

Racialism, from Clyde Fitch to Vaudeville

In the opening chapter of Edith Wharton's novel *The House of Mirth* (1905), the Jew, Sim Rosedale, appears as an omen of things to come. Lily Bart, the novel's protagonist, encounters him on Madison Avenue after she has had a tête-à-tête with the eligible bachelor Lawrence Selden—a meeting which Lily would prefer remain discreet. From the moment of her chance encounter with this "plump, rosy man of the blond Jewish type," Lily's existence begins to undergo a precipitous social and economic decline from fixture of the upper-class social scene to struggling shopgirl and desperate drug addict. Later in the novel, when faced with Rosedale's advances, she resists his offer of marriage, despite the fact that such a union would restore her economic standing, even while it would raise the racial standing of the upwardly mobile Rosedale's own progeny. If Lily systematically plunges down the social ladder over the course of the novel, she nevertheless honorably resists submitting her pedigreed bloodline to a parallel decline.

I start with *Mirth* here because it is a widely read work which, it seems to me, demonstrates the racialist politics of its day—a novel that plays out the anxieties of a class that perceives itself in decline and sees itself threatened from without by social and economic forces represented by "foreign" parvenus like Rosedale. In fairness to Wharton, the novel does paint a complex picture of Lily's world, documenting how a corrosion of values from within ultimately renders her social class worthless and hollow; in contrast to the blatant hypocrisy of many of Lily's high society soul mates, Rosedale's blunt candor is refreshing and serves to partially redeem the reader's impression of the Jew. Rosedale's qualified redemption, however, does not alter the fact that Lily contemplates the possibility of sexual union with the Jew with evident disgust: "There were certain things not good to think of, certain midnight images that must at any cost be exorcised—and one of these was the image of herself as Rosedale's wife." Lily's fall from grace then, exposes her to the prospects of ethnic mixing, even if the novel opts for the segregationist solution of having her reject such a union and perish alone in poverty and purity, her Old World sensibility intact, her Old World bloodline untarnished.[4]

Mirth also has its connections to the stage. A best-seller, the novel was quickly converted into a play that made it to Broadway within a year of its release, in an adaptation penned by one of the most accomplished and successful American playwrights of the day, Clyde Fitch (1865–1909). In addition to his dramaturgical expertise and a long string of successes, Fitch was a logical choice for handling the adaptation, as he not only shared Wharton's upper-class background and perspective but also had experimented with Jewish characters. Fitch's first major success, *Beau Brummel* (1890), describes a similar arc to the one Wharton developed fifteen years later in her novel. The play tells the story of an eighteenth-century upper-class English dandy who, having lived beyond his means, experiences a precipitous decline toward shabbiness and untimely death, though he neither loses his instinctive honor nor sells himself out in the descent. Like *Mirth*, the play also features a Jew in its opening scene, in the person of the moneylender Abrahams who aggressively demands repayment from Brummel on his IOUs. Unlike Rosedale, however, Abrahams does not reappear. His brief stage moment serves merely as a similar omen; he is the threatening messenger, an embodiment of the economic forces of the future who foreshadows the decline that the Old World Brummel is about to undergo.[5]

As represented by these works, Wharton and Fitch are part of this same network of anxiety about the eroding power of a once dominant class; they are two artists among many whose works play out the politics of perceived social and economic decline. In the Progressive Era, however, as in these plays, social decline implicated the possibility of racial decline, and vice versa; the two went hand in hand. Though it was an era which saw important social reforms as correctives to the excesses of the Gilded Age, it was also an era when the imagination of the arts and sciences fixated itself on the idea of race.

What has been called racialist or eugenicist sociology gradually rose to prominence in America during the first decades of the twentieth century, with the widespread application of Darwin to a variety of social issues and the appearance of such influential tracts as Prescott F. Hall's *Immigration and Its Effects Upon the United States* (1906), Alfred P. Schultz's *Race or Mongrel* (1908), and Madison Grant's *The Passing of the Great Race* (1916). Rooted in the nineteenth century's increasing interest in race as a defining way of understanding nature and civilization, these works traced an increasingly vociferous argument for racial regulation and separation. Hall, for example, advocated applying Darwin's theory of natural selection to human breeding, noting that "we have here in the United States a unique opportunity to try the effect of hybridizing race-stocks upon an enormous scale."[6] Schultz, in contrast, argued that such hybridization portends the downfall of the nation: "One cause only is sufficiently powerful to cause the decay of a nation. This cause is promiscuousness. A nation is decayed that consists of degenerates when it no longer constitutes a distinct race. A degenerated race is one that has no longer the same internal worth which it had of old, for the reason that incessant infusions of foreign blood have diluted and weakened the old blood."[7] Schultz supported this polemic on the undesirability of mongrels with the examples of great historical civilizations that he contended, went into decline through decadent crossbreeding. A decade later, Grant followed Schultz's racialism with similar bio-historical arguments, all grounded in the thesis that "race lies to-day at the base of all the phenomena of modern society."[8] By the time of H. Fairchild's *The Melting-pot Mistake* (1926), eugenicists were likening race mixture to "a pound from which no dog was ever rescued, and which all the dogs were free to interbreed at will."[9] Mongrelization had thus become both cause and symptom of a nation's decline.

It is not my purpose here to detail racialism and its attendant direct and indirect cultural manifestations, including martialism, neo-medievalism, and the anti-modern ethic in general, all of which emerged in an era in other ways characterized by increasingly progressive politics.[10] The social policy implications of such thinking, however, remain relevant. Racialists tended to advocate prohibiting or severely restricting immigration from Eastern and Southern European countries and segregating those groups who had already arrived in order to prevent further inbreeding that would further cause the decay of the nation. Some, like Schultz, added the additional caveat that "people that are now in the United States [should] not become 'Americanized' too quickly. Children of foreign parentage should know their mother tongue as well as English. Losing it, they become inferior to their ancestors."[11] In most cases, the racialists argued that culture was the direct outgrowth of biology, and consequently, that in the breeding of peoples lay the story of all human civilization.

This thinking had a variety of implications for American views on Jewish immigration, as Robert Singerman and others have already made clear. The notion that Jewish men were morally debased or effeminate had already been circulating for centuries. Progressive Era racialism, however, coalesced these traditions into the notion that Jews, as a race, were biologically weak and degenerate. The objective fact that Jews tended to be slighter of stature than individuals of Northern European descent prompted these generalizations. However, in their incessant quest to link biology and history, the racialists readily conflated Jewish physical characteristics with moral and social attributes. In 1903, Robert Mitchell, in taking note of the "physical degeneration" of Jews, for example, included poverty as symptom of this physical inferiority: "In a great measure the poverty to be found in the 'Ghetto' is due to disease or lack of physical strength. Jewish immigrants of a military age who could pass army requirements are relatively rare." He went on to specify the "moral deterioration" which accompanies the Ghetto Jew's physical deficiencies.[12] In a similar vein, Grant managed to conflate in the same sentence the Polish Jew's "dwarf stature, peculiar mentality, and ruthless concentration on self-interest," seeing these interrelated qualities as threatening the nation.[13]

Again, this decay that the Jews threatened was nothing new; nineteenth-century European anti-Semitism, as Sander Gilman has made clear, regularly linked Jews to decadent cosmopolitanism and emotional illness.[14] The new century, however, brought into focus the physical (that is, racial) manifestations of this decadence, as if the external vitality of individual bodies clearly signaled internal strength. In America, after all, this was an age in which the Victorian ideal of the cultivated, sedentary male was repudiated in favor of the robust athleticism of a Teddy Roosevelt.[15]

The peculiar contradictions of racialism's views of the Jews became evident in the way these men who claimed authority as scientists confronted and elided a variety of statistics which challenged their assumptions of Jewish weakness. First, most of the racialists accepted the notion that Jews demonstrated unusual cerebral facilities, as borne out by the sort of intelligence testing and anecdotal observation upon which these writers thrived. If a race's physical stature directly implicated its mental abilities, how then to explain the case of the Jews, where, by the standards of these scientists, the former seemed so clearly inferior and the latter, so clearly superior? It was a contradiction the racialists acknowledged and dismissed. Mitchell, for example, simply observed that "the mental standard of the Jewish immigration fails to offset the physical inferiority when brought into active competition with other elements of our cosmopolitan population."[16] Such a dismissal seemed consistent for the racialists since, when it came to biological evolution, physical characteristics superseded intellectual ones. Besides, intellect was not to be equated with righteousness; the Jews' apparent mental acumen did not obviate the race's perceived moral degeneracy.

More troubling to the racialists was the fact, strongly supported by statistics, that Jews tended to live longer than gentiles of similar backgrounds. If longevity was a sign of vigor—in fact, the clearest temporal marker of a species' survival—how could a race so physically weak produce individuals who endured so long? Such statistics challenged the era's notions of what sorts of bodies represented strength and weakness. In the face of these disturbing facts, a eugenicist like Paul Popenoe reapplied Darwin to create a paradigm to suit his assumptions: "In a community of rascals, the greatest rascal might be the fittest to survive. In the slums of a modern city the Jewish type, stringently selected through centuries of ghetto life, is particularly fit to survive, although it may not be the physical ideal of an anthropologist."[17] The explanation succeeded in its time, for its purpose, for its audience. Social scientists today, with different purposes and different audiences, have largely repudiated the racialist view; they account for Jewish immigrants' longevity by citing cultural factors, including health, hygiene, and child-rearing practices.

The racialist response to Jewish immigration was not uniformly anti-Semitic. For some, the seeming anomalies above emphasized not only the superiority of the Jewish race but the validity of racialist principles as well. Schultz insisted, for example, that the Jews had succeeded precisely because, through their traditional aversion to intermarriage, they had demonstrated the importance of racial purity and preservation, thereby proving that "the blood that courses in the veins of the individual is more sacred than gold, silver, territory, flag and country."[18] A 1913 study praised the Jews for having kept themselves "a distinct and distinguished Asiatic race."[19] Moreover, many Jews themselves, especially in Europe, if they did not exactly share the racialists' assumptions, applied their biology to matters of culture. Max Nordau, for example, called for a physically fit "muscle Jew" to supplant the excessively cerebral ghetto Jew of European tradition, and many of the leaders of the Zionist movement trumpeted the emergence of a new physically vital, sexually healthy Jewish culture which would be neither debased nor degenerate.[20]

Whether anti- or philo-Semitic, the racialist response generally condemned the mixing of Jewish and gentile blood. For the most part, the racialists tended to view Jewish blood as unwholesome and debilitating, postulating that ethnic mixing would only serve to weaken or dilute what was perceived as the American master race. The Jews constituted a particular threat because, according to writers like Grant, "the cross between any of the three European races and a Jew is a Jew."[21] The Jews, in this view, were the ultimate mongrels who reduced all races with whom they mixed to the status of mutt. Even for those like Schultz who viewed the Jews as quintessential purebreds, the very strength of the Jewish bloodline implied its inherent ability to overwhelm any ancestry with which it mixed, and hence, its danger.

The racialist response, with its obsession with blood, tended to equalize the Jew and Jewess. In nineteenth-century thinking, after all, these two figures had been positioned by gentiles in distinctive ways: he was the preying animal and she the exotic prey. In the age of biological strength and weakness however, it became clear that since the same blood coursed through the veins of both female and male, sexual union with her threatened racial purity as clearly as did the attacks of the lecherous Jew. In fact, precisely because she was a figure of temptation, the Jewess potentially posed a greater threat than her male counterpart who, if lascivious, at least repeatedly proved ineffectual in his lust. Mere conversion could not diminish the threat she posed to the strength of the bloodline of the dominant American race.

Though Fitch was a member of this race, he was far from a strapping specimen of robust, Rooseveltian masculinity. Sickly health curtailed much of his writing for the last decade of his life and resulted in an untimely death, when he was still near the peak of his power. More to the point, in dress and demeanor, Fitch's performance of himself was a self-conscious affront to such a Progressive Era masculine ideal. This eternally "eligible bachelor" (as journalists sometimes called him) and dandy flaunted his effeminate behavior and resembled, in the view of at least one reporter, his own renowned fop, Beau Brummel.[22] Fitch's perceived defects in masculinity led some critics to take backhanded snipes at his work; one evaluation written shortly after the playwright's death praised Fitch for his female characters but lamented: "It is difficult to recall a single male character who is not either commonplace or defective in manly qualities."[23] Fitch, it seems, was not a manly enough writer for the standards of his age, which preferred rugged literary figures like Stephen Crane, Jack London, and Frank Norris, even if all three of these authors, in another example of life disproving paradigms of vigor, passed away even more prematurely than did Fitch.

However degenerate a male figure Fitch may have represented in Progressive Era America, where the counter model of Oscar Wilde enjoyed little currency even in the theater community, the playwright nevertheless partook indirectly of the racialism of the time. His outlook may have partially been connected to his background; he haled from an old Connecticut family, attended Amherst College, and abandoned a genteel law practice early in his career in order to try his hand at playwriting. More importantly, Fitch's notions of the Jewish presence in America, as reflected in characters in his plays from *Brummel* to *Mirth*, typify the attitudes of his social class. However, in the Jewish performances he creates, Fitch supersedes many of his peers. Wharton's invidious Rosedale, for example, at least possesses the saving grace of candor, which makes him a refreshing, if still repugnant, part of *Mirth*. In Fitch's adaptation of the novel however, Rosedale loses many of his redeeming qualities; he becomes an aggressive blackmailer, a "pushy" and "fatuous" little man who "brutally" presses his sexual advances against Lily, lunging forward at one point to squeeze her waist, a gesture he never attempts in the pages of the book, where he comes across in contrast as a more restrained and diplomatic manipulator.

The irony of Fitch's *Mirth* is that in fleshing Rosedale out with many of the attributes of the stage sheeny, he created perhaps the script's most playable character. A number of reviewers called Albert Bruening's performance in the role the only memorable aspect of a play filled with "hopeless, brainless, inconsequential figures."[24] The production itself flopped. While Wharton's novel had formulaic elements that echoed the continental well-made play, its subtle gradations of character and incident did not suit the tightly constructed society dramas for which Fitch was famous. Fitch had trouble, therefore, finding the sorts of stage bodies with which to make intricate, oblique characters like Lily and Selden compelling on the commercial stage. In the case of Rosedale, however, both Fitch and his audience had the long tradition of the stage sheeny to draw upon for ready reference. Thus even a naturalized, modified embodiment of the sheeny found a way to invoke these codes and perform itself with clarity.

Fitch's most significant stage Jew was no secondhand borrowing from an established novelist, but rather, his own creation: Louis Klauffsky in *The Woman in the Case* (1905), one of the biggest hits of the playwright's career, which ran for four months on Broadway and enjoyed a successful national tour. *Woman* is mostly a conventional drama which transplants the formulas of traditional melodrama into a "realistic" New York high-society setting. Dapper young society gent Julian Rolfe finds himself unjustly jailed for the murder of his friend, Phillip Long. Julian's bride, Margaret, played in the original production by Blanche Walsh, goes to extraordinary lengths to prove the innocence of the man she has just married. Though a cultivated lady of high social standing, Margaret decides to pose as a vulgar, working-class girl in order to extract the truth from Claire Forster, the tawdry young woman whose lies have framed Julian for the murder.[25]

The play's third act, which made the production a sensation, is set in Margaret's Fifty-second Street flat, where for two months she has been posing as a "Mrs. Darcy" and securing the confidence of Claire, who lives next door. Julian's case goes to trial the next day, making Margaret desperate to pry the truth from Claire before the night is over. The actual focus of the scene's interest, however, lies in the titillating spectacle of Margaret, this refined figure of upper-class womanhood, acting like and consorting with a gaudy floozy in order to achieve her aims. The tacky furnishings of Margaret's flat emphasize her "acquired vulgarity," as the script puts it; its brass chandelier, imitation palms, popular sheet music, and multi-colored sporting pennants accentuate how effectively Margaret has staged her own drop in social status, a decline as degrading as Lily Bart's, if less scandalous only because the audience knows it is but the deftly executed performance of an incorruptible society lady.

The tacky setting, it turns out, comes outfitted with a tacky Jew, Klauffsky, who symbolizes this decline just as surely as Abrahams and Rosedale signal Beau Brummel's and Lily Bart's respective plummets to tawdriness. Klauffsky is Claire's "gentleman friend," and the couple show up at Margaret's apartment after a night out on the town. A cheerful fellow who speaks with a slight accent, Klauffsky regularly breaks out singing loudly and vulgarly, in imitation, for example, of the over-sized actress Marie Dressler:

> A great big girl like very truly yours,
> Is a very pretty sight to see.
> They always make a pet
> Of a stingy faced soubrette
> Nit a great big girl like me.

Klauffsky caps off this song by dancing "in a ridiculous fashion with his hands over his head in imitation of a ballet girl," thus underscoring the way he performs himself as a feminized jolly good fellow.[26]

In addition to acting the mock-effeminate, Klauffsky also presents himself as a possessive lecher, who follows "every movement" of the supple young Claire with his eyes and deports himself "as though he were the owner of the house." As he gets progressively more inebriated during the course of the scene, though, his possessiveness extends beyond Claire to Margaret, whom he repeatedly attempts to kiss and grope. When Margaret tactfully finds ways to rebuff him, Klauffsky returns his attentions to Claire, whom he salutes in a final toast before exiting: "To the beautiful and sweet-tempered little girl beside me—who eats up a lot o' money but who's cheap at the price." The toast sums up all the attributes of the stage Jew whom Klauffsky embodies: gaudy spendthrift, tightfisted cheapskate, and lascivious preyer upon gentile flesh, for whom sex and money are inseparable, based as they are upon the same acquisitive spirit.

However, while earlier stage Jews maintained their primary relationship to money, Fitch's Klauffsky, in contrast, has a primary relationship to sex. Much of his stage time involves the way he lusts after the two gentile women who are clearly younger and more attractive than he. Money, rather than an end in itself, is the means by which the Jew manages a sexual relationship with a gentile. Whereas earlier stage Jews floundered comically when lusting after such a liaison, Klauffsky succeeds marvelously in purchasing ownership of Claire, although she may be no more than cheap gentile merchandise, the whore to his john.

The scene indirectly reflects many of the racialist anxieties of the day. Margaret, the upper-class gentile woman, finds herself stuck in this horror shop of degradation where she has fallen so low in social environment that she ends up getting pawed at by a Jew. In this vulgar arena where people act like animals, it seems that only the basest elements will survive. However, by descending to these animals' level and playing their games, Margaret ultimately proves to be the fittest, since, at the scene's end, she extracts a drunken confession from Claire and vindicates her husband, although the process of doing so leaves her bedridden and emotionally exhausted at the end of the play. Having won the day by teetering on the brink of disgrace within touch of the Jew's corrupting sexuality, Margaret is able return to her proper environment where, with Julian's help, she will regain her strength. Degradation has been avoided and the future seems to be assured, as the curtain comes down on what one critic called "one of those strong virile plays," high praise in an era when strength and virility were cardinal virtues in all forms of cultural expression.[27]

If *Woman* obliquely manifests racialism, *Husband* (1910), which features a Jewess named Rebecca Levine, amounts to a self-conscious tract on the topic. Though I can find no evidence of the play ever having received a major New York production, the piece nevertheless possesses both cultural and theatrical significance. Not only was the play published by a major house like Houghton Mifflin, but its author, John Corbin (no relation to Manhattan Beach's Austin Corbin), served three different tenures as chief drama critic for the *New York Times* between 1902 and 1924, before becoming a leading editorialist for that same publication. In the 1930s he became infamous for a *Scribner's* piece that lambasted the Jewish influence on theater. One does not have to read *Husband* in the light of this later evidence of Corbin's anti-Semitism, however, to see the way it promotes racialism.

Set in New York, *Husband* dramatizes the story of Tony Wayne, a high-minded, idealistic lawyer of old Anglo stock, who labors under the thumb of his domineering wife, Clora. Under the influence of Rebecca, a legal aid worker, Tony has involved himself in left-leaning political causes that have brought him into conflict with his upper-class circle of friends, who nostalgically long for the good old pre-muckraking days of the Gilded Age. Meanwhile, Tony and Clora's marriage starts to fall apart: he gets immersed in running for municipal office, and she becomes involved with a European aristocrat. After a fierce rupture, the Waynes reunite with a newly pledged passion. At the curtain, Tony wins the election but vows never to neglect Clora again.

In the published introduction to *Husband*, Corbin makes clear his ideological purpose in relating this fable. He condemns the "mannish activity" of the New Woman, pointing out the pitfalls that plague her aspirations to equality with men. Biology, Corbin asserts, makes such equality impossible. Invoking the rhetoric of Darwin, he underscores how women have been specialized for motherhood. Influential playwrights like Ibsen have deceived themselves into forgetting this fact, he argues; as a result, the world today has become filled with absurd "outdated Noras" who dedicate themselves to the work to which they are by nature least suited.

Here is where racialism comes in. Cut off from "their ancient productivity," modernized English, American, French, and German women have contributed to a profound decline in the quality and quantity of Western European biological stock. We cannot, he states, "recruit the future mainly from the lower ranges of our life—the ill-begotten, uneducated, ill-bred children of diseased or embruted parents." He stresses that women of Western European descent need to return to procreative fecundity in order once again to create "human thoroughbred[s]" like Ben Franklin, one of seventeen children.[28]

In the context of this introduction, the sexual politics of *Husband* come into sharper focus. The socialist activist Jewess Rebecca embodies, on one hand, the New Woman gone astray, usurping the role of the man as she aggressively "scolds" Tony into his political positions. At the same time, this "lithe, feline" creature, with jet black hair and "dark, red and amber" cheeks, radiates the vital life force of somebody sure of herself—a vitality reflected in the fact that she has mothered a love child with one of her radical comrades.

The Waynes, in contrast, embody the anxieties of the master American race contemplating its own decline; Tony is the domesticated, passionless husband, while Clora is the domineering, independent wife who no longer supports her husband's interests. Emblematic of their race's decline, the Waynes have been unable to produce any children. In the climactic argument which leads to their final reconciliation, Tony laments to Clora that "once there were women in this land—the wives of strong men, and the mothers. The sons they bore tamed the wilderness, framed the laws of a great nation. In you and the millions like you to-day their spirit is dead. The race of Americans has vanished!" In contrast, women like the "prolific Levine . . . are our conquerors." This stinging rebuke leads Clora to acknowledge, "a woman is—a woman. I never knew one of us but deep down in her heart she was mortally ashamed to be childless." Reunited in the end as husband and wife, they wake up to the "reality of things" and, at curtain, take each other "forcibly" into an embrace, the implication being that their newfound passion will plant the seeds of another great race of Americans. *Husband* thus posits the rejuvenation of the American bloodline, in response to the anxiety that, in their fecundity, recently arrived immigrant groups were numerically threatening to supersede "native" Americans.[29]

The Jewess appears as a symptom of this anxiety. Though not the object of Tony's affections, Rebecca diverts his passions and thereby subtracts the sexual energy that this patrician should be investing in his own race's survival; she and the teeming, feminine world of "dark alleys and filthy holes" from which she comes represent a malicious power that distracts Tony from the responsibilities he owes his race, class, and gender. By preventing the gentile man from performing his proper role of husband, the

Progressive Era Jewess here distinguishes herself from the exotic belle juive of the romantic stage, whose grandeur represented the liberating force of romantic love. This Jewess offers not salvation but degradation. As a direct source of fecundity who readily bears love children, she represents the most direct threat to the future of America. Fortunately, in the end, Tony finds a way to reinvigorate his seed without betraying the progressive politics for which both he and the Jewess stand.

If racialist attitudes characterized some legitimate drama, they also found their way into vaudeville which, in its open-ended diversity, had room for all points of view. Typically, these concerns were played out in sketch comedy through a scheming Jewish man who attempted to marry a wealthy gentile widow. William A. Quick's *Cohen's Courtship* (1907), for example, has a "stout Hebrew" showing up at the residence of a Mrs. Elliott, whom he takes to be a wealthy lady. The sketch features the Jew's aggressive sexual pursuit, in which he takes the widow's hand, squeezes her waist, and like Klauffsky before him, dances wildly and eccentrically when he feels he is close to cornering his prey. When, in the end, he discovers that her wealth lies entirely in trading stamps, he "staggers and drops to the floor in a faint."[30]

Kinder and gentler is Junie McCree's *Hebrewing and Shewooing* (1909), which features the "professional bridegroom" Isidore Zizzlebaum's pursuit of a widow named Mrs. Anna Himmelspeck ("Divine Bacon," hence forbidden fruit). As in many of these pieces, the humor comes as much at the expense of the widow as of the Jew, the implication being that any gentile who would subject herself to a sexual liaison with a Jew must be either stupid, desperate, or ugly. In any case, from the start, the sketch presents intermarriage as a ridiculous proposition. It opens with Mrs. Himmelspeck reading a letter from a suitor:

> Dear Madame: If you and I married and had children and they grew up and found out that we were their parents, they would laugh themselves to death.
>
> Yours, Solomon Gladt[31]

This sheeny speaks here on behalf of the racialists, for whom the progeny of Jew and gentile embodied a ludicrous vision of America's future.

The Melting Pot, from Israel Zangwill to Tin Pan Alley

If racialism found itself reflected in and perpetuated by plays and performances, it was a play itself, ironically by an Anglo-Jewish author, that popularized and disseminated the American melting-pot ideal. Israel Zangwill's *The Melting-pot* (1909) became one of the hits of the New York season and most talked about plays of its generation. If the concept of the melting pot, discredited as it may be, remains an influential metaphor for American acculturation, then one can posit Zangwill's play as one of the most influential events in the history of Broadway.

The origin of the term "melting pot" itself has been the subject of much recent scholarly interest. Most writers agree that Zangwill neither coined the term nor created the concept. Arthur Mann has noted, for example, that the ideal has roots as far back as the eighteenth century, and that Emerson later invokes a similar ideal when he envisions a "new race" of diverse peoples who will eventually make up America. Similar ideas, Mann suggests, can be traced through the historiography of Frederick Jackson Turner and the politics of Teddy Roosevelt.[32] Werner Sollors has argued that the notion of "consent," implicit in most melting-pot paradigms, has been a fundamental aspect of the American cultural tradition, though it has always hovered in dialectical antithesis to the race-based, tradition-centered notion of "descent," which values the importance of ancestry over an individual's freedom to alter her own identity.[33] Still, deep as the concept may course, nobody disputes that Zangwill made the melting pot a household term by both dramatizing a nation's anxiety and positing a paradigm that seemed to resolve it. Almost a century later, the anxiety remains, and so does the term, empowered by the very fact that it remains the paradigm that many still labor to reject.

In 1909, Zangwill (1864–1926) was already a well-known figure to many Americans. Born in London to poverty-stricken Eastern European parents, he had published a number of widely read books and produced one major play in New York, *Children of the Ghetto* (1899), based upon his series of prose vignettes by the same name. (It starred Wilton Lackaye, who had recently triumphed as Svengali.)[34] He was seen as an unconventional literary figure and political activist who held a strong disgust for traditional religion and bourgeois institutions, as represented by his widely publicized marriage in 1903 to the Christian feminist activist Edith Ayrton. It is instructive that at least one critic, when reviewing the very conventional *Auctioneer* in 1901, specifically contrasted this play's rosy view of the immigrant world with what he saw as Zangwill's distasteful, rabble-rousing work.[35]

More than any of the other personalities I have examined here, then, Zangwill associated himself with the politically engaged fringe of the progressive reform tradition. To those familiar with the era, it will not be surprising that Zangwill was a vociferous advocate of the realistic problem plays of Ibsen and Shaw which, in the first decade of the century, had cast but a tiny shadow on the English-language theater in America, despite the fact that artists like Belasco and Fitch imported aspects of this style into commercial Broadway.[36] As a playwright then, Zangwill aligned himself more with Shavian continentalism than Broadway commercialism. It seems likely as well that, in fashioning *The Melting-pot*, Zangwill was influenced by Heijermans's groundbreaking but little noticed *Ghetto*, which had briefly played New York in a weak adaptation a month before Zangwill's more lauded *Children of the Ghetto*.[37]

In spite of Zangwill's pretenses to the new realism, *The Melting-pot* nevertheless goes a long way to recommend itself as turgid melodrama. Set in New York, the play focuses on the romance between David Quixano, a talented young Jewish composer, and Vera Revendal, a high-minded gentile settlement worker of Russian extraction. Mendel Quixano, David's devoted uncle and guardian, cannot abide his nephew's interest in a gentile woman and bitterly turns him out of the house, shouting, "Go out and marry your Gentile and be happy. . . . Go! You have cast off the God of our fathers!" Distanced from his family, David discovers that Vera's father, the Baron Revendal, played a key role in the Russian massacre of Jews at "Kishineff" [sic], at which both David's mother and sister lost their lives. The Baron pleads forgiveness from his daughter, and offering David his pistol, asks his potential son-in-law to kill him. Unable to reconcile himself to a union with a woman whose ancestors have so oppressed his own people, David goes back to live with his uncle, thinking that the "river of blood" which separates him from Vera can never be traversed, not even in America. At a Fourth of July concert though, David's symphony, inspired in the ideals of the new races of the new world, makes a glorious debut. After the concert, in a settlement house's rooftop garden, Vera begs David's forgiveness for her race's sins against his. David, in turn, begs forgiveness for having prejudged her for the sins of her fathers. At the play's end, as the sun sets over the expansive city, David and Vera reconcile, kissing "three times on the mouth as in ritual solemnity," the way Russians kiss at Easter.[38]

The theme of ethnic blending presents itself throughout *The Melting-pot* in a variety of ways. The Quixanos, for example, live in a modest Staten Island home that the stage directions describe as a "curious blend of shabbiness, Americanism, Jewishness, and music." Through a variety of characters who embody this curious blend, the play expands upon this idea. There is Kathleen, the dimwitted but big-hearted servant of the classic stage Irish type, who at one point puts on a false nose and dances joyfully around in a Purim skit; by the end of the play, she has even mastered long snatches of pseudo-Yiddish. Paralleling Kathleen's case is the example of Herr Pappelmeister, an expansive, jolly orchestra leader of a classic stage German type who is learning to adapt himself to American musical and business practice. Both Kathleen and Pappelmeister assume their blended cultural identities through performance: Kathleen by doing Jewish folk dances and Pappelmeister by conducting American music. Performance both symbolizes and embodies the very process of acculturation.[39]

The Melting-pot's thematic concern with ethnic blending is brought didactically to the surface in the play's final moments, when David and Vera reconcile in the rooftop garden. Zangwill places some of his most powerful rhetoric in the mouth of his Jewish protagonist, who has just kissed Vera beneath the "burning flames" of the sky:

> *David:* It is the fire of God round His Crucible. (He drops her hand and points downward.) There she lies, the great Melting-pot—listen! Can't you hear the roaring and the bubbling? There gapes her mouth (He points east)—the harbour where a thousand mammoth feeders come from the ends of the world to pour in their human freight. Ah, what a stirring and a seething! Celt and Latin, Slav and Teutonic, Greek and Syrian—black and yellow—
> *Vera:* (Softly, nestling to him) Jew and Gentile—
> *David*: Yes, East and West, and North and South, the palm and the pine, the pole and the equator, the crescent and the cross—how the great Alchemist melts and fuses them with his purging flame! Here shall they all unite to build the Republic of Man and the Kingdom of God. Ah, Vera, what is the glory of Rome and Jerusalem where all nations and races come to worship and look back, compared with the glory of America, where all races and nations come to labour and look forward. (He raises his hands in benediction over the shining city.) Peace, peace, to all ye unborn millions, fated to fill this giant continent—the God of our *children* give you peace.

As twilight falls over the city, and the musicians and vocalists in the settlement below join in "My Country, 'Tis of Thee," the curtain comes down. Heavy-handed yet moving, the finish remains almost too powerful for the stage; it is a final flourish almost cinematic in conception. If Zangwill fails at Shavian social realism, he succeeds at Hollywood myth-making. In the final analysis, he may be closer to Frank Capra than Henrik Ibsen.[40]

In its own way, *The Melting-pot* seethes with self-conscious racial politics as much as does Corbin's *Husband*. After all, as Mann has pointed out, the play is centered around the racial implications of the union between David and Vera. When David speaks to Vera of the "our children," he is referring figuratively to the coming generation but also specifically to the children which his sexual union with Vera will produce. Zangwill infuses the play, too, with racial rhetoric: the lovers readily refer to the "river of blood" and "call of our blood" which separates them. Only something as powerful and disruptive as a fiery crucible, the play makes clear, can meld these separate bloodlines into one race. Zangwill then, like his racialist peers, construes culture in terms of race, though his vision for America's future is not degeneration through mongrelization but celebration through mixing.[41]

This message, along with many elements of *The Melting-pot*'s paradigm in general, became distorted when appropriated and performed in other venues. As Sollors has documented, by 1916 the Ford Motor Company English School was staging ritualistic rebirths for its immigrant workers, in a ceremony which enacted the melting out of ethnic difference. Though this Americanization-through-deculturation may always have been implicit in the very metaphor of the melting pot (the alchemical roots of which suggest the conversion of worthless material into something valuable), when appropriated across a generation, the melting pot came to be seen as a process by which immigrants would lose their differences as they conformed to a higher, more valorized standard of "American-ness." As Mann has deftly suggested, it is an ideology which speaks to the same anxiety over foreign presence in America as does racialism and posits a parallel strategy for neutralizing the threat of difference posed by Eastern and Southern European immigrants. Both racialism and the melting pot then, devised paradigms for preserving American purity, one by separating out impurities, the other by melting them away.[42]

Zangwill's play, however, presents a melting-pot metaphor more radically de-centered than the concept of the effacement of difference which the melting-pot idea came to encompass. First, his play makes clear that the process, as implicit in the notion of a crucible, is difficult and painful, involving violent confrontations between generations and erecting painful though ultimately surpassable boundaries between lovers. Ultimately, this mixing is preferable only because that "nightmare of religion and races" in conflict through the European centuries looms as a bloodier alternative. No happy naturalization ceremony for foreign workers is part of Zangwill's plan. Moreover, as a critic for the *Times* pointed out in a disparaging review, the only "native" American in Zangwill's play, Quincy Davenport, proves to be an unctuous, spoiled snob.[43] The union the playwright dramatizes is not between Jewish and gentile American, but rather, between two recently arrived immigrants. The play thus resists presenting a new ideal body or solid center of America. Rather, it offers only the dynamic metaphor of process, as represented by the melting pot, performed through an encounter between a Russian Jew and a Russian Christian, who are not to be servants of an American ideal but the creators of it.[44]

I do not want to overstate my case here. Certainly, *The Melting-pot* does not de-center American identity to the point where it expects Mendel Quixano to adopt the brogues of his servant, or Pappelmeister's orchestras to prefer German music, or David's adoring public to start learning Yiddish. In fact, it seems naive for Zangwill to imagine an America not dominated by a hegemonic center, to assume such a blatant absence of power. The metaphor itself elides the issue of who owns the pot itself, of whose hand is guiding this American alchemy. The melting pot, after all, is not a verb: it is a noun to be possessed, a site to be occupied, a place to be controlled. Zangwill does not pose the question of who will have the power to effect this possession.

Almost immediately, *The Melting-pot* stirred controversy. Aware of Zangwill as one who had apparently strayed from the faith, some Jews were particularly offended by its endorsement of intermarriage as both romantic and sociological ideal. The Jewish press perceived the problematics of such a sanguine view of assimilation in America. "It is all the worse for you and me, brother," wrote the *American Hebrew*, "who are to be cast into and dissolved in the crucible." The Jewish writer Horace Kallen preferred a different metaphor for America: an orchestra, with each ethnic group (instrument) playing in its own separate tonality, collectively resulting in a harmonious whole.[45] The *Times*, in two separate reviews that appeared the week the play opened, rejected the play as "cheap and tawdry," dismissing it as the work of a "neurotic sentimentalist." Some of the criticism was well-founded: the play, indeed, was "awkward in structure, clumsy in workmanship," and included many "forced and false" elements, such as German accents on the tongues of the Russian characters.[46] But the vociferousness of some of the criticism suggests that the play had struck an uncomfortable chord by explicitly advocating racial union in an age of rising racialism.

The Melting-pot was not soundly rejected by all who saw it. It quickly became a commercial success. The progressive reform community embraced the play. Roosevelt himself, to whom Zangwill dedicated the play, praised it. Jane Addams went on record in support of it.[47] For all the dangerous territory it explored, *The Melting-pot* managed to succeed and perpetuate itself as a model. Sollors credits Zangwill with shaping the debate over American immigration for subsequent generations by naturalizing the ideology of "consent" as romantic, sacred, and eternal while downplaying "descent" as temporal, hard, and unfeeling, thus opening up "an immensely pliable middle ground between ethnic believers in the immutability of descent, radical cultural critics, and American critics of immigration."[48] Both these polarized groups, strange bedfellows in their opposition to racial mixing, now found themselves in the minority in the face of this new centrist paradigm to which many immigrants and Anglo-Americans now felt they could more readily subscribe. Much of twentieth-century America has since situated itself in this middle ground which Zangwill stakes out in his play.

The Melting-pot both reflected and gave new impetus to the theme of Jewish-gentile romance. The year 1909 saw at least three other major Broadway productions centering on issues of intermarriage: J. Hartley Manners's *The House Next Door* (a British import), Roy Horniman's *Idols*, and Thomas Addison's *Meyer and Son*. Plays in succeeding years also dealt with the theme, whether comically, such as in Charles Klein's *Maggie Pepper* (1911), in which a Jewish salesman proposes marriage to the title character, inviting her to "change over—it's easy. . . . Ain't that business?;" or more dramatically, as in Maurice Donnay's *Return from Jerusalem* (1912), a French import about an affair between a freethinking Zionist and her gentile lover.[49] Generally, these "melting-pot" plays performed intermarriage as a laudable development of progressive, open-minded society, as represented by the deft light comedy of Manners's play, in which an irascible anti-Semite eventually consents to his son's marriage to his Jewish next-door neighbor's daughter. The play, which was received as "wholesome," full of "tenderness and sentiment," easily elided the controversy which accompanied the more tendentious *Melting-pot*.[50]

If the melting pot became a persistent theme in legitimate Broadway, it also expressed itself forcefully in other genres. Starting in 1906 or so, for example, a wave of fascination with Jewish-American subject matter swept through the professional song-publishing industry. Edward B. Marks, veteran songwriter and publisher, attributed the start of the Jew-song craze to the impact of Irving Berlin's hit "Yiddle on Your Fiddle" (1909), but my research suggests that Marks may be overstating "Yiddle"'s importance due to its lasting popularity, linked to the international fame of its composer. In fact, I have come across an array of pop songs with Jewish themes, many dating from 1907 and earlier.[51]

Like the routines of the vaudeville Hebrews, these songs, though often written by Jews for largely immigrant audiences, contain much that we would find problematic if not downright offensive today. Many years later, when a revue of his old songs was in the works, Berlin wrote to Groucho Marx that "there are some songs I would be tempted to pay you not to do;" presumably, they could no longer be taken in the spirit in which they had been written.[52] It may also have been that, during that mid-century stretch characterized by the effacement or softening of ethnicity in popular performance, any such public reminder of his ethnic affiliation made this Jewish composer of "White Christmas" uncomfortable.

In any case, certain thematic concerns emerge repeatedly in these Tin Pan Alley lyrics. Most of the songs, in one way or another, dwell upon the incongruity of Jews in various situations: Jew as cowboy ("I'm a Yiddish Cowboy," "Yonkele the Cowboy Jew"); Jew in unusual geographical locations ("Moshe from Nova Scotia"); Jew as dapper hotshot ("Abie the Sporty Kid"); Jew as passionate lover ("Yiddisha Nightingale," "Rebecca," "Under the Matzos Tree"); Jewess as singer ("Yiddisha Nightingale").

Perhaps the most prominent recurring interest in these songs, however, is that of romance between Jews and gentiles. If these melting-pot songs revel in the incongruity of two profoundly different ethnic types in love with each other, they also express conflicted sentiment as to the nature of the sexual transactions these young American lovers are about to undergo. On one hand, such forays into the melting pot could meet with downright failure and ridicule, thereby suggesting that Jews were better off resisting racial mixing and sticking to their own kind. "Yonkele the Cowboy Jew" (1907), for example, leaves his family and pawnshop business to try his fortunes as an outlaw in the Wild West, where he meets a "pretty cowboy girl" who makes his "Yiddish brain" go wild. The cowgirl's beau proves tougher than the Jew, and with a few well-aimed shots from his pistol, chases Yonkele the tenderfoot out of town. "Marry a Yiddisha Boy" (1911) tells of Abie Rosenthal, who begs his beloved Sadie not to fool around with a gentile, warning her that she should "know what will the goy will do." In this song, too, the boyfriend beats up the Jew, but the results are also calamitous for the would-be couple, since the police wagon ends up carting off all parties involved.

"That's Yiddisha Love" (1910), the most negative depiction of the ramifications of ethnic mixing, follows the fate of young Morris, who elopes with an Irish girl named Maggie, in spite of his parents' warnings. The marriage fails: Maggie wears a wig, spends too much money, flirts with other men, and eventually runs away. Morris learns his parents' lesson well: marry a nice Jewish girl who has plain tastes and a willingness to help out with the business. Then,

> If she's honest and frank
> And has money in the bank
> Oi! Oi! that's Yiddisha love.

More commonly, however, these intermarriage songs perform more positive, if still humorous, possibilities for America's melting pot. "I'm a Yiddish Cowboy" (1908) deals with an affair between the newest of the new Americans, the Jew, with the oldest of the old Americans, the Native American, as if in the meeting and mating of these two grotesque extreme anomalies lay all the myriad possibilities of the nation (see Appendix Av). Levi marries the "blue blood Indian maiden" he loves and ends up receiving the blessing of her father, Big Chief "Cruller Legs," even if he does have trouble inhaling the good chief's peace pipe. "It's Tough When Izzy Rosenstein Loves Genevieve Malone" (1911) details the plight of two star-crossed lovers, while lamenting that "there's no Juliet in the Irish set / For Izzy." This is no mere novelty gag song, but rather, a sentimentalized account where youthful love is valorized at the expense of ancestral tradition. "Yiddisha Luck and Irisha Love" (1911) explores a similar situation more optimistically through the romance between Sadie Rosenbaum and Michael Kelly, even if the title suggests a pairing which brings out the worst in both worlds (see Appendix Av).

That is not to say that Tin Pan Alley did not also engage the old metaphor of performance as a symbol for cultural mixing in America. If Jewish-gentile love comes across as one prevailing theme in these songs, the other such primary concern is the position of Jewish men as performers, notably musicians and actors. "When Mose with His Hand Leads the Band" (1906) chronicles the curiosity of a Jewish marching band, something normally associated with Irish urban fraternal organizations and therefore as seemingly a contradictory bunch as a Jewish rap group might seem today. "Abie, Dot's Not a Business for You" (1909) tells of the Jew who decides to become an "actor man" and thereby risks getting called a "ham" by his kosher family. Finally, the famous "Yiddle on Your Fiddle" (1909) revels in the novelty of a Jew who delves into the world of ragtime.

Certainly, the concept of a Jewish artist performing American idioms constitutes a tentative way of hinting at the possibilities of melting-pot culture without engaging the issue of sexuality; it represents a way of eliding racial issues and exploring a middle ground between fusion and segregation. However, the particular fixation on this motif after 1907 or so seems to have other motivations as well. In the legitimate dramas I consider here, for example, the key male player in the sexual transaction almost always turns out to be a performing artist or musician, whether Jewish or not. Manners's Cecil Cotswold, for example, is a musician, while Zangwill's David Quixano is a composer. From "Abie Singer, the tenor singer" on up, these men are creators of one sort of another—imaginative individuals who are somehow directly engaged in fashioning the future of society. The creative ferment of their artwork and their performances thus not only stands in for but also parallels the sexual ferment of their interracial love affairs. As imagined by these performances, these creative men seem to be planting the seeds of future generations in more ways than one.

Whether Jewess or gentile, the women who partake of these sexual encounters are performed as playing a far more passive role in this melting-pot ferment. This fact may be as much a reflection of reality as a statement of ideology; women in 1910 continued to be discouraged and excluded from many of the arts. It is significant, however, that it is the racialist plays which cast the female parties to these transactions as performers. *Woman*'s Claire Forster, for example is a Broadway showgirl, while *Glickman*'s Charlotte Russe is an actress. The implication here is precisely the reverse of the plays where the men are artists. These pieces draw upon the traditional association between the actress and the prostitute. In these pieces, the women who sexually consort with Jews come across as little better than whores who are degrading both themselves and their race.

Whether idealistic young male musicians were leading willing female partners into a future promising evolution into higher forms, or loose showgirls were threatening the quality of their bloodline by flirting with debased Jews, the future generations of America were at stake in these couplings. If racialism gradually lost ground after 1920 as a way of defining these future generations, it did so only because the idea of the melting pot that many Americans eventually embraced incorporated many racialist assumptions. In the new middle ground, intermarriage remained rare, but rapid cultural assimilation achieved the same ends, as mixing came to be constructed in cultural rather than racial terms. The effect of this new middle ground was decreased visibility for Jewish figures in popular culture.

CHAPTER 6

Getting Reformed

THE TRANSITION TOWARD JEWISH
INVISIBILITY IN POPULAR PERFORMANCE

*"[The Russian Jews'] absorption by the American people will remove
many if not most of these peculiarities, but it will tend to preserve the humor
and intellectual quickness which are such striking characteristics of the race."*
—David Warfield, c. 1901[1]

$\mathcal{L}$egend has it that the comedian Willie
Howard made a key breakthrough in his career one night when he found
himself in a difficult predicament. As Bernard Sobel relates the story,
Howard (born William Lefkowitz) was preparing to take the stage at a
smalltime burlesque venue, circa 1902, when rowdy stagehands ripped off
his crepe whiskers, which were requisite for Hebrew comedy. Under the
pressure of the moment, and still smarting from the attack, Howard had no
choice but to go on beardless. When the manager saw Howard preparing to
take the stage without the crepe, he was upset: "If you don't wear a beard
the audience won't know you're a Jewish comedian." Howard went on
without the beard anyway, putting his act over so successfully that he apparently decided to keep his Jew beardless for future performances. This
"cleaned-up" Hebrew became for a time the centerpiece of Howard's successful vaudeville turn with his brother Eugene, starting a counter-trend of
Hebrew comedy that was less grotesque than the acts represented by performers such as Warfield and the Welch brothers.[2]

I start with Howard's breakthrough here because it usefully represents the beginnings of a trend in performing Jewishness, increasingly evident after 1905 or so, in which some vaudeville Jews cleaned up their acts
and became less grotesque in the performance of ethnicity. Especially after

1910, the grotesque stage Jew, burdened by heavy beard and butchered dialect, began to disappear, after more than a decade of headlining burlesque revues, providing comic relief in musical comedies, and appearing prominently in vaudeville bills. Audiences apparently were increasingly ready to recognize and accept Jews without their beards, the concerns of Howard's manager notwithstanding.

Yet it seems appropriate that the impetus for Howard's taking off the crepe was not the voluntary act of the performer but the violent act of another. To clean oneself up, to reform one's image into something more naturalized and palatable, can be a sign of empowerment but also an action taken under duress. To take a step toward invisibility, to adjust one's body to suit the neutrality of the melting pot appearances, is not necessarily an act of liberation. Performing oneself as a Jew-without-a-beard is, after all, the requisite first step toward performing oneself as no-Jew-at-all. Indeed, this new type of Jewish body signaled the beginning of an era where ethnic visibility in general and Jewish visibility in particular were no longer desirable. In its place came invisibility, as Jewish characters became less frequently seen on major American stages.

Trends and ideologies which I trace in the preceding two chapters impacted and reflected this gradual disappearance. First, the growing presence of Jews behind-the-scenes in show business reflected a dynamic in which Jewish men found a comforting creativity by fashioning and promoting theatrical works that featured others. The more that Jews were able to contribute artistically as producers and writers, the less they were required to risk the onus of having to perform themselves in a larger culture in many ways antithetical to Jewish traditions. Second, the ideal of the melting pot gradually came to posit an ideal American body through a process of assimilation that would somehow purify immigrants of visible ethnic difference, remaking them in the "neutral" image of Americans of Western European descent.

I am not arguing that after 1910 Jewish characters could no longer be found on American stages. In fact, the 1910s continued to see performances of Jewish characters of all types. However, these years were marked by two developments that in historical perspective signal the transition toward decreased Jewish visibility. The first development was the occasional appearance of the exemplary, upstanding Jewish male protagonist, as represented by two major plays of 1911: Louis Parker's *Disraeli* and Augustus Thomas's *As a Man Thinks*. Second, and far more importantly, these years saw the "whitening" of the Jewish comedian into a body less grotesque than in previous generations, as represented most prominently by the hit play *Potash and Perlmutter* in 1913. Through these new types of performances during this era of reform, the stage Jew was indeed effectively "re-formed" in ways which resulted in decreased visibility in popular performances.

Exemplary Jews

In discussing the prototypes of Jewish characters in English literature, Edgar Rosenberg has outlined two basic categories. One is the Jewish villain, rooted in medieval tradition, popularized by Marlowe, Shakespeare, and Dickens. The second, less common type is the saintly Jew, first convincingly dramatized by Richard Cumberland through the character Sheva in his 1794 play *The Jew* (shortly after German playwright G. E. Lessing created his exemplary Jew in *Nathan the Wise* in 1783).[3]

As Rosenberg notes, these exemplary Jews rarely were as interesting characters as their more malicious counterparts, which may partially explain why such high-minded Jews rarely showed up in American performances during the era I examine in this book. Despite the occasional philo-Semitic play like *Ben Israel*, a failure in New York in 1876, the examples of "serious" plays in which Jewish male or female characters were noble humanitarians were few and far between. The most redeeming male characters, as I have shown, were almost invariably linked to vaudeville and musical comedy traditions that directly compromised their grandeur. Arguably, the most heroic of all these characters, the Jewesses of turn-of-the-century biblical dramas like *Judith*, maintained a terrifying edge that compromised their saintliness, even while their biblical settings effectively distanced them from connections to the contemporary immigrant experience.

With *Disraeli* and *Thinks* in 1911, however, two exemplary Jewish protagonists appeared in serious plays for the legitimate stage. Both plays depicted Jewish men in positions of power and influence acting benignly for the good of society. The fact that two plays with such exemplary characters appeared apparently independently of each other's influence in the same year seems too good to be true for the historian. However, I do not want to overstate the trend they represent or argue that they signal a revolution in performance. Nor can I pinpoint their appearance to any localized event or issue of 1911. My point, rather, is more modest: that they appeared at a moment when it was first becoming possible to universalize the

Jewish man into a heroic humanitarian, and have an audience accept the characterization as such.

Created as a vehicle for the multi-talented George Arliss, *Disraeli* readily manipulates British history and the circumstances of the prime minister's purchase of the Suez Canal. The commanding protagonist is described by one character as having an "extraordinary personality. Sort of man you feel come into a room, even if you don't see him." Fending off anti-Semites and spies (and working with the former when necessary to achieve his aims), the witty and brash Disraeli successfully manages the purchase of the canal for England, using his influence with Jewish bankers to advantage. When Probert, one of the play's chief schemers, threatens Disraeli, asserting, "I am not to be ordered about by an . . . alien Jew," Disraeli calmly replies, "Ah, but the alien Jew happens to be the better citizen." As a reward for his courage and tenacity, Disraeli and his wife ultimately end up regaled in a magnificent ceremony where the couple is to be honored personally by the Queen.[4]

Disraeli went on to become one of the major hits of the decade. Arliss toured the play in the United States to great success for many years, eventually starring in a film of the same name; it was the role with which he became forever associated. Whatever its relationship to historical reality, the play depicted the wheeling-dealing, unflappable Jew as the play's unquestioned hero, charmer, and voice of reason: a literate and sophisticated imperialist mastermind for an age of high-minded imperialism (when Panama, not Suez, was transparently the canal at issue). In other words, a Jewish character took the lead in a play that was neither a comedy nor specifically about Jewishness. Jewish power was performed as actively patriotic, as the play emphasized above all Disraeli's love of country. Any threat of difference was diffused.[5]

Thomas's *Thinks* unites the intermarriage theme to the style of the realistic problem play. A number of stories intertwine obliquely in its tangled plot, set among the privileged classes of New York. In one subplot, the Jewess Vedah Seelig pursues a love affair with the gentile sculptor Julian Burrill, despite the disapproval of her father, Dr. Samuel Seelig, who prefers that she marry Benjamin de Lota, a Sephardic Jew. De Lota, it turns out, was romantically involved years before with Dr. Seelig's friend, Elinor Clayton; the social pressures of anti-Semitism, however, prevented the romance from developing. Moreover, Elinor's husband, Frank, wrongly suspects his own son of being the half-Jewish progeny of his wife and De Lota. Much of the play's action centers on Dr. Seelig's counseling and intercession, which helps Frank realize that he has applied a double standard in condemning his wife for imagined peccadilloes that he himself has actually committed. Meanwhile, Vedah and Julian elope. When Dr. Seelig hears the news, he broods for a moment, only to rush out to treat a medical emergency, ever ready to do his noble duty as self-sacrificing surgeon and friend to all humanity. Just before the final curtain, Elinor, in a memorable theatrical gesture, takes the Doctor's head in her hands and kisses him out of sheer gratitude. Love and rational understanding thus win out over oppression and irrational fear.[6]

At the time of the play's debut, Thomas already enjoyed a reputation as one of the foremost playwrights of his generation. In 1908, before *The Melting-pot* had been staged in New York, he went on record saying that the next great American play would be about Jews, "not the Jew of persecution, as he has been heretofore pictured, but the great Jew of America, philanthropic, far-seeing, and above all, sweetly domestic."[7] In seeming to speak so prophetically, Thomas was probably talking about the play that he no doubt was already conceiving. The following year, he joined people like Roosevelt and Addams in praise of *The Melting-pot*. When *Thinks* finally debuted at the Thirty-ninth Street Theater in 1911, with the prominent actor John Mason in the lead role of Dr. Seelig, it was a concept which had therefore already been a number of years in gestation.

Unlike Israel Zangwill's Quixanos, the Seeligs are a family denuded of most ethnic markings. Their only explicit connection to their heritage lies in Dr. Seelig's abstract philosophical speculation as to how "the belief in one God is given in trust to the Jew." This thin link to the past, however, has racial implications for the Doctor, who believes that "for the world to grow," the Jews must maintain this unique view by conserving themselves as a distinct tribe; monotheism for him is "the precious idea of which every Jewish woman is custodian and which to transmit the Jew suffers and persists." Aside from this philosophy, however, there is nothing in behavior, language, taste, or outlook which distinguishes the Seeligs from their gentile neighbors of the same class. Their very Jewishness is only subtly stated throughout the first half of the play; at intermission, an audience member could easily be left confused as to the family's ethnicity. Thomas, then, has melted the traditional markers of difference out of his Jews. All possible cause for anxiety has been distilled out of this admirably upright family.

In fact, it is only in their near-perfection that the Seeligs differ significantly from their gentile peers. Dr. Seelig performs himself not only as ideal father but also as moral compass for the play's other characters, who freely consult him with their problems. Even Frank, who harbors anti-Semitic feelings, describes the doctor this way: "Wonderful man with children, this Seelig. . . . He's at the head of the hospital for crippled children but great in diagnosis—medicine—anything. . . . His heart makes him a doctor. If I ever go to Heaven and that old Jew isn't there I'll ask for a rain check." This old Jew, it turns out, quotes Jesus Christ on the subject of goodwill and forgiveness to his Christian friends, who attentively listen to the Doctor as he regrets that the "Nazarene" is no longer taken at his word. At one curious moment, Seelig even laments not having become a priest. He embodies, it seems, not so much the exemplary Jew as the exemplary Christian, thus bearing the burden of having to prove his race's worth to others by treading the edge of divine perfection. It is not his Jewishness then, that redeems him, but his ability to prove himself indistinguishable from (and even better than) any Christian. If his daughter and her lover promise to effect one sort of melting through their union, then Seelig effects another sort of melting, where the pain of the American crucible ends up concealed beneath the smile of this Christ-like man.[8]

Both *Disraeli* and *Thinks* allay any anxiety over Jewish power by casting these influential, upper-class characters so idealistically. Whether through the inspired nationalism of Disraeli or the generosity of spirit of Dr. Seelig, Jewishness poses little threat, embodies little difference. In so reforming the Jew to perfection, these performances perched on the transitional point between an earlier era of grotesque visibility and a latter one of greater invisibility. Both eras made such idealized performances unlikely for sharply different reasons. In the earlier era, the Jewish man could not be universal. In the later era, the universal man could not be specifically Jewish.

Cleaning Up Jewish Comedy

The generalized "decline of the racial comics" in vaudeville and variety theater has been ably described by Paul Antonie Distler. As Distler makes clear, it was not just the Hebrew comedians who started to become far less prevalent after 1910 or so. Traditional stage Irish and stage Dutch also fell out of view, and the roughhouse comedy of violence epitomized by Weber and Fields was replaced by a more verbal, urbane humor.

Distler offers a number of cogent, localized explanations for this phenomenon, including the changing tastes of an increasingly bourgeois audience and the rise of musical comedies whose more fully integrated book and lyrics tended to squeeze out ethnic character comedy, which normally depended upon set routines and monologues and as such resisted assimilation into a unified whole. Additionally, Distler points out, with the gradual assimilation of immigrants and their children, and the arrival of fewer new ones to take their places after the passage of stricter immigration laws following World War I, fewer models of striking cultural difference presented themselves in the population for performers to parody or audiences to recognize. If the last explanation seems the most obvious, its apparent power depends on shared assumptions about how immigrants should be assimilated. Such assimilation is by no means a universal way of absorbing immigration, but rather, a process specific to its American time and place. If performances seem to be mimicking this process, they are not so much reflecting historical inevitability as they are making this history possible.[9]

The fourth reason Distler offers for the disappearance of immigrant racial comedy is the one I want to consider briefly here: the rise in the 1910s of pressure groups that actively campaigned against Hebrew comedians. For Jewish-American performances, the key year for the emergence of these associations was 1913, which saw the birth of both the Anti-Stage Ridicule Committee, which organized a boycott in Chicago against what it perceived to be the most invidious Jewish performances, and the Anti-Defamation League of the B'nai B'rith, which devoted itself to fighting anti-Semitism of all types.[10] Around 1913, too, older organizations of the Reform Jewish establishment, including the Central Conference of American Rabbis and the Associated Rabbis of America, started to involve themselves actively in campaigns against "derogatory characterization of the Jew" in the theater, as Rabbi William S. Friedman put it in a letter to the *New York Times*.[11]

By pressuring theater managers and song publishers, by writing letters to newspapers, by sponsoring public forums, and by encouraging their constituencies to boycott theaters that permitted offensive performances, these watchdog organizations waged a "war on ridicule," in a campaign empowered by the fact that many theater producers and patrons were themselves Jewish. The collective efforts of these groups led almost immediately to the toning down and elimination of the more grotesquely marked stage Jews. By 1918, according to Distler, such performances were virtual relics of the past. History arcs ironically here. In 1879, anti-Semites like Corbin had organized the first boycott against Jewish performers. In 1913, Jewish groups themselves organized the second boycott, now as a way of battling anti-Semitism.

These campaigns had a variety of objectives and targets. Generally, they centered on the mass entertainment milieus, including vaudeville, legitimate theater, and sheet-music publication—industries where Jews had notable presence. Areas of cultural production where Jews had less impact, such as publishing, tended to be overlooked. The boycotts claimed to target only those performances that promoted "race hatred" and "social harm," such as portrayals "of the Jew as a mean, slinking individual, given to vulgarity and villainy." Prominent spokespersons reiterated that they were not against Jewish representation as such. Professor Ernest Freund, an activist in New York, proposed, for example, that a line be drawn between "the harmless and the vicious."[12] Judge Hugo Pam stated during the Chicago boycott of 1913: "Do not think that we must not have any jokes on the Jew. He is as susceptible to jokes as the German, Irishman or the American, but we want present day jokes reformed, and to have the stings which are now carried with the stage Jew removed."[13] "Reform" was a magic word in this age of reform, and Pam's invocation of this concept helps to position these campaigns as part of a larger political network.

The targets of these groups' campaigns, however, were sometimes more widespread and reflected the class-based cultural politics of a leadership composed of prominent, highly educated individuals from an assimilated Jewish elite. They sometimes equated, for example, all Jewish representation in "lower" forms with offensiveness itself; song-publishing firms, for example, were asked to discontinue all "low comedy songs" about Jews, as if such tunes were inherently repugnant.[14] Along similar lines, sweeping boycotts were at some points urged against all comedians who did a Jew routine. Moreover, there was a consistent moral tincture to the crusade, which railed, it seemed, not only against racial comedy but raciness as well; they condemned shows that constituted "flagrant transgressions of the laws of decency."[15] In Chicago, for example, organizers sought to boycott, along with stage Hebrews, "the introduction of immoral songs and questionable speeches."[16] The notion of what was offensive, however, could be extended to fit many performances; one leader asserted that *The Melting-pot* and plays like it "had done more to injure the race than the lampoons of low comedy."[17]

While I admire these groups' resolute push toward more dignified Jewish representation, I also acknowledge that their efforts sometimes ended up amounting to a regularization campaign in favor of a specific cultural ideal. Derogatory representations of Jews and other immigrant groups were their primary targets, but they ended up serving the broader purpose of agitating for more decorous, respectful performances that reinforced haute-bourgeois notions of propriety. It is instructive, for example, that the leadership of these campaigns came primarily from the comfortable, bourgeois German-Jewish elite—judges, lawyers, doctors—who were far more established in the United States than the "greenhorn" Eastern European immigrants. Their religious practice itself had been denominationally "Reformed" for a number of generations, in contrast to the new immigrants who were generally either far more traditional in worship, or on the other extreme, socialist freethinkers.

It is instructive, too, that the first and most prominent campaign took place in Chicago, a city then somewhat removed from New York's poverty, immigration, and intercultural conflict, as well as from the very industries which produced this entertainment. Ethnic differences which could not be so readily made invisible in the Lower East Side seemed most to offend those middle-American Jews who were modeling themselves into middle-class and upper-middle-class Americans. Ironically, despite the centralization of the show business industry in New York, it was groups located geographically and culturally in Middle America which most successfully pushed for this reformation, so to speak, of the Jewish body on stage.

Some of the top Hebrew comedians from the turn of the century now found themselves in disfavor. Julian Rose had to go overseas beyond the melting pot, to pursue his career, enjoying a second wave of popularity in the British music halls of the 1920s, where racial typing continued to be the rage.[18] Joe Welch's Hebrew act was one of the specific targets of the 1913 boycott. He defended himself in these terms: "We ought to be broad enough to recognize our own racial eccentricities and to laugh with other peoples when their angles are emphasized purely for amusement purposes. But we ought also to protest when the low comedian debases the character and presents a type that does not in any respect typify the race. But if we were to remove from the stage the Hebrew character in comedy roles, the stage would lose much."[19] Welch lost much. Lacking the versatility of a Warfield, he had no effective way of passing himself off as gentile, of regularizing his grotesque comedy. The boycotts effectively put an end to his career. Welch was committed to a mental institution shortly before his death in 1918 at the age of forty-nine.[20]

The few remaining vaudeville performers who specifically structured their acts around a stage Jew did so with what was called the "cleaned-up" version of the character—that is, a character cleaner-shaven, lighter complexioned, less racially and culturally different. The prototypes for this cleaned-up Jew had appeared earlier, near the turn of the century, in the bodies of gentiles like Jess Dandy. Howard popularized this style; others, like Andy Rice, furthered it. Harry Cooper, for example, handled Jewish comedy with the Empire City Quartette, circa 1909, wearing, according to Joe Laurie, Jr., "no make-up except for an over-sized derby which he kept tipping to imaginary women in the audience."[21]

Ironically, it was in 1913, the signal year of boycotts and watchdog groups, that one of the most successful plays featuring stage Jews, *Potash and Perlmutter*, reached the boards. The terms of its success, however, underscore the changing cultural politics of the day. The play was inspired by a series of stories recently published by the Anglo-Jewish writer Montague Glass. Glass's stories detail the exploits of a pair of crass but endearing Jewish immigrants who run a clothing business together in New York; though they argue perpetually with each other, they remain affectionately bonded together, like some long-married couple. A pointed sense of irony distances the author from his two characters, making Glass more the urbane satirist than the bourgeois sentimentalist. Still, on the whole, his Abe Potash and "Mawruss" Perlmutter come across in the stories as humanized Jews in the tradition of Warfield's Simon Levi; each effects a tightfisted exterior but lets this facade crumble at the slightest prodding to reveal a heart of gold.

Given the relationship of Glass's stories to the stage Jew tradition, it is not surprising that the stage version of *Potash and Perlmutter* became a collaboration between many major figures associated with the tradition. The show's producer was Al H. Woods, who had created *Fast Life in New York* for Julian Rose in 1905. Charles Klein (1867–1915), whom Woods commissioned to adapt the stories, had performed key dramaturgical duties for *The Auctioneer*, in addition to collaborating with David Belasco on *The Music Master*, another Warfield vehicle. To play Potash and Perlmutter, Woods hired the actors Barney Bernard and Alexander Carr. Carr was a Russian-born variety veteran; in burlesque, he had built an act around an imitation of David Warfield, and in vaudeville, had been part of the team of Carr and Parr. The Polish-Jewish Bernard, while known primarily as a comedian, had even once played Shylock.

The production had significant political pressure, however. It opened in August 1913, just four months after the Chicago-based boycott went into effect. Klein's Jewish friends were pressuring him to drop the project all along. Though Klein did complete the script, he attempted to sever all public connection to it. The initial program acknowledged only Glass as its author.[22]

Potash and Perlmutter, however, managed to negotiate its way around controversy. It immediately won rave reviews for its "natural and human sentiment" and ran for over 400 performances on Broadway before enjoying an equally successful run in London.[23] It spawned four Glass-inspired sequels between 1915 and 1923, by a variety of adapters, with a variety of Perlmutters, but always featuring Bernard as Potash. Propelled by this success, Glass continued to turn out more books of Jewish-American humor, one of which, *Object, Matrimony*, in 1916 also made it to the stage.

Clues in production suggest how *Potash and Perlmutter* managed to negotiate the delicate terrain of 1913 so successfully. First of all, Bernard and Carr's Potash and Perlmutter represented, in physical aspect, two Hebrew comedians who were very much cleaned up. Based upon photos in the published version of the play, both forsook the beards and excessive make-up of earlier days; in place of baggy pants and over-long coats, they attired themselves in sharply fitted business clothes and vests. Of the two characters, Bernard's Potash was stouter and more balding, and in subtle ways, the more visibly "ethnic" of the two. In contrast, Carr cut a more lithe, dapper figure as the "good-looking dynamic" Perlmutter, who was supposed to be about ten years younger than his partner. This physical typing represented a departure from the implication of Glass's stories, where the two salesmen are nearly identical in demeanor, except for the fact that Potash, as "outside" man, tends to be more aggressive and fast-talking, while Perlmutter, the "inside" man, comes across as more subdued and whimsical. Through the less ethnically different body of Carr then, the production created a more striking visible contrast between the partners, fashioning Perlmutter as the more handsome and dynamic of the duo.

Potash and Perlmutter, like *The Auctioneer*, features an almost negligible plot that serves mainly as a framework for the salesmen's shtick. The thin story involves the plight of a bookkeeper, Boris Andrieff, a Russian refugee who has fallen in love with Potash's daughter; the play has him eventually successfully managing to resist extradition from the United States. On stage, the ironic edge and literary pretensions of Glass's stories dissolve into the more heavy-handed conventions of the commercial stage comedy, replete with melodramatic plot turns, love interest, supporting characters drawn in broad strokes, and constant vaudeville-like banter and bickering between the two protagonists (see Appendix Avi). With most of the markings of the Jewish comedian toned down, with understated make-up and just a hint of dialect, Potash and Perlmutter were left largely with a verbal comedy of wordplay, malapropisms, and conflict with which to perform their Jewishness.

This wordplay was rooted in Hebrew and other ethnic vaudeville routines, where language itself had increasingly become the source of much humor, as madcap verbal gaming gradually usurped ethnic dialect comedy proper. When traced out across the subsequent development decades, Jewish dialect comedy resulted in a curious irony. The once ethnically specific comedy of Jewish dialect fed directly into a new tradition of humor much less tied to characters' ethnicity. This new tradition of crazy punning and madcap linguistic wordplay, as epitomized in the 1920s and 1930s by the Marx Brothers, no longer had clearly visible ties to the stage Jew. What was once a key marker of stage Jewishness became a way of accessing the Hebrew comedian's legacy without stepping into his body, in an era when, as Distler has noted, violent verbal humor gradually replaced violent physical humor on the stage. Potash and Perlmutter thus straddle this transition between comic styles—between Weber and Fields on one hand and Groucho Marx on the other.[24]

In terms of the Hebrew comedian's sexuality, *Potash and Perlmutter* also represents a new generation of performances. Perlmutter, in contrast to previous stage Jews, becomes the object of love interest from the "tall, blonde and beautiful" Ruth Snyder, played in the original production by the prominent comedienne Louise Dresser. Ruth falls in love with Perlmutter; as if to confirm the Jew's ascension out of the ridiculous and depraved in the areas of romance, she tells him after a passionate embrace, "Morris, you are a man that needs no pity, a real man, a business man."[25] With this validation of the stage Jew as real man, the play effaces a decades-long tradition of the stage Jew, who never before had attracted this interest from a beautiful, apparently gentile woman, let alone from one embodied by so prominent a stage personality as Louise Dresser.

This pairing of Perlmutter and Ruth further foregrounds the way the stage Jew was being cast into the melting pot. Miss Snyder, after all, does not seem to be Jewish; the union being proposed, one assumes, is an intermarriage. The play, however, does not present the intermarriage as problematic; unlike *The Melting-pot*, it sidesteps the issue entirely, locating the relationship safely in the apolitical conventions of stage comedy. The intermarriage subplot between Boris and young Irma Potash is also equally unproblematic in the play, despite the fact that such a union between Russian and Jew, like that between Vera and David in *The Melting-pot*, carries the potential for agonizing intercultural and intergenerational conflict. The play, then, elides all potential conflict that would arise out of such relationships.

Potash and Perlmutter then, valorizes the paradigm of the melting pot so completely that it creates a stage world where Jews, in the context of sexual relationships, avoid invoking their own Jewishness; where intermarriage is apparently the norm; where characters are free to romance whomever they want, outside all social, historical, and cultural parameters. The play thus represents the first step toward the "absorption" Warfield speaks of in this chapter's epigraph, where "humor and intellectual quickness" would be the only differentiating elements left to the Jewish man in his performance of himself. *Potash and Perlmutter* thus represents the most assimilated bodies Hebrew comedians could inhabit and still remain visibly marked as Jewish.

The situation of Jewish female performances differed from the male comedians in this age of assimilation and reform. Now that the heyday of the belle juive had largely passed, the Jewess was already marginalized and invisible, a secondary or tertiary figure (when present at all) in most shows including Jewish subject matter. In fact, one could make the case that the more that Jewish men occupied prominent positions in show business, the less Jewish women were visible on stage. In intermarriage plays written by Jews, the gentile woman most readily became object of desire, to be paired with the Jewish man. Meanwhile, a female Jewish body seemed virtually incompatible with the context of vaudeville.

The relative invisibility of the Jewish woman rested partially in the fact that, in these male-dominated industries, the female body was itself a significant enough sign of difference that to compound it with grotesque ethnicity was redundant or contradictory. Illustrations to old sheet music covers indicate this disjuncture between Jew and Jewess in the age of vaudeville. The male figures, from Yonkele the Cowboy Jew to Mose the Band Leader, are ugly, grotesque, or ridiculous. In contrast, the Jewesses, from the elegantly dressed Rebecca to the smiling young woman on the cover of "Moshe from Nova Scotia," cut more traditional figures of gentile feminine beauty, attired in mainstream fashions of the time.[26] It seems that the Jewish men who shaped this industry desired gentile ideals of feminine beauty in their lovers, even while continuing to posit themselves as grotesque buffoons.

This long-standing, informal tradition which discouraged comedy and ethnicity from being joined in the body of a Jewess led, for many years, to the absence of Jewish comediennes. When the occasional Jewess needed to be played in a comedy sketch, she tended to be performed by a gentile, such as Earle Remington, who starred in the vaudeville sketch "Our Pawnshop" with her partner, William Hines, throughout the 1890s. It is significant, too, that the first female Jewish performer to become a national sensation in vaudeville, Nora Bayes, did so by effectively concealing her ethnicity from her audiences, who had little reason to suspect that this figure of poise, the on-stage partner and off-stage lover of the debonair Jack Norworth, was actually born Dora Goldberg.[27] Though Bayes suppressed most elements of ethnicity from her stage persona, when asked about the key to her success, she replied that it was her "absolute sincerity," that "endeavor to give the best and most truthful part of yourself to your friend."[28] If by "friend" she meant her audience, these friends were denied the "absolute sincerity" of Dora Goldberg. They got, instead, the lilting "Shine On, Harvest Moon" of Nora Bayes.

If Bayes played out the old contradictions which suppressed the female Jewish comedy, the next Jewish comedienne to star in vaudeville and musical comedy, Fanny Brice, embodied new possibilities. As a youth, Brice (Fania Borach, 1891–1951) informally trained herself in the tradition of the Hebrew comedians. In amateur shows in the mid 1900s, she even took the stage doing imitations of well-known performers like Joe Welch.[29] In a key moment in 1909, though, the little-known Brice found a way to perform a youthful, female comic Hebrew by featuring Irving Berlin's "Sadie Salome, Go Home" in her act in a small-time benefit show. Her success with the number won her a prominent spot in the "College Girls Show" revue, which led in 1910, to a featured position in the Ziegfeld Follies, which led, in turn, to a long and successful career.

One of the period's many Jew-craze songs, "Sadie Salome" features in its lyrics the twist of a Jewish woman in the position of comic incongruity previously only reserved for men. It tells the story of a greenhorn immigrant girl who neglects her boyfriend when she becomes obsessed with the "Salome" cooch-style dancing craze (which had been sweeping the country since 1907). Mose begs her:

> Don't do that dance, I tell you Sadie,
> That's not a bus'ness for a lady!
> Most everybody knows
> That I'm your loving Mose,
> Oy oy oy oy—where is your clothes?[30]

Brice performed the piece in Yiddish dialect in a white sailor suit, gathered up at the crotch; her wriggling and shimmying, while full of sexual innuendo, made clear this eighteen-year-old Jewish girl with rolling eyes was incompetent both as exotic dancer and sex object. In her own way, she was as ridiculous as any trumpet-playing or gun-toting Jew: as problematic a female as the Hebrew comedians were problematic males. Brice's performance of the song then, represents a Jewish woman finally succeeding at a comic, self-deprecating performance of herself.

The performance's quoting of "Salome" also subverts older performance traditions. While the stage and literary figure "Salome" was not always coded as a Jewess per se, she came embedded in the oriental, biblical trappings which allowed some to see her as young Jewish vixen; in any case, Salome invoked the fin-de-siècle mystique of the alluring and dangerous oriental woman in which the tragic Jewess was implicated.[31] Through Berlin's song then, Brice not only debunks, as Barbara W. Grossman has noted, the entire grandiose Salome tradition, but succeeds in inverting the Jewess's relationship to it.[32] Brice's performance then, closes the door on any notion of the exotic Jewess, and under the title of "Sadie" (the standard name of the homespun immigrant girl), domesticates the Jewess's sexual trappings to the point of rendering them ludicrous.[33]

Brice's later career also reflected the contradictions of the first generation of melting-pot performers. After all, her stage act of the 1910s did not revolve around her Jewishness; while brimming with Yiddish sounds and sensibilities, it implicated but rarely focused on her ethnicity, foregrounding instead her femaleness. Brice's Jewishness, however, manifested itself more strongly in other ways. In sharp contrast to Bayes, Warfield, and many of the other Jewish stars who preceded her, Brice went out of her way to overstate her ghetto roots. She learned her Yiddish, not at home, but for the specific purpose of bolstering her stage act; moreover, while Brice was indeed born in poverty on the Lower East Side, she spent most of her childhood in relative comfort in suburban Newark, where her mother ran a small business. Her ethnicity, in a sense, was a tool she controlled and manipulated as a way of asserting power, in contrast to Warfield, who asserted his power by voiding himself of ethnicity.[34]

Based on the contrasting examples of Brice and Warfield, it seems that women were expected to reassert their roots in old traditions and folkways, whereas men were expected to transcend or deny them. The men whitened themselves into exemplary Americans, the heroes of assimilation success stories. Brice balanced her own considerable success with a performance of self that established her comfortingly within a world of ethnic difference, tying her to the domestic sphere in a way that performers like Warfield were not.

Into the Melting Pot

In a larger culture where Jews might have exercised a more dominant presence, the boycotts and developments of the 1910s might have resulted across the board in more lasting and enlightening Jewish performances in popular venues. However, Jewish-American power, significant as it was in certain narrow genres of the performing arts, was ultimately limited and insecure in American society as a whole. The result was the gradual elimination rather than the transformation of Jewish comedy. The alternatives posed in America ultimately became not a choice between complementary and derogatory ethnic performance, but rather, between expressed and suppressed ethnic difference.

My focus here therefore ends with the 1910s, which I assert as the last decade (until recent times) in which markedly Jewish characters were commonplace in American popular performance. While Jewish characters by no means disappeared from the American stage after 1920, they became less visibly present in mass culture. The performances I examine in this chapter then, can be positioned as the start of this trend away from openly performing Jewishness on major American stages.

By no means am I arguing that Jewish performance disappeared after 1920. *Abie's Irish Rose* (1922) and *Awake and Sing!* (1935) are but a few prominent examples of plays that deal explicitly with Jewish issues. In film, *The Jazz Singer* (1927) stands out as a history-making performance which foregrounds Jewish subject matter. However, for the most part, when Jewishness asserted itself in performances of the later 1910s and into subsequent decades, it increasingly played itself out in oblique ways, many of which have been well explored. It expressed itself indirectly through the tantalizing "coon" songs of Sophie Tucker (Sonia Kalish); through the efforts of muscle of Harry Houdini (Erich Weisz); through the neurotic zaniness of Eddie Cantor (Isidore Itzkowitz); through the anarchic comedy of the Marx Brothers (Julius, Adolph, Leonard, and Herbert); and in a thousand other performances that have long since been forgotten.[35]

With the passing of time, these expressions became increasingly masked, indirect, invisible, as Jewish bodies seemingly vanished into the air, leaving Jewishness less present to the eye but still floating in the air, audible through aggressive verbal wit or ventriloquized through the bodies of gentile characters, both black and white. By the middle decades of the century, this presence had become a seeming absence in popular culture, cloaked under other types of bodies, as what had once been a grotesque visibility gradually transformed itself into a generalized invisibility. In the era of the melting pot, these stage types performed and created new ideals of Jewish-American assimilation, resulting in a decades-long popular-culture disappearing act.[36]

What is one to make of this disappearing act? The history I have explored here certainly foregrounds the painful alternatives of both visibility and invisibility when Jewish ethnicity has been performed on American stages. On one hand, when Jewish difference was asserted in opposition to some ideal body, it ended up performing itself grotesquely or exotically, inscribed in ways that perpetuated humiliation, degradation, and marginalization. On the other hand, when difference was suppressed in the face of this ideal body, it led to varieties of self-denial that obliterated the realities of Jewish difference and presence.

Negotiating this chasm between visibility and invisibility, between racialism and the melting pot, means treading difficult terrain, especially in an America, where these two polarities have often fused to uphold essentialist notions of racial difference under a thin veneer of cultural assimilation. For ethnic groups of color—that is, Americans who have been classified in opposition to whiteness—this fusion has often had oppressive consequences and made it necessary for many to posit an alternative authenticity denied in mainstream representation.[37]

The Jewish-American experience, however, is unique because, in my view, it has not been characterized by the same levels of overt oppression and disempowerment that have shaped, for example, the performances of African Americans from minstrelsy to the television situation comedy. Because of the presence of many Jewish men in the commercial show business industry, the Jewish situation in twentieth-century America cannot readily be understood through us-them, insider-outsider, Same-Other, domination-resistance binaries which more readily seem to hold for other groups. The contradictions of the Jewish-American experience has coupled growing power, most particularly in the type of representations I look at here, in the context of a larger culture that has often been alien to Jewish traditions and aspirations.

I hope this history offers an empowering self-critique which explains many of the performances by which Jews and gentiles alike have come to understand Jewishness. If we are indeed finally "beyond the melting pot," by looking clearly at our past, we can more meaningfully shape the Jewishness of the future.

APPENDIX A
Selected Shtick from Comic Performances
Featuring Jewish Characters

i. Frank Bush Songs (circa 1880)

"THE JEW PEDDLER"[1]

Oh! ladies and gents, now who vants to buy?
I wouldn't cheat you, no more would I lie;
I zells cheap for cash, I never give 'time;'
Of you want a necktie, take it for a dime.

Chorus:
Neckties! Suspenders! I zell drough de town;
Buy a pair of my 'braces' und your pants von't come down.
Neckties! Suspenders! Und who is der next to buy! to buy!

I stand on der corner undil I'm most froze,
Und dey say, 'Look at Sheeny mid a hump on his nose.'
But I care not for dot, of my goots I do zell,
Und ven zey pass me by I loudly do yell—"

Chorus

"MY SON MOSES"[2]

The boy I'm going to sing about, he is a son of mine
He's working in a clothing store, they use him for a sign.
He looks the image of myself, although he's not so stout
And I use him for a walking stick whenever I go out.

Chorus:

My son Moses he is the boy
I dress him like a five-cent toy
And you know my only joy is my son, Moses.

My Mosey is a tough young man, he wears his hair like me,
His nose and chin they both do meet and he looks like a Chinee.
The girls they call him darling Moses for he dresses up so fine.
And he says he'll put me in his place for I'd make a better sign.

Chorus

ii. From **Sam'l of Posen** *(1881) by George Jessop*[3]

Scene: Winslow's jewelry store

Sam'l: (Entering with his sales tray) You want to buy some shoulder-braces? Three pair for a dollar.

Mr. Fitzurse: No, sir. I don't care for any.

Sam'l: Well, everybody knows his business best. If you want to buy any Boston garters, two pair for a quarter. They have brass buckles and attach at both ends. They never break to pieces. (Business) You want to buy?

Fitzurse: I don't care for them.

Sam'l: You don't want them? Everybody wants them. Everybody wears them. How do you keep your stockings up without garters?

Fitzurse: I don't wish for any, I tell you.

Sam'l: Well, everybody knows his business best. Would you like some rolled plate collar buttons? I'll sell you three for ten cents.

Fitzurse: No, I don't wear them.

Sam'l: Don't wear them? How do you keep your shirt on without collar buttons?

Fitzurse: You are a horrid fellow.

Sam'l: A horrid fellow? "New est mis och vecht." Can't I sell you some patent suspenders with double-end nickel buckles and brass pulleys on both sides? Made of the best India rubber? I tell you, you can go out and shovel dirt from morning to night with these suspenders. Two pair for a half a dollar.

Fitzurse: (Aside) I'll buy them to get rid of this fellow. (Gives money to Samuel)

Sam'l: And I'll stick to him till I have got his money.

Fitzurse: Let me have them.

Sam'l: (Aside) Everybody knows his business best. (Aloud) Thank you. For a half a dollar you've got a bargain. (Aside) They cost me a dollar a dozen. (Enter Quinn)

Fitzurse: (To Quinn) Here. I will make you a present of them.

Quinn: (Takes suspenders) I thank you, sir. (Bows; goes down right)

Sam'l: You want to buy some socks with double heels and double toes, warranted not to rip or tear? The longer you wear them, the thicker they get. Four pairs for half a dollar.

Quinn: No, I have all the socks I want.

Sam'l: I'll give you ten cents for those suspenders.

Quinn: I think you're too sharp.

Sam'l: How do you know? I pay half a dollar a dozen for a dozen of the same.

Quinn: If that's the case, you can have them. (Hands them to him)

Sam'l: For nothing?

Quinn: For ten cents.

Sam'l: (Gives money; Aside) I bet I made money on dem shoulder braces.

iii. "Levinsky at the Wedding" by Julian Rose[4]

It was very cold when I started for Abe's wedding last night. I got in the car and found myself sitting next to one of these Irishmen. He wasn't cold. He had a nice blanket around him. "Must be fine to have a fine blanket to sit inside and keep warm," I said to him. "Wish I could have one like that." Then he said, "Why don't you take mine?" As I reached over for it, he said, "You do, and I'll give you a wallop in the eye." So unreasonable, those people. If I'd had a pistol I'd have slapped his face. Then he poked his finger in my eye and I got out, because that's not healthy.

Well, I guess Abe's lucky, now he's married. I'd like to do it, too, but every time I fall in love with a girl I find she's got no money, so what can I do? One thing I didn't like about Abe's wedding was right away it said at the top, "your presents is requested." They can't wait to let you know you must help pay the expenses. And down at the bottom was "please come in evening dress." Ikey Blatt wore his pajamas.

Mrs. Cone was there with her hair in a lufly physic knot. Her teeth are beautiful—both of them. She had her dress ripped open at the knee—directory. The groom had it a new suit, made for his brother when the brother got married. When Abe sat down in it he stood up. His gift from the bride was a fine watch, Swiss cheese movement.

Three little girls held up the bride's dress, but the groom used a safety pin for his trousers. Then the rabbi told him, "There are three incidents in a man's life: he is born, he is married, he dies. Now all you have to do is die."

Inside that little hot room everybody was crying, except big fat Mrs. Bloom. She perspired. Mrs. Bauman was dressed to kill, but no wonder, her husband's a butcher. Four little Wolffs were there, and oi, how they did eat! Now I know why it is always said keep the wolfs away from the door.

Mrs. Iberg was telling about awful romantic pains in her arm. She said she painted 'em with eiderdown. Always something the matter with that woman. Last spring she was at the hospital, on account she ate a sick fish. Before that she had hardening of the artillery.

We had so much to eat I was a stuffer. First we had menu, but I didn't get any of that. I guess they ran out of it early. Then was to-mato surprise. But it was no surprise to me. I ate 'em before lots of times. Irving Blatt emptied a whole bottle pickled onions in his pockets. He thought they were camphor balls.

The janitor of the apartment, Mickey McCann, calls himself superintendent, and he was there, too. He gets forty-five dollars month wages and neighbors' milk. He got noisy and hit Cone with a bottle. It was a good thing Cone got in the way, or the bottle would have broken a window.

Then Milton Bloom started to sing, "Why Did They Sell Killarney?", and that Irish loafer McCann blamed it on Milton, and started to muss him all up. McCann didn't know it was a song. He thought Killarney was really sold, and jumped on Milton because Milton deals in real estate. They had to open a window and let in some climate.

A cop walking by called Mickey over to the window and asked what's going on in there. Mickey told him he was cleaning up a Jewish wedding, and the cop shook hands with Mickey and lent him his club.

By the time they arrested Bloom he didn't have a stitch to his back. But they had to take three in his head. I was hit with a cowardly tomato. That's the kind which hits you and runs. Then there were several old shoes thrown at me—one with a foot in it.

I had to go outside, on account I couldn't stand any more. I was under a table so long, almost to suffocation. Outdoors I met my old friend Lepinsky. I invited him to take a little drink, and he said sure, so we went across the street, he put in five cents, I put in five cents, and together we had a good time.

We stepped across the room to the free lunch, and there was a roast chicken just put on the table. Lepinsky grabbed the whole chicken by the neck and brought it to our table.

"Lepinsky," I said, "You can't have that chicken all alone to eat."

"You're right," he says, "I'll go back to the table and get some potatoes to go with it."

iv. From **The Auctioneer** by Lee Arthur and Charles Klein (1901)[5]

Scene: Simon Levi's auction house

Levi: (Escorting his assistant Mo and customer Dorkins into clothing department). Now, what kind of dress suit would you like? (Turning to Mo) Mo—bring me suit No. 8764. Now you're going to see a garment—something fine. (By this time Mo has brought the coat to Levi. Levi takes the coat—letting it hang before him on his finger—so that Dorkins gets a sort of bird's-eye view.) Look it. Is that a garment? See how it hangs. Look. Look—that garment was made on Third Avenue. That's only two blocks from Fifth Avenue. Them goods are so valuable we ought to keep them in a safe.

Dorkins: Well, sir—I should prefer something very cheap, if you please.

Levi: (Cutting him short) Nothing cheap for a gentleman like—Mo, would you recommend anything cheaper than a $15.00 suit for such a gentleman?

Mo: No, sir.

Levi: No—look at that figure. And that chest—(Pointing to Dorkins's stomach). It would be an insult to your physic. Say—Mister—do me a favor?—Try it on. It won't cost you nothing. Go in the dressing-room. (Dorkins starts looking around, not knowing where to make the change.) Mo—take him to the dressing-room. (Dorkins continues looking around.) Mo—take him to the dressing-room. (Dorkins goes up to front of mirror. Mo pulls cloth, and he and Levi hold it up before Dorkins while he changes coat. Dorkins then comes forward. Business of Levi admiring coat.) Say something—No. I can't speak. My goodness—I didn't believe a suit could fit a man like that. Look at that leppel? (Pronounced like "apple") And look at that button-hole. That button-hole was imported. My, you look—Mo, does he look like a gentleman? You couldn't tell the difference.

Dorkins: Don't you think the sleeves are a trifle long, sir?

Levi: (All seriously gets down in front of Dorkins to critically examine the length of the sleeves). No, sir. N-n-n-n————o. No: that's how they wear them now . . . just till the first knuckle. (With an air of reassurance) If that suit wasn't A-1 I wouldn't have it in my emporium.

Dorkins: Oh—I believe that's all right, sir. But how is it in the back? It's a little loose—isn't it? (Turns his back to audience)

Levi: (Business of examining the wrinkle in the back of the coat). What is it mit—(To Mo)—Eh? I dunno—that's the latest wrinkle. Of course, if you don't like it I can fix it in a few minutes.

Dorkins: (Turning around) Have you a looking glass?

Levi: Huh? Oh—don't look. Take my word for it. It's alright. Say—Mister—I like so well on you—I'm going to make it for you a bargain. Take it for nothing—fifteen dollars—ten off for cash. Thirteen-fifty. Mo, don't tell my wife I'm making such a bargain. (Dorkins tries to speak.) Sh——sh——sh——sh——sh. Don't say nothing—

Dorkins: (Pulling out a one dollar bill from his pocket) I——I——I'm obliged to say, sir, that I can't pay for it now, sir. Here's all I've got, sir. (Holding out bill, which Levi does not take).

Levi: You expect a dress suit for a dollar?

Dorkins: Well . . . no, sir. But I'll tell you how it is, sir. I've been drinking a drop too much lately, sir. And—I have a chance to do better now. I'll make good. Why—I've served in the best families and restaurants in New York—Delmonico's, Sherry's—and Shanley's—

Levi: Oh! You are a waiter?

Dorkins: Yes, sir.

Levi: Well, I don't know—but—say—you come to my address next week some time. I'm going to move from here—up to #97 Lexington Avenue. You come up Tuesday or Wednesday—And I speak mit you.

Dorkins: (Starting to go) Yes, sir. Thank you very kindly, sir. Thank you.

Levi: That's alright.

Dorkins: My name's Dorkins, sir, Charley Dorkins.

Levi: All right, Charley. Mo, let him have the suit.

v. Tin Pan Alley Songs[6]

I'M A YIDDISH COWBOY (TOUGH GUY LEVI)"
BY EDGAR LESLIE, AL PIANTADOSI, AND HALSEY K. MOHR (1907)

Way Out West in the wild and woolly prairie land,
Lived a cowboy by the name of Levi,
He loved a blue blood Indian maiden,
And came to serenade her like a "tough guy."
Big Chief "Cruller Legs" was the maiden's father
And he tried to keep Levi away,
But Levi didn't care, for ev'ry ev'ning
With his Broncho Buster, Giddyap! Giddyap!
He'd come around and say:

Chorus:
Tough guy Levi, that's my name, I'm a yiddish cowboy.
I don't care for Tomahawks or Cheyenne Indians, oi, oi.
I'm a real live "Diamond Dick" that shoots 'em till they die,
I'll marry squaw or start a war, for I'm a fighting guy.

Levi said that he'd make the maiden marry him
And that he was sending for a Rabbi,
The maiden went and told her father,
He must not fight because she liked the "tough guy,"
"Cruller Legs" gave the "Pipe of Peace" to Levi
But Levi said I guess that you forget,
For I'm the kid that smokes Turkish Tobacco,
Get the Broncho Buster, Giddyap! Giddyap!
Go buy cigarettes.

Chorus

"YIDDISHA LUCK AND IRISHA LOVE (KELLY AND ROSENBAUM, THAT'S
MAZELTOFF)" BY ALFRED BRYAN AND FRED FISCHER (1911)

Last year Sadie Rosenbaum she married Michael Kelly-o.
Oi, oi, oi, oi, what a joy!
He treats her like a princess and he's just as sweet as jelly-o.
Oi, oi, oi, oi, that's a boy!
The wedding was the finest that you have ever seen,
The organist played "Mazeltoff" and "Wearing of the Green."

They thought the bride was Irish 'cause she wore a veil that day,
Till Izzy Rosenbaum stepped up and gave the bride away.

Chorus:
Yiddisha luck and Irisha love,
Yiddisha moon shining down from above;
Corn-beef and "Gefillte Fish"
Mixed together, that's a dish.
How'd you like to board with me?
Irisha man the baby carriage to push,
Yiddisha girl to handle the cush,
Oi! such a luck! and Oi! what a love!
Kelly and Rosenbaum,
That's Mazeltoff, that's Mazeltoff.

Maybe they ain't happy now, they've got a lovely baby-o.
Oi, oi, oi, oi, what a dream!
Toblitsky says they ought to call it Isador or Abie-o.
Oi, oi, oi, oi, it's a scream!
One half the baby's Irish, the other half is Jew;
We'll call it "Patrick Isador," said uncle Mike McCue.
Its father said, "We'll call it Dan O'Connell Oscar Wilde."
But she just called it Sadie 'cause it wasn't that kind of a child.

Chorus

vi. From **Potash and Perlmutter** *by Montague Glass (1913)*[7]

Scene: Offices of Potash and Perlmutter's clothing company

Perlmutter: Listen. Feldman the lawyer has got the cutter and designer
   who created the Averne Sack to promise to come and see us, now—
   what we lose on Pinkel we make up on him.
Potash: By golly, Mawruss, that's fine. We'll get him to design for us
   no matter what it costs.
Perlmutter: My, my, my, what's going to happen? For ten years we been
   partners—this is the first time you don't give me an argument.
Potash: Well, why should I give you an argument—Max Pinkel is a rot-
   ten designer.
Perlmutter: Well, you hired him, not me.

Potash: But you introduced him to me as a first-class man.

Perlmutter: Introducing is one thing, and hiring another.

Potash: All right, I hired him—but you wanted him.

Perlmutter: I wanted him? Abe, honestly, you've forgotten how to tell the truth already.

Potash: That one partner should live to call the other partner a liar. (Rising) It was you who said to me—

Perlmutter: It was me—call it to my face—go on—call it—it's all right—I don't mind.

Potash: No, Mawruss, I wouldn't call you a liar, even if I thought so. Here's a fine cigar that Malinsky gave me. Smoke it. What's the use of having arguments all the time? Arguments—(Sits L. desk)—arguments—arguments—

Perlmutter: (Takes cigar; chews it) Abe, I would rather you call me a liar than give me this. (Squeezes cigar)

Potash: What's the matter with it?

Perlmutter: What's the matter with it? If you get another one like this give it to your wife's brother. (Rising, throws cigar in waste basket, stands behind desk).

Potash: Ah, Mawruss! Vot a disposition you got—the milk of your kindness has turned into acid—no wonder you got rheumatism.

Appendix B
American Productions of Plays with Jewish Characters, 1860–1920

Dates given are of first New York performance. For shows that never appeared in New York, American premieres are given. Asterisks indicate a play or production imported from England or the Continent. I have also included other significant theatrical moments noted in this book.

This list does not include short vaudeville or variety sketches; it also excludes published plays when I could find no evidence of production. Nor is the list meant to be exhaustive; it excludes, for example, many revivals of standard repertory pieces like *Merchant of Venice*, *Leah, the Forsaken*, and *Oliver Twist*. I have included revivals only when they seemed like significant theatrical events (debuts, new adaptations, attention-getting events, etc.) that provide useful context for the purposes of this book.

I am indebted to Edward Coleman for much of the information in these lists, which I have augmented with my own research.

1860
Joseph and His Brethren. Biblical epic produced at Barnum's Museum.

1862
The Jew of Notre Dame.

*Ruth by John Thomas Haines. Revival of old British play, featuring characters of Jabez Grimani and his daughter Leah.

1863
Games; or, The Jewish Mother.

*The Jew of Southwark by Edward Stirling. Revival of old British play known as *The Mendicant's Son!*, involving poor but heroic Jew.

Leah, the Forsaken, translated/adapted/produced by Augustin Daly, from Salomen Hermann von Mosenthal's old German play *Deborah*. Kate Bateman plays title role.

Leah, the Forsook. Burlesque featuring Dan Setchall as Leah.

*My Noble Son-in-Law, translation of play by G.V.E. Augier. G. F. Browne and C. T. Parsloe play Salomons and Isaacs.

*The Ticket-of-Leave Man by Tom Taylor. Humphrey Bland plays Melter Moss, henchman.

1866

*Society by Tom Robertson. G. F. Browne plays Moses Aaron, bailiff.

1867

Fanny Janauschek appears in Mosenthal's *Deborah* in German.

Edwin Booth's first major production of *Merchant of Venice*.

*Flying Scud by Dion Boucicault. Charles Fisher plays Mo Davis, henchman.

1868

*After Dark by Dion Boucicault. E. Coleman plays Dicey Morris, henchman.

The Lottery of Life, a Story of New York by John Brougham. Charles Fisher plays Mordie Solomons, villain.

1869

Much Ado About A Merchant of Venice by John Brougham. Burlesque of Shakespeare's play, with Brougham as Shylock.

1872

Kate Bateman appears in revival of *Leah*.

The Bells, adapted from Emile Erckmann's French play *The Polish Jew*. Features J. W. Wallack as Mathias, whose conscience is haunted for murdering a Jew.

1873

Fanny Janauschek's English-language debut in *Leah*.

E. L. Davenport appears in production of *Merchant of Venice*.

*The Wandering Jew, adapted and translated by Leopold Lewis from Eugene Sue's French play. J. W. Jennings and Cyril Searle play Jewish parts.

1874

Last documented New York performance of an *Ivanhoe* adaptation. Ione Burke and Edwin Thorne play Rebecca and Sir Isaac.

Revival of *Oliver Twist*, produced by Augustin Daly. Charles Fisher plays Fagin.

1875

Clara Morris appears in Augustin Daly's revival of *Leah*.

1876

Ben Israel by Edward Tullidge. Philo-Semitic play set in Restoration England.

Moses, a Dealer in Second-Hand Clothing. Musical melodrama.

The Phoenix by Milton Nobles. George Ketchum plays comic broker Moses Solomons for New York premiere, a role later held by Alonzo Schwartz.

1877

Revival of *Oliver Twist* with McKee Rankin as Fagin.

1878

Frank Bush starts to gain notice for his variety-hall Jew routine.

1879

Jew Trouble at Manhattan Beach by George Stout. Sketch part of variety bill
at Tony Pastor's concert saloon, with J. F. Peters as Levi Mendathall.

1881

Lawrence Barrett appears in *Merchant of Venice*.
Sam'l of Posen; or, The Commercial Drummer by George Jessop. Vehicle for
M. B. Curtis in title role.

1882

Mordecai Lyons by Edward Harrigan, who flops in title role. Tony Hart plays
Leon Mendoza.
My Hebrew Friend by Frank Dumont.

1883

*Henry Irving's first tour of *Merchant of Venice*. His New York season also
features him in *The Bells*, in an adaptation by Leopold Lewis.
Never Too Late to Mend, adapted by Cyril Searle from Charles Reade's novel.
H. A. Weaver plays upstanding Isaac Levy, secondary character.
Siberia by Bartley Campbell. Georgia Cayvan and Blanche Mortimer play
half-Jewish sisters who suffer in pogroms.

1884

Mr. Moses Myers by Frank Dumont.
On Hand. Features a Jewish peddler in secondary role.

1885

Spot Cash by Ed Marble and M. B. Curtis. Another Sam'l Plastrick vehicle
for Curtis.

1886

Margaret Mather's first appearance in *Leah*.
Caught in a Corner by W. J. Shaw. Another vehicle for Curtis, this time as
Isaac Greenwald.
The Leather Patch by Edward Harrigan. Includes song and dance of Jewish
old clothes men.

1888

David Warfield debuts as Melter Moss in California production of *Ticket-of-
Leave Man*.

1889

An Iron Creed by Charles Stow. J. F. O'Brien and Marie Cross play the
wealthy David Belmont and his daughter Ruth.

1890

Beau Brummel by Clyde Fitch, as vehicle for Richard Mansfield. W. H. Crompton plays Abrahams, creditor.

*Judah by Henry Arthur Jones. E. S. Willard plays title role of half-Jew.

The Last Word, translated and adapted by producer/director Augustin Daly, from Franz Von Schoenthan's play. Frederic Bond plays minor role of Moses Mossop, operator.

Men and Women by David Belasco and Henry De Mille. Frederick de Belleville plays Israel Cohen, high-minded banker.

The Shatchen by Charles Doblin Dickson. Another vehicle for Curtis, this time as Meyer Petowsky.

1891

Edwin Booth's last production of *Merchant of Venice*.

1892

*Sarah Bernhardt brings her adaptation of *Leah* to New York.

*The Cabinet Minister by Arthur Wing Pinero, produced by Augustin Daly. Sidney Herbert and Edith Crane play Joseph Lebanon and Mrs. Gaylustre, money-lender and his sister.

1893

Richard Mansfield debuts his *Merchant of Venice*.

1894

On the Bowery by R. N. Stephens. Frank Bush plays Jewish huckster in secondary comic role.

1895

*A Bunch of Violets by Sydney Grundy. Charles Allan plays Jacob Schwartz, grafting labor leader.

Down the Black Cañon by Forbes Heermans. Performed in Salt Lake City this year, though published in 1890. Features character of Solomon Goldstein, sheriff.

The Great Diamond Robbery by Edward M. Alfriend and A. C. Wheeler. Fanny Janauschek plays vicious fence Frau Rosenbaum.

Trilby, adapted by Paul Potter from George Du Maurier's novel. Wilton Lackaye plays Svengali.

1896

*Herbert Beerbohm Tree brings his *Trilby* to New York.

A Girl Wanted by R. N. Stephens. Frank Bush plays small Jewish comic role.

1897

Nance O'Neil starts touring *The Jewess*, a version of *Leah*.

In Gay New York by C.M.S. McLellan (Hugh Morton). Warfield plays Solomon McCarthy in revamped version of earlier Casino Company revue.

1898

Augustin Daly produces/directs *Merchant of Venice*, with Sidney Herbert as Shylock.

*The Christian by Hall Caine, adapted from his own novel. Edgar Norton plays Rosenberg, theatrical manager.

The Dreyfus Affair by Vera DeNoie and A. D. Hall.

Hurly Burly by Edgar Smith and John Stromberg. Warfield plays Solomon Yankle in Weber and Fields musical.

*Trelawny of the "Wells" by Arthur Wing Pinero. Mrs. Thomas Whiffen plays Mrs. Mossop, owner of theatrical rooming house.

1899

Jess Dandy and Julian Rose start to gain notice for their vaudeville Jew routines.

Children of the Ghetto by Israel Zangwill, produced by James A. Herne. Wilton Lackaye plays Reb Shemuel, Blanche Bates plays Hannah. By an English playwright, but first professionally produced in United States.

*The Ghetto, adapted by Chester Bailey from Herman Heijermans's Dutch play. Joseph Haworth, Sidney Herbert, and Mrs. McKee Rankin play major Jewish parts.

Helter Skelter by Edgar Smith. David Warfield plays Isidore Nosenstein in Weber and Fields musical.

Whirl-i-Gig by Edgar Smith. David Warfield plays Sigmund Cohenski in Weber and Fields musical.

1900

Joe Welch starts to gain notice for his vaudeville Jew routine.

*The Degenerates by Sydney Grundy. Lillie Langtry vehicle includes small Jewish role.

Fiddle-Dee-Dee by Edgar Smith. David Warfield plays Shadrach Leschinski in Weber and Fields musical.

*Hearts Are Trumps by Cecil Raleigh, produced by Charles Frohman. Includes the character of Leopold Klowitz, villain.

The King of Rogues by James H. Wallick. Features the characters of Levine and Silver, Jewish villains.

When We Were Twenty-one by Henry Vernon Esmond. Thomas O'Berle plays David Hirsch, thief.

1901

Nat Goodwin appears in *Merchant of Venice*.

The Auctioneer by Lee Arthur and Charles Klein. Vehicle for David Warfield as Simon Levi, produced by David Belasco.

Under Two Flags, adaptation by Paul Potter of Ouida's novel, produced by David Belasco and Charles Frohman. Albert Bruening plays secondary role of Baroni, shopkeeper.

1902

Iris by Arthur Wing Pinero. Oscar Asche plays Maldonado, handsome Jew who courts gentile title character.

The Peddler by James "Hal" Reid. Vehicle for Joe Welch as Abraham Jacobson.

Sally in Our Alley by George Hobart. Marie Cahill as big-hearted immigrant title character.

1903

*Henry Irving's last New York production of *Merchant of Venice*.

Jacob Adler production of *Merchant of Venice*. Adler plays in Yiddish opposite English-speaking cast.

Nance O'Neil tours adaptation of Paolo Giacommetti's *Judith*.

Child Slaves of New York by Charles Blaney and Howard Hall. Frank Opperman plays Abraham Levy.

The Girl from Kays by Ivan Caryll. Sam Bernard plays likable wealthy "Piggy" Hoggenheimer.

Rachel Goldstein by Grace White, adapted from Thedor Kremer's book. Louise Beaton plays immigrant title character.

1904

Cohen's Luck by Lee Arthur. Vehicle for Joe Welch.

Judith of Bethulia by Thomas Bailey Aldrich, as vehicle for Nance O'Neil.

Leah Kleschna by C.M.S. McLellan (Hugh Morton). Minnie Maddern Fiske plays title role, vaguely Jewish thief reformed by high-minded lover.

Letty by Arthur Wing Pinero, produced by Charles Frohman. Arthur Playfair plays Bernard Mandeville.

The Pit, adapted by Channing Pollock from Frank Norris's novel. Richard Manuel plays secondary role of Hirsch, a stock trader. Wilton Lackaye stars.

1905

Revival of *Trilby* with Wilton Lackaye.

Revival of *Siberia*.

Charles Frohman's revival of *Oliver Twist*, with J. E. Dodson as Fagin.

The Conspirators by Maurice Douglas Flattery. Russell Bassett plays Joe Leavitt, renegade. Produced in Boston.

Fast Life in New York by Al H. Woods. Features Julian Rose.

The Shepherd King by Wright Lorimer, who also plays title role of King David in Biblical epic.

The Woman in the Case by Clyde Fitch. Samuel Edwards plays lecherous Louis Klauffsky.

1906

The House of Mirth by Clyde Fitch, adapted from Edith Wharton novel. Albert Bruening plays upwardly mobile Sim Rosedale.

Mizpah by Ella Wheeler Wilcox and Luscombe Searelle. Elizabeth Kennedy plays Queen Esther.

Old Isaacs from the Bowery by Charles Blaney. *Auctioneer* rehash.

The Rich Mr. Hoggenheimer by Harry B. Smith. Sam Bernard plays title role in follow-up to *Girl from Kays*. Includes music by Jerome Kern.

The Stolen Story by Jesse Lynch Williams. Stephen Wright and Charles Nevil play secondary characters Jake Shayne and Sam Nordheimer, grafters.

1907

Revival of The *Peddler*, with Samuel Tornberg in lead role.

The Money Lender by James "Hal" Reid. Samuel Tornberg plays Abraham Jacobson, heroic sweatshop worker.

The Shoemaker by James "Hal" Reid. Joe Welch plays title role.

When Knights Were Bold by Harriet Jay, produced by Charles Frohman. George Irving and Margaret Gordon play Isaac Isaacson and his daughter Sarah. Comic retake of *Ivanhoe*.

1908

Lady Frederick by W. Somerset Maugham. Orlando Daly plays Captain Montgomerie, usurer, secondary character in play starring Ethel Barrymore.

Samson, translation of French play by Henri Bernstein. William Gillette plays self-destructive millionaire.

1909

Fanny Brice debuts "Sadie Salome" routine, built around Irving Berlin song.

The House Next Door by J. Hartley Manners. Thomas Findlay plays Sir Isaac Jacobson in intermarriage play.

Idols, adapted by Roy Horniman from William J. Locke's novel. Leonore Harris plays Minna Hart in intermarriage play.

Israel by Henri Bernstein, produced by Charles Frohman. Edwin Arden plays elderly Jewish banker.

The Melting-pot by Israel Zangwill. Walker Whiteside plays David Quixano in intermarriage play. By an English playwright, but set in United States and frequently produced there before first English professional production.

Meyer and Son by Thomas Addison. William Humphrey and Nathan Ritchie play title roles in intermarriage play.

New Lamps and Old, adapted and translated by Oscar Leonard from Ronetti Roman's play. Wilton Lackaye plays Manasse, patriarch of Jewish family. Produced in St. Louis.

On the Eve, adapted by Martha Morton from Leopold Kampf's play. J. Adelman plays Tantul Vlasador, Russian revolutionary.

The Passing of the Third Floor Back by Jerome K. Jerome. A. G. Poulton plays Jake Samuels, rogue.

The Third Degree by Charles Klein. George Barnum plays Dr. Bernstein, secondary role.

1910

The Country Boy by Edgar Selwyn. Arthur Shaw plays Joe Weinstein, fast-talking theater ticket speculator and gambler, secondary role.

*Smith by W. Somerset Maugham. Jane Laurel plays Mrs. Otto Rosenberg, social butterfly, secondary role.

1911

As a Man Thinks by Augustus Thomas. John Mason plays Dr. Samuel Seelig, high-minded Jewish doctor, in intermarriage play.

Disraeli by Louis Parker. George Arliss plays charismatic title role.

Excuse Me by Rupert Hughes. Frank Manning plays Max Baumann, secondary role.

The Faun by Edward Knoblock. Lionel Belmore plays Maurice Morris, moneylender, secondary role.

Maggie Pepper by Charles Klein. Leo Kohlmar plays Jake Rothschilds, salesman, secondary role.

1912

Revival of *Oliver Twist*, adapted by J. Comyns Carr, featuring Nat Goodwin as Fagin.

*Bella Donna by James Bernard Fagan, adapted from Robert Hichens's novel. Charles Bryant plays Meyer Isaacson, secondary role.

*The "Mind the Paint" Girl by Arthur Wing Pinero. Lee Cooper plays secondary role of Sam de Castro, backstage lecher. Includes two Jerome Kern interpolations.

*Return from Jerusalem, translated by Owen Johnson from French play by Maurice Donnay. Mme. Simone plays Henriette de Chouze, freethinking Jewess who loves a gentile man.

1913

Jewish organizations start to protest anti-Semitic characterizations.

*Forbes Robertson brings his production of *Merchant of Venice* to New York.

Revival of *The Auctioneer*, starring David Warfield, directed by David Belasco.

*The Five Frankforters, adapted and translated by Basil Hood from Carl Roessler's play about Rothschild family. Mathilde Cottrelly plays grandmother Gudula.

*The Great Adventure by Arnold Bennett, produced by David Belasco. Edgar Kent plays Ebag, picture dealer, secondary role.

*Grumpy by Horace Hodges and T. W. Percyval. Lenox Pawle plays Isaac Wolfe, small role.

The Heart of a Child by Julia Frankau. Robert Graceland plays Joe Aarons, lecherous theatrical manager.

The House of Bondage by Joseph Byron Totten, from Reginald Wright Kauffman's novel. Agnes Kelly plays Carrie Berkowitz, prostitute, in white-slavery play.

Potash and Perlmutter, adapted by Charles Klein from Montague Glass's stories. Barney Bernard and Alexander Carr play title roles.

The Tongues of Men by Edward Carpenter. Sheridan Block plays Herman Geist, opera manager, secondary role.

1914

The Show Shop by James Forbes. George Sidney plays Max Rosenbaunm, likable theatrical manager.

1915

Revival of *Trilby* with Wilton Lackaye.

Abe and Mawruss (later known as *Potash and Perlmutter in Society*), adapted by Roi Cooper Megrue from Montague Glass's stories. Barney Bernard and Julius Tannen play title roles.

The Bargain by Herman G. Scheffauer. Modernized retake of *Merchant of Venice*.

*The Doctor's Dilemma by George Bernard Shaw. Wright Kramer plays Dr. Schutzmacher.

Our Mrs. McChesney, adapted by George Hobart from Edna Ferber's stories. Thomas Reynolds and Jack Kingsberry play Greenebaum and Perlman.

Young America by Frederick Ballard. Joseph Berger plays Isaac Slavensky, secondary role.

1916

Mine Eyes Have Seen by Alice Dunbar Nelson. Jewish labor leader character appears.

Night by Sholem Asch. Yiddish play in translation, produced by East-West Players.

Object, Matrimony by Montague Glass and Jules Eckert Goodman.

Turn to the Right by Winchell Smith. Jewish tailor and pawnbroker characters appear briefly.

With the Current by Sholem Asch. Yiddish play in translation, produced by Neighborhood Playhouse.

1917

Revival of *Disraeli* with George Arliss.

Business Before Pleasure, adapted by Jules Eckert Goodman from Montague Glass's stories. Barney Bernard and Alexander Carr as Potash and Perlmutter.

Lombardi Ltd. by Frederic and Fanny Hatton. Harold Russell plays Max Strohn, cheap theatrical manager, secondary role.

1918

The Gentile Wife by Rita Wellman. D. Powell plays David Davis in intermarriage play.

A Little Journey by Rachel Crothers. Paul E. Burns plays Leo Stern.

Penrod by Edward Everett Ross, from Booth Tarkington's stories. Henry Quinn plays Maurice Levy, gang member.

1919

Gibson Upright by Booth Tarkington and H. L. Wilson. George Somnes plays Frankel, labor leader. Produced in Indianapolis.

His Honor Abe Potash, adapted by Jules Eckert Goodman from Montague Glass's stories. Barney Bernard plays title role.

1920

Poldekin by Booth Tarkington. Edward G. Robinson plays Pinsky in play starring George Arliss.

The Unwritten Chapter by Samuel Shipman and V. Victor. Louis Man plays Haym Solomon.

The Wandering Jew by E. Temple Thurston. Produced by David Belasco.

Welcome Stranger by Aaron Hoffman. George Sidney plays Isidor Solomon.

NOTES

Introduction

1. "Thirty-five Years of Stage Fright," *Pictorial Review*, February 1926, in the Warfield file of the Billy Rose Collection of the New York Public Library. The paragraphing here is my own. William C. Young, in *Famous Actors and Actresses*, specifies the time and place as Napa, California, 1888. On the subject of Warfield's reputation as a great actor, see *Outlook*, 26 October 1912. As late as the film *Gold-diggers of 1933*, a character could admiringly mention Warfield in the same breath as the heralded George Arliss—another actor who became famous playing a Jew. See my discussion of *Disraeli* in Chapter Six.

2. On Warfield's not being Jewish, see Paul Antonie Distler, "Rise and Fall of the Racial Comics," 171. Sources give a variety of spellings for Warfield's family name, including "Wollfeld," but "Wohlfelt" is the one I have come across most often and the one I use here. Immigrant families themselves sometimes spelled their English names inconsistently or gradually changed the spelling over time.

3. Sander Gilman and Stephen T. Katz, *Antisemitism*, 18.

4. Landa laments that at the beginning of the twentieth century the Jew remained an "enslaved buffoon" but also suggests that the future might bring more positive portrayals of the Jew. See 308–310. Ellen Schiff's *From Stereotype to Metaphor* (1982) suggests that the modernist revolution indeed brought about such a liberation, making it possible for the Jewish character to "play any role intended for a human being," 247.

5. Edgar Rosenberg, *From Shylock to Svengali*, 297.

6. While Mayor descends at times into a mere catalogue-like listing, in its ambitious scope it remains an impressive piece of scholarship that has been of great use to me.

7. Judith Butler, *Gender Trouble*, 140–141.

8. Dwight Conquergood, "Rethinking Ethnography," 184.

9. Albert Sonnenfeld, "The Poetics of Anti-Semitism," 84. Sonnenfeld also articulates how Jews have been perceived in relationship to economic and political practices. On the position of Jews in America, see Albert S. Lindemann, *The*

Jew Accused, 209. On the many meanings of Jew, see George M. Kren, "The Jews: The Image as Reality," 285–287.

10. Distler's unpublished dissertation, "Rise and Fall of the Racial Comics," is the one pioneering survey, but it does not pretend to go into detailed analysis and confines its scope to a specific era of variety theater.

11. In making this generalization, I do not want to reduce the complexity of pre-Holocaust Jewish immigration to the United States to two simple waves. There were, for example, Sephardic Jews living along the eastern seaboard as early as the seventeenth century; there were many Eastern European Jews who arrived before 1881; there were some German Jews who arrived after 1881; there were Central European Jews arriving throughout this era who do not fit so neatly into one category or another. Hasia R. Diner has particularly emphasized the diversity of the mid-nineteenth century arrivals throughout *Time for Gathering*.

12. As is clear from Nahma Sandrow's *Vagabond Stars*, there was no single "Yiddish theater" in America; it was a highly diverse network of institutions spanning a broad range of styles, appealing to a wide variety of audiences. When extended to the international level, the whole question of Yiddish theater becomes even more complex.

13. Historians often refer to a large portion of this era as the "Gilded Age," but I prefer the term Victorian because it better reflects the time frame and conjures up the cultural milieu with which I am concerned than do other terms. If it reflects an Anglo-centrism, then it accurately reflects the stage world I am looking at, which was directly impacted by many English and Irish artists, as I make clear in Chapter One. The emergence of Jews in the theater, which I trace in Part Two, can thereby be seen as representing a departure from this Victorian era.

14. Some would argue that to use the term American to refer to the United States (as I do here) unfairly appropriates an entire hemisphere (the Americas) for a single and rather atypical country within that region. At the moment, however, I cannot find another adjective which so usefully serves my purposes and so I continue to use it, though I welcome others using it for their purposes as well. From having lived in Mexico, I know that, while I was a "norteamericano" to some of my Mexican friends, I remained an "americano" to the vast majority.

15. Heinz Kosok deals with this issue in greater depth in "Dion Boucicault's 'American' Plays."

16. In determining what is significant, I have exercised subjective judgment, influenced by the size of audience, length of run, and relevance to the issues I am discussing. In particular, I have excluded works by established British playwrights like Jones, Maugham, Pinero, and Shaw which, despite their importance in the history of dramatic literature, received mostly brief productions in the United States. On the other hand, Herbert Beerbohm Tree's production of *Trilby* cannot be ignored. Israel Zangwill's *The Melting-pot* receives extended treatment; though Zangwill was English, the play was not only set in the United States, but had its first production there and significantly shaped the public conversation on immigration.

17. For more detailed examinations of the rise of modern anti-Semitism, see Judith

Marion Halberstom, "Parasites and Perverts," 101; Lindemann, *The Jew Accused*, 16; Kren, "The Jews: The Image as Reality," throughout.

CHAPTER 1   ***Making the Jewish Villain Visible***

1. Cited in Kirk Mallory Reynolds, "A Stage History," 222.
2. "The Larks," *The Shakespeare Water-Cure*, 4.
3. For related observations about the representation of the Jewish man in German culture, see Sander Gilman, "Salome, Syphilis, and Sarah Bernhardt," 195.
4. Of course, Shylock is rooted in older, medieval conceptions of the Jew, which are beyond the scope of my inquiry. See Edgar Rosenberg's *From Shylock to Svengali* and John Gross's *Shylock* for more detailed analysis of the character's antecedents in theater and elsewhere.
5. Examples of this are legion and demonstrate the power of stage performances and literary creations to shape reality. To take one recent example, Hector Mendez, a civilian rescue hero of the 1985 Mexico City earthquake, criticized the perceived inaction of the predominantly Jewish owners of clothing factories that had collapsed during the disaster: "You've read Shakespeare? *The Merchant of Venice*? You remember Shylock, right? Well, Shylock is the portrait of the Mexican Jew." From Elena Poniatowska, *Nada, nadie* (Mexico City: Ediciones Era, 1988), 189. Translation is my own.
6. Gladys Veidemanis, "Reflections on 'The Shylock Problem,'" 370–371.
7. Among the many works linking Shylock to a larger tradition of anti-Semitism, two recent books are notable. Gross's *Shylock* comes to a similar conclusion as mine (see page 321, for example): that whatever humanistic touches and complexities the character may possess, Shylock cannot be dissociated from the history of anti-Semitism; his villainies are traditional Jewish villainies. In *Shakespeare and the Jews*, 119–130, James Shapiro has artfully speculated on the connections between circumcision and Shylock's pound of flesh while resisting the notion that *Merchant* is anti-Semitic.
8. Along these lines, Marlowe's *Jew of Malta*, which features a far less naturalized and more invidious Jew, makes a useful point of comparison that puts Shakespeare's work in perspective.
9. On the trend toward a sympathetic Shylock, see Reynolds, "A Stage History," 399. The same point is clear throughout Gross's *Shylock*.
10. Louis Harap, *Image of the Jew*, 205.
11. Gross, *Shylock*, 126. My estimate of the frequency of productions is based on those that received reviews in the *New York Times*, as indexed in the collection of *Times* theater reviews from these same years.
12. Albert Sonnenfeld, "The Poetics of Anti-Semitism," 79.
13. M. J. Landa in *The Jew in Drama* devotes an appendix to refuting Kean's Jewishness. On abridgments made to the text, see Reynolds, "A Stage History," 398. For an excellent, opinionated overview of the contributions of the elder Kean and Booth to the role, see William Winter, *Shakespeare on the Stage*, 137–150.
14. Winter, *Shakespeare on the Stage*, 152.

15. Adah Isaacs Menken, "Shylock."

16. Again, these numbers are derived from my survey of *Times* theater reviews.

17. Richard Lockridge, *Darling of Misfortune*, 101.

18. Reynolds, "A Stage History," 195–196.

19. Toby Lelyveld, *Shylock on the Stage*, 72.

20. Booth's style as both actor and manager not only catered to the respectable American white bourgeois audience that emerged in the mid-1800s, but in fact, helped to create such an audience, which welcomed women as respectable theatergoers and also established an emerging decorum related to the process of attending and watching plays that has largely persisted to this day. Bruce A. McConachie's *Melodramatic Formations* details cultural and economic factors that led to the emergence of new types of theaters.

21. Reynolds, "A Stage History," 205.

22. Winter, *Shakespeare on Stage*, 158.

23. *New York Tribune*, 16 February 1896.

24. *Century*, January 1892, 320, 333.

25. Jacob A. Riis, *How the Other Half Lives*, 112.

26. Robert Mitchell, "Recent Jewish Immigration," 340.

27. William Dean Howells, "An East-Side Ramble," 107.

28. Reynolds, "A Stage History," 198.

29. Winter, *Shakespeare on Stage*, 156.

30. Eleanor Ruggles, *Prince of Players: Edwin Booth*, 120.

31. Edwina Booth Grossmann, *Edwin Booth*, 259, 264.

32. Daniel J. Watermeier, *Between Actor and Critic*, 256.

33. Cited in Lelyveld, *Shylock on the Stage*, 69.

34. Grossmann, *Shylock on the Stage*, 269.

35. For the account of an actress who saw Booth in the role in 1889, see Katherine Goodale, *Behind the Scenes with Edwin Booth*, 312.

36. For a discussion of the possible Jewish roots of the Booth clan, see Stephen M. Archer, *Junius Brutus Booth: Theatrical Prometheus*, 4.

37. In 1883, Irving's fame stemmed partially from another role associated with the Jewish question, that of Mathias in Leopold Lewis's *The Bells*, a translation-adaptation of Emile Erckmann's French melodrama *The Polish Jew*. Since 1871, Irving had been mesmerizing audiences with this tale of a German burgomaster haunted by the memories of a wayfaring Jewish traveler whom he murdered fifteen winters before. With the introduction of Shylock into his repertory then, Irving added a second Jewish-related play to his international reputation.

38. Bram Stoker, *Personal Reminiscences of Henry Irving*, 1:84.

39. Laurence Irving, *Henry Irving*, 333.

40. Quotations are from Winter, *Shakespeare on Stage*, 180. Winter offers an excellent discussion of the costuming and other staging elements, 177–189.

41. Cited in Lelyveld, *Shylock on the Stage*, 91.

42. Cited in Lelyveld, *Shylock on the Stage*, 82–83.

43. For more details on the touches Irving brought to the role, see Reynolds, "A Stage History," 227; Winter, *Shakespeare on Stage*, 186–189; Irving, *Henry Ir-*

ving, 338–344; Lelyveld, *Shylock on the Stage*, 82–84. Also, I refer the reader to Gross's *Shylock* for its outstanding section on how Irving reconceived the part, and the controversy in which this characterization sometimes embroiled him.

44. Winter, *Shakespeare on Stage*, 193, 196.

45. For a thoughtful examination of the relationship between anti-Semitism and Gothic monsters, see Judith Marion Halberstom, "Parasites and Perverts." In this context, Stoker is a fascinating part of this network, since he links Irving to Dracula.

46. For an excellent analysis of how the Jew traced a similar course in nineteenth-century England, see Shearer West's "Construction of Racial Type."

47. On different genres of melodrama and their relationships to specific audiences, the definitive work is McConachie, *Melodramatic Formations*. David Grimsted's influential *Melodrama Unveiled* is also useful. Both these works deal primarily with the earlier part of the century; there is no comprehensive examination of the varieties of melodrama, 1860–1920, which is perceived as a period of decline for the form.

48. For a more detailed analysis of Fagin, including Dickens's reading of him, see Rosenberg, *From Shylock to Svengali*, 116–137. J. E. Dodson and Nat Goodwin are two early twentieth-century actors who played both Shylock and Fagin. It seems appropriate that their Shylocks were more in the malevolent tradition of Macklin and less in the sympathetic one of Irving.

49. Forbes Heermans, *Down the Black Cañon*, 4.

50. Charles Townsend, *Jail Bird*, 4, 7. Townsend (1857–1914) was a Buffalo-born playwright and actor who turned out some fifty plays for his company, a number of which feature stage Jews in secondary parts. Probably he had an actor in his troupe adept at these roles. See also his *Golden Gulch* (1893), *Iron Hand* (1897), and *Perils of a Great City* (1899).

51. Townsend, *Jail Bird*, 9.

52. On the Jew as petty capitalist, see Louise A. Mayor, *Ambivalent Image*, 90–91, 181; Albert S. Lindemann, *The Jew Accused*, 207; David A. Gerber, "Cutting Out Shylock," 225.

53. Mayor, *Ambivalent Image*, 19, 181.

54. Gerber, "Cutting Out Shylock," 219.

55. Frank Bixby, *The Little Boss*, 6.

56. On deviant Jewish male sexuality, see two works by Gilman: *Jewish Self-Hatred*, 75; *The Jew's Body*, 122–124.

57. Cited in Bram Dijkstra, *Idols of Perversity*, 221.

58. Townsend, *Jail Bird*, 15, 42.

59. Bixby, *The Little Boss*, 44.

60. My quotations from *Lottery of Life* come from the holograph in the Billy Rose Collection of the New York Public Library.

61. Chase (1857–1920), who sometimes published under the name Abel Seaman, was associated with the Boston theater. He published many vaudeville-style vignettes, a number of which featured Jews.

CHAPTER 2   *Taming the Exotic Jewess*

1. Quotations cited are in Louis Harap, *Image of the Jew*, 109–110.
2. For an excellent overview of the belle juive, see Ellen Schiff, *From Stereotype to Metaphor*, 22–23.
3. I do not deal with *Ivanhoe* at length here, since it has been well covered by other authors. See, for example, Edgar Rosenberg, *From Shylock to Svengali*, 73–115.
4. I base this final date on Gerald Bordman, *American Theatre: A Chronicle*, 76.
5. It is no secret that Daly's script is actually a translation by W. Benneaux. Daly had an active hand in adapting the translation for its initial American production and managed to parley this power into legal authorship. For more of these details on the production and its reception, see Marvin Felheim, *Theater of Augustin Daly*, 47, 159, 162. This appropriation of authorship, which in the twentieth century reads like plagiarism, was common practice in the nineteenth-century American theater, especially before the enforcement of international copyright laws; as Felheim makes clear, Daly probably served as little more than collaborator on many of the plays that today bear his name.

   An interesting angle on *Leah*, beyond the scope of my inquiry, is how it was received as a commentary on slavery. *Harper's Weekly*, for example, cited the timeless message of the play, linking the villagers' inhumane treatment of Leah to the inhumane treatment of slaves in the American South. "Go and see Leah," its critic wrote, "and have the lesson burned upon your mind, which may help to save the national life and honor." (7 March 1863)
6. The preceding quotations are from Augustin Daly, *Leah, the Forsaken*, 5, 19, 33–34, 36, 12, 15, 4. Much of Nathan's venom is the original contribution of Daly; perhaps as a way of catering to American audiences' taste for melodrama, he took Mosenthal's less-prominent Nathan and elevated him into a commanding villain whose cunning drives the action of the play.
7. Though just twenty years old at the time, Bateman already enjoyed international acclaim, having made her debut at age four as a child prodigy under the management of her father, the actor and impresario H. L. Bateman. In 1862, Daly was serving as the Batemans' publicist. His scripting of *Leah* amounted to his helping the elder Bateman fashion a vehicle for his daughter to show off her talents, not as child prodigy or youthful ingenue, but as grand tragedienne in the continental tradition. For more details, see Felheim, *Theater of Augustin Daly*, 7, 159. For an excellent analysis of how Daly manipulated women to remake himself in the image of late nineteenth-century controller of nature, see Kim Marra, "Taming America."
8. Clara Morris, *Life of a Star*, 180, 174.
9. For further details on the life of Menken, see Wolf Mankowitz's *Mazeppa*. For fine analysis of the contradictory ways in which Menken was received by her audiences, see Elizabeth Reitz Mullenix, "Neither Fish, Flesh Nor Fowl."
10. In including Bernhardt here, I want to make clear that the performer made a tremendous impact on America. She toured the United States nine times be-

tween 1880 and 1918, logging hundreds of performances not only in major metropolises but in many secondary cities as well, sometimes performing to crowds so massive that they had to be accommodated in enormous tents.

11. On anti-Semitism in Paris during Bernhardt's early years, see Cornelia Otis Skinner, *Madame Sarah*, 12.

12. Arthur Gold and Robert Fizdale, *The Divine Sarah*, 275.

13. *New York Dramatic Mirror*, 28 March 1879.

14. Cited in Skinner, *Madame Sarah*, 13.

15. Gold and Fizdale, *The Divine Sarah*, 198.

16. *New York Times*, 21 April 1892. The adaptation Bernhardt employed highlights Leah's position at the expense of Rudolf and other characters who share her spotlight in the Daly and Mosenthal versions. Bernhardt's *Leah* also features an extended scene of pathos between the Jewess and her father, Abraham, while they huddle in the forest, dreaming of a future of freedom and equality in a "great land of liberty, where Love and Duty do not conflict." Whether by virtue of such reworking of the text, or by the way that text was transacted through the body of Bernhardt, American critics perceived the production as having a more explicitly philo-Semitic message than it had been associated with in the past. In the citation above, the *Times* saw her Leah, in contrast to Bateman's, as "the representative of a cruelly-wronged race, the living symbol of its passion, its pain, and anger."

17. Gold and Fizdale, *The Divine Sarah*, 13.

18. On Bernhardt as "consumptive sublime," see Bram Dijkstra, *Idols of Perversity*, 46.

19. *New York Dramatic Mirror*, 9 January 1886.

20. *San Francisco Bulletin*, 30 December 1902; *Boston Evening Transcript*, 19 February 1904. Both clippings are in the O'Neil file of the Billy Rose Collection of the New York Public Library.

21. Unidentified, undated clipping in O'Neil file of the Billy Rose Collection.

22. *Denver Daily News*, 15 April 1903. In O'Neil file of the Billy Rose Collection.

23. For thoughtful analysis of the *Ben Hur* sensation, see Paul Gutjahr, "Solid Puritans."

24. Aldrich (1836–1907) was one of the last representatives of the fading genteel New England literary tradition. Though famous as a poet and novelist (he authored an epic poem based on the Judith story), he had an intense interest in the theater and had been a close friend of Edwin Booth. Adah Isaacs Menken also wrote a poem on Judith, published in Mankowitz, *Mazeppa*, 248–250.

25. Thomas Bailey Aldrich, *Judith of Bethulia*, 21, 97.

26. For more on Judith as fin-de-siècle icon, see Dijkstra, *Idols of Perversity*, 376–379.

27. For more on the relationship between Bernhardt and Salome, see Sander Gilman, "Salome, Syphilis, and Sarah Bernhardt."

28. McLellan also wrote musical comedy under the name Hugh Morton, where he collaborated on some of the early David Warfield revues that I document in Chapter Four.

29. *Metropolitan Magazine*, March 1905. In Fiske file of the Billy Rose Collection.
30. The two rare, short films are available at the National Center for Jewish Film at Brandeis University. In including these three films, I should make clear the direct connections between early silent movies and the stage. Many of the actors and some of the directors of early film were trained, like Griffith, as members of touring combination companies. Moreover, as Roberta E. Pearson argues in *Eloquent Gestures*, early silents relied heavily on the stock conventions of stage melodrama both for their stories and acting techniques, and thus established a continuity between the two media.
31. Tom Gunning, *Outsiders as Insiders* (unpaginated pamphlet).
32. *Biograph Bulletin*, 25 October 1908.
33. Jacob A. Riis, *How the Other Half Lives*, 104.
34. *Cohen's Fire Sale* is available at the National Center for Jewish Film.
35. Unidentified, undated clipping in Janauschek file in the Billy Rose Collection.
36. As a touring piece, without Janauschek, *Diamond Robbery* held the stage into the next century. Movie versions were produced in 1912 and 1914.
37. The preceding quotations are from Edward M. Alfriend and A. C. Wheeler, *The Great Diamond Robbery*, 85, 79, 91.

CHAPTER 3   *Becoming a Jolly Good Fellow*

1. See Neal Gabler, *Empire of Their Own*, especially the Introduction, for an excellent account of the Jews who shaped Hollywood. Many of them, like Adolf Zukor, for example, entered show business after already having had experience in various retail industries.
2. Louis Harap, *Image of the Jew*, 202.
3. On the specifics of anti-Semitism in this era, see Louise Mayor, *Ambivalent Image*, 92–108; Leonard Dinnerstein, *Anti-Semitism in America*, 34–40. Dinnerstein cogently argues that this period represents the first major era of American anti-Semitism, starting a trend that continued until the second part of the twentieth century.
4. *New York Times*, 23 July 1879.
5. Dinnerstein, *Anti-Semitism in America*, 40.
6. *New York Times*, 24 July 1879.
7. The playbill is in the Pastor file of the Theatre Collection of the Humanities Research Center, the University of Texas at Austin.

   I use the term "variety" the same way it is generally used by theater historians: to describe the mixed-bill, mostly working-class entertainments of roughly the 1860s through 1880s, before the term "vaudeville" (connoting a more regularized circuit for largely middle-class audiences) came into common usage to describe mixed-bill entertainment.
8. M. J. Landa, *The Jew in Drama*, 22.
9. Clara Morris, *Life on the Stage*, 242–243.
10. William Winter, *Shakespeare on Stage*, 197.
11. Both quotations appear in the introductory pages of Milton Nobles, *The Phoenix*.
12. *New York Times*, 17 August 1880. The issue comes up of Nobles' ethnicity.

Lacking evidence to the contrary, I take him to be gentile, though his name suggests the possibility of Jewish origins.

13. This number is given in the *New York Dramatic Mirror*, 21 August 1880.
14. *New York Dramatic Mirror*, 5 January 1884.
15. *New York Times*, 17 August 1880.
16. Nobles, *The Phoenix*, 104, 107.
17. In *Phoenix* file of the Billy Rose Collection of the New York Public Library.
18. The preceding quotations are from Nobles, *The Phoenix*, 4, 106, 112, 120, 139.
19. Nobles, *Shop Talk*, 94, 103.
20. Joe Laurie, Jr., *Vaudeville*, 319.
21. Douglas Gilbert, *American Vaudeville*, 73.
22. Richard Moody, *Ned Harrigan*, 72.
23. In the Pastor file in the Theatre Collection of the Humanities Research Center.
24. Edward B. Marks, *They All Sang*, 14–15. Of the many raconteurs who have nostalgically recorded the days of variety, vaudeville, and Tin Pan Alley, Marks remains the most engaging.
25. Gilbert, *American Vaudeville*, 288.
26. Frank Bush, *Pesock the Pawnbroker*, in the Harris Collection, Brown University.
27. Bush, *O! Moses* in the Harris Collection.
28. Bush, *Pesock the Pawnbroker*, in Harris Collection.
29. For a fuller discussion of the violent comedy of variety and early vaudeville, see Paul Antonie Distler, "Rise and Fall of the Racial Comics," 16.
30. Bush, *Pesock the Pawnbroker*, in Harris Collection.
31. See entry on Bush in Gerald Bordman, *Oxford Companion*.
32. *Illustrated American*, 27 February 1882, in Curtis file of the Billy Rose Collection of the New York Public Library.
33. The preceding quotations are from George Jessop, *Sam'l of Posen*, 159, 162.
34. *Spirit of the Times*, 21 May 1881.
35. *New York Dramatic Mirror*, 21 May 1881.
36. *Spirit of the Times*, 20 June 1881.
37. *New York Dramatic Mirror*, 21 May 1881.
38. *New York Times*, 18 May 1881.
39. *New York Daily Graphic*, 17 May 1881.
40. On *Mordecai Lyons* and its influences, see Moody, *Ned Harrigan*, 70, 132; Warren T. Burns, "Plays of Harrigan," 58–59. The play, whose promptbook survives in the Library of Congress Manuscript Edition, is a fascinating, unwieldy mix of melodrama and variety comedy, with a plot involving not only intermarriage but also a potential incest, which gets averted at the last minute.
41. *New York Times*, 27 February 1883.
42. Noted in George C. D. Odell, *Annals*, Volume 12, 100.
43. Undated clipping from the *New York Dramatic Mirror* in Curtis file in the Billy Rose Collection.
44. The typescript is in the Library Congress, Rare Books Division. Though less structured than its predecessor, *Spot Cash* is far more dynamic and engaging a script, though it also makes no literary pretensions.
45. The souvenir card can be found in the *Sam'l of Posen* file in the Theatre

Collection of the Museum of the City of New York. The booklet is in the Harris Collection.

46. *San Francisco Examiner*, 16 October 1893.
47. In the Curtis file of the Billy Rose Collection.
48. Much of what I have been able to piece together about Curtis's later career comes from clippings in the Curtis file of the Billy Rose Collection and in the *San Francisco Herald*, especially 9 April 1894. M. J. Landa, *The Jew in Drama*, 201, makes a thoughtful reference to the 1895 London engagement. A strand to the homicide/extortion story is that in December of 1893, Curtis purchased the Driskill Hotel in Austin, Texas in exchange for $350,000 and property near Fresno. The *Austin Evening News*, 7 December 1893, reported that Curtis had fallen "in love" with the city and hoped to make it his home; he had plans, too, for building a first-class opera house downtown. I can find no evidence, however, that Curtis ever moved to Austin; in a few years, at any rate, the Driskill was in another proprietor's hands. The whole transaction may have been Curtis's scheme to cut all ties to California, where his life and property were no longer safe.

Chapter 4   *Managing Power*

1. Harry Lee Newton, *Dinkle and Pinkle*, 4.
2. *Life*, 12 May 1898.
3. On the Syndicate's emergence and its relationship to black performers, see Thomas L. Riis, *Just Before Jazz*, 18–19. I have yet to find a thorough work on the Syndicate itself, which despite its importance, has been avoided by most scholars like the plague.
4. Cited in Louis Harap, *Image of the Jew*, 207.
5. Irving Howe, *World of Our Fathers*, 55.
6. Lawrence Senelick, "Variety into Vaudeville," 2.
7. Leonard Dinnerstein, *Uneasy at Home*, 25. The Jewish presence becomes evident by leafing through old issues of *Variety*. The appendixes to Joe Laurie, Jr., *Vaudeville*, are also useful in this regard. Of course, a name not sounding Jewish does not eliminate the possibility of the subject being Jewish, particularly in this era.
8. On Jewish women as theatergoers, see Kathy Peiss, *Cheap Amusements*, 145. Overall, Peiss is an outstanding source on the gender dynamics of audiences at this time.
9. This anecdote is recounted in John E. DiMeglio, *Vaudeville, USA*, 67–68.
10. Albert F. McLean, *Vaudeville as Ritual*, 113. In "Variety into Vaudeville," Senelick suggests that this stylistic distinction between variety and vaudeville cannot be so easily drawn.
11. Howe, *World of Our Fathers*, 558.
12. Neal Gabler, *Empire of Their Own*, 6–7.
13. Stephen J. Whitfield, *American Space, Jewish Time*, 45.
14. *New York Times*, 12 March 1895.
15. For an excellent analysis of how Tree made his Svengali more Jewish, as well

as for speculation on Tree's possible Jewish heritage, see George Taylor, "Svengali: Mesmerist and Aesthete," 108–109. Taylor also offers insightful commentary on Tree's work in the 1914 film version of the play. By contrast, Lionel Barrymore's performance in the 1931 film, while clearly inscribed with many of the traditions of the Jewish villain, refrains from explicitly making Svengali Jewish.

16. For more on Svengali, see Edgar Rosenberg, *From Shylock to Svengali*, 234–261; Elaine Showalter, *Trilby*, Introduction.

17. Armond and L. Marc Fields, *Bowery to Broadway*, 52–53, 33. This book offers the most detailed account of not only Weber and Fields's career but those of other entertainers of the era as well.

18. Fields and Fields, *Bowery to Broadway*, 92, 132.

19. Felix Isman, *Weber and Fields*, xi.

20. Craig Timberlake, *Bishop of Broadway*, 13, 69–77.

21. David Belasco and Henry C. De Mille, *Men and Women*, 314.

22. From playbills and programs in Pastor file in the Theatre Collection of the Humanities Research Center, University of Texas at Austin.

23. On Jewish comedians in burlesque, see Irving Zeidman, *The American Burlesque Show*, 61; Bernard Sobel, *Burlycue*, 142. On the gradual development of burlesque from musical extravaganza into tawdry strip show, the outstanding work is Robert C. Allen, *Horrible Prettiness*.

24. Paul Antonie Distler, "Rise and Fall of the Racial Comics," 82.

25. Distler, "Rise and Fall of the Racial Comics," 166, 178.

26. Zeidman, *The American Burlesque Show*, 56.

27. For more on Joe Welch, see Laurie, Jr., *Vaudeville*, 176; Distler, "Rise and Fall of the Racial Comics," 163.

28. Distler, "Rise and Fall of the Racial Comics," 80, has ably documented the Jewish type.

29. *Toledo Examiner*, 20 January 1907. In Dandy file of the Billy Rose Collection of the New York Public Library.

30. *New York Times*, 3 November 1903.

31. The unpublished typescript of *Hebraic Types* is in the Library of Congress, Rare Books Division. In addition to scripting sketches, McCree also managed, produced, and acted in vaudeville acts; he died prematurely in 1918. Hoffman went on write the important play, *Welcome Stranger* (1920), which Ellen Schiff has recently included in her anthology *Awake and Singing*. See Schiff, 3–5, for more details on Hoffman's life and work.

32. DiMeglio, *Vaudeville, USA*, 105.

33. *New York Times*, 30 August 1902.

34. These novelty acts are noted in Laurie, Jr., *Vaudeville*, 223, 219; Zeidman, *The American Burlesque Show*, 57. On the Wandering Jew tradition, see Rosenberg, *From Shylock to Svengali*, 187–205. Rosenberg sees Svengali as having elements of the Wandering Jew, which suggests that Joe Welch's forlorn comedian and Du Maurier's sinister manipulator were not only contemporaries of each other but closer cousins than they may have first appeared.

35. On Jewish audiences and Julian Rose, see Distler, "Rise and Fall of the Racial Comics," 158–159, 166.
36. Unidentified clipping, 22 September 1901, in Warfield file in the Billy Rose Collection.
37. Warfield's appeal to Lederer is recounted in an unidentified clipping, 1901, in Warfield file in the Billy Rose Collection.
38. Unidentified clipping, 1902, in Warfield file in the Billy Rose Collection.
39. Isman, *Weber and Fields*, 239.
40. On Belasco's initial approach to Warfield, see Timberlake, *Bishop of Broadway*, 206.
41. The promptbook for the 1913 revival of *The Auctioneer* is in the Library of Congress, Manuscript Collection, where it was deposited in 1915. I can find no evidence of the survival of the 1901 script. From plot descriptions, however, the only major departure appears to be that in the original version, Isaac's intrigue involves bad stock, while in the 1913 script, it revolves around a phony diamond necklace.

    An interesting sidelight on *The Auctioneer*, beyond the scope of my inquiry, is that in 1905 the play and its authorship became the subject of lawsuits involving Belasco's attempt to break the Syndicate's monopoly. The play therefore was not only about the struggle between Jewish brothers but also became the subject of struggle between Jewish producers. Its authorship was a classic example of script doctoring, with Belasco first commissioning Arthur, then calling in Klein for an emergency rewrite. See Gerald Bordman, *Chronicle*, 483, for a brief summary.
42. Kenneth McGowan, "How an Actor Gets Into Your Heart," *Colliers*, 23 February 1924. In Warfield file of the Billy Rose Collection.
43. The preceding quotations are from David Warfield, "How I Discovered Levi," unidentified, 22 September 1901, in Warfield file in the Billy Rose Collection. Warfield's denials are recorded in an unidentified clipping, 14 December 1901, in same file.
44. The bicycle anecdote is recounted in an unidentified clipping, 1902, in Warfield file in the Billy Rose Collection.
45. *Chicago Post*, 30 April 1902.
46. Unidentified clipping, 28 September 1901, in Warfield file in the Billy Rose Collection.
47. William Winter, *Shakespeare on Stage*, 199.
48. Cited in Lulla Rosenfeld, *Bright Star*, 309.
49. For more on Adler's performance, see John Gross, 254; Joel Berkowitz, "True Jewish Jew," 76–82. Berkowitz thoughtfully compares Adler's Shylock to two other Yiddish Shylocks: Rudolf Schildkraut and Maurice Schwartz.
50. *New York Times*, 16 May 1905.
51. *New York Times*, 22 December 1922.
52. *New York Times*, 7 January 1923.
53. For more on Warfield's Shylock, see Timberlake, *Bishop of Broadway*, 371; Gross, *Shylock*, 167.

54. Timberlake, *Bishop of Broadway*, 371.
55. Warfield's fruitful partnership with Loew was no secret and is noted in many sources. Fields and Fields, *From Bowery to Broadway*, 291, briefly describe its roots.

CHAPTER 5 *Breeding New Generations*

1. John Corbin, *Husband*, 216.
2. On Jewish attitudes toward and frequency of intermarriage, see Jena Weissman Joselit, *The Wonders of America*, 49–51. Joselit also makes excellent reading for the way in which Jewish traditions were reconfigured in America.
3. Jules Chametzsky, "Beyond Melting Pots," features a provocative discussion of the relationship between multiculturalism and essentialism.
4. The preceding quotations are from Edith Wharton, *House of Mirth*, 16, 258. Christine Riegel, "Rosedale," 233, downplays Wharton's anti-Semitism, arguing that the author merely shared the views of many of her contemporaries. The same argument, often made for Shylock, is generally reserved for writers whose work has garnered literary cachet (in Shakespeare and Wharton's cases, certainly with merit).
5. *Brummel* was essentially a vehicle for Richard Mansfield (1854–1907) who, three years later, became the most notable American Shylock of the 1890s, as I discuss in Chapter Four.
6. Prescott F. Hall, *Immigration and Its Effects*, 322.
7. Alfred P. Schultz, *Race or Mongrel*, 258.
8. Madison Grant, *Passing*, xvii.
9. Cited in Robert Singerman, "Jew as Racial Alien," 112.
10. On fertility-related anxiety, see Miriam King and Steven Ruggles, "American Immigration;" on anti-modernism, see T. J. Jackson Lears, *No Place of Grace*; on neurasthenia, see Tom Lutz, *American Nervousness*; on militarism and patriotism, see Michael Pearlman, *Democracy Safe*.
11. Schultz, *Race or Mongrel*, 329.
12. Robert Mitchell, "Recent Jewish Immigration," 342.
13. Grant, *Passing*, 16.
14. Gilman, *Difference and Pathology*, 154.
15. On Roosevelt and masculine ideals, see Pearlman, *Democracy Safe*, 16–24. The irony is that Roosevelt, sickly as a youth, actively had to remake his own image and body.
16. Mitchell, "Recent Jewish Immigration," 342.
17. Cited in Singerman, "Jew as Racial Alien," 113.
18. Schultz, *Race or Mongrel*, 41.
19. Cited in Singerman, "Jew as Racial Alien," 110.
20. On attempts to construct a new Jewish cultural ideal, see Gilman, *Difference and Pathology*, 157; David Biale, "Zionism as an Erotic Revolution," 283–286. In these contexts, Zionism can be seen as an explicit attempt to repudiate a supposedly feminized, Yiddish, Diaspora culture.

21. Cited in Singerman, "Jew as Racial Alien," 115.
22. Unidentified clipping in Fitch file in the Billy Rose Collection of the New York Public Library.
23. *Life*, 25 March 1909.
24. *New York Dramatic Mirror*, 3 November 1906. Bruening had already played a stage Jew, in Belasco and Charles Frohman's co-production of *Under Two Flags* in 1901.
25. Walsh (1874?–1915) had resisted another groping stage Jew a decade earlier when she played Mary Lavelot in *The Great Diamond Robbery*, opposite Fanny Janauschek's Frau Rosenbaum.
26. All my quotations come the *Woman in the Case* promptbook in the Billy Rose Collection.
27. Unidentified, undated clipping in Fitch file in the Billy Rose Collection.
28. The preceding quotations are from Corbin, *Husband*, xxv, xxvii, xxx.
29. The preceding quotations are from Corbin, *Husband*, 10, 214, 216, 220, 233. This anxiety over reproduction rates was founded in a statistical misreading which applied biological rather than cultural criteria to the birthrates of first generation immigrants and therefore overlooked the fact that the children of these immigrants, once assimilated, actually reproduced at rates comparable to or lower than "native" stock. See King and Ruggles, "American Immigration," 354.
30. The unpublished typescript for *Cohen's Courtship* is in the Library of Congress, Manuscript Collection.
31. The unpublished typescript for *Hebrewing and Shewooing* is in the Library of Congress, Manuscript Collection.
32. Arthur Mann, *One and the Many*, 118–122.
33. Sollors's excellent *Beyond Ethnicity*, in which he lays out these competing ideals of consent and descent, is another useful way of framing culture in a way that avoids essentialism. In this respect, he follows in the tradition of William Boelhower's *Through a Glass Darkly*, cited in my introduction.
34. Lackaye (1862–1932) ranks as one of the foremost players of Jews in drama if, in addition to *Trilby* and *Children of the Ghetto*, one includes *The Pit* (1904) and *New Lamps and Old* (1909). It seems likely that his success as Svengali legitimized him as the actor to be sought when a commanding Jew needed to be played.
35. Unidentified clipping, 1901, in Warfield file in the Billy Rose Collection.
36. Foreign-language theater in America was another matter; the playwright Jacob Gordin, for example was turning out Ibsen-esque problem plays for the Yiddish-language theater in New York before the turn of the century, in the same decade when critics were praising Edward Harrigan as the foremost proponent of American realism. Nahma Sandrow, *Vagabond Stars*, is the basic English-language reference for the international scope of Yiddish theater.
37. The possible influence of *The Ghetto* upon *The Melting-pot* is based not upon independent evidence, but rather, my own reading of the two plays, which both

feature temperamental Jewish sons who are in love with gentile women and who battle hardheaded, traditional father figures. Per his American setting, Zangwill creates a more optimistic conclusion about the possibilities of love triumphing over tradition (in Sollors's terms, consent over descent). At the very least, the plays represent the worldviews of two independent-minded Jewish intellectuals, in many ways at war with their own heritage.

38. The preceding quotations are from Israel Zangwill, *The Melting-pot*, 103, 166, 198.
39. Zangwill, *The Melting-pot*, 2.
40. Zangwill, *The Melting-pot*, 198–199.
41. For more on *The Melting-pot*'s view of race, see Mann, *One and the Many*, 115.
42. For more on the meanings of the melting-pot ideal, see Sollors, *Beyond Ethnicity*, 92–94; Mann, *One and the Many*, 108–115.
43. *New York Times*, 12 September 1909.
44. An interesting point of comparison here is Mira Nair's film *Mississippi Masala* (1992), which may be the closest recent retelling of Zangwill's fable, in that it also posits a decentered notion of American ethnicity through two romantic leads, neither of whom come from dominant American cultures (Indian Ugandan and African American) and both of whom struggle against the weight of a parental authority that, while lovable, is presented as outdated. It is significant that, in one of the film's final shots, the camera shows the young couple romping through a cactus-filled fantasy land of the American West (not unlike the fantasy world evoked by Zangwill in the rhetoric of David's final speech). This visionary, liberating, ahistorical space seems to be the only place that such a couple can be imagined as inhabiting.
45. For these and other Jewish responses to the play, see Mann, *One and the Many*, 113; Chametzsky, "Beyond Melting Pots," 7–8. Note that the orchestra metaphor elides the issue of who will be conducting.
46. *New York Times*, 7, 12 September 1909.
47. Mann, *One and the Many*, 110.
48. Sollors, *Beyond Ethnicity*, 74.
49. Charles Klein, *Maggie Pepper*, 62. Klein is the same influential figure who collaborated on *The Auctioneer* and *Potash and Perlmutter*. Ellen Schiff discusses the anti-Semitism of the Donnay play in *From Stereotype to Metaphor*, 23–25, contextualizing it in the tradition of the belle juive.
50. *New York Times*, 4 April 1909. One reason the play circumvented controversy is that it presented the wealthy Jewish family as thoroughly assimilated members of the English upper-middle-class elite; only a bigot could have objected to the intermarriage it dramatizes.
51. All the titles that I cite (except the well-known "Yiddle") had recently come into the Harris Collection of Brown University when I was there in November 1992. The iconography of the sheet-music covers itself is a topic that would make for fascinating analysis.
52. Cited in Irving Howe, *World of Our Fathers*, 162.

CHAPTER 6   *Getting Reformed*

1. Unidentified clipping in Warfield file of the Billy Rose Collection of the New York Public Library.
2. The anecdote is recounted in Bernard Sobel, *Burlycue*, 143.
3. For more on these polarized types and the work of Cumberland, see Edgar Rosenberg, *From Shylock to Svengali*, especially Part One.
4. Louis Parker, *Disraeli*, 24, 65.
5. I want to emphasize the American nature of *Disraeli*. Despite its British setting, the play never succeeded in that country, precisely because its audiences would have recognized its simplification and telescoping of recent history in ways that clearly lacked verisimilitude.
6. For analysis of *As a Man Thinks* as an important transitional work in the development of American realism, reflected in its controversial theme and colloquial syntax, see Brenda Murphy, *American Realism*, 94–98. It is a far more subtly stated piece of dramatic writing than either *The Melting-pot* or *Disraeli*, both of with which it may be usefully compared.
7. "Next Great Play About the Jews," *New York Evening Telegraph*, 8 May 1908.
8. The preceding quotations are from Augustus Thomas, *As a Man Thinks*, 111, 89–90.
9. Paul Antonie Distler, "Rise and Fall of the Racial Comics," 188.
10. Distler, "Rise and Fall of the Racial Comics," 250–251.
11. *New York Times*, 26 March 1912.
12. Distler, "Rise and Fall of the Racial Comics," 191; *New York Times*, 25 April 1913.
13. *Chicago Tribune*, 25 April 1913.
14. *New York Times*, 26 March 1912.
15. Cited in Distler, "Rise and Fall of the Racial Comics," 189.
16. *New York Times*, 25 April 1913.
17. *New York Times*, 25 April 1913.
18. Distler, "Rise and Fall of the Racial Comics," 178.
19. Cited in Distler, "Exit the Racial Comics," 250.
20. Edward D. Coleman, writing in the 1930s, echoes the boycotters by criticizing Welch for having done "incalculable harm to the Jewish name throughout the country." See *Jew in Drama*, xvii.
21. Joe Laurie, Jr., *Vaudeville*, 76. See 76–82 for more on these cleaned-up Jews.
22. The London-born Klein (1867–1915), in addition to writing plays with Jewish characters such as *Maggie Pepper* and *The Third Degree*, also collaborated on *The Auctioneer*, making him perhaps the most influential scripter of stage Jews of the era. Though never a great writer, he had a deft sense for comedy and dramatic construction, which served him in his frequent role as playreader for the producer Charles Frohman (a key player in the Syndicate). He died on the *Lusitania*. As I write, his papers have recently been acquired by the Theatre Collection of the Humanities Research Center, University of Texas at Austin.
23. *New York Times*, 17 August 1913.

24. On the transition to verbal comedy, see Distler, "Exit the Racial Comics," 252–253.
25. Montague Glass, *Potash and Perlmutter*, 104.
26. Sheet music in the Harris Collection at Brown University.
27. Various sources give Bayes's (Goldberg's) first name as Eleanor or Leonora.
28. Cited in Charles W. Stern, *American Vaudeville*, 268.
29. Herbert G. Goldman, *Fanny Brice*, 37.
30. Cited in Irving Howe, *World of Our Fathers*, 562.
31. For more on Salome, see Bram Dijkstra, *Idols of Perversity*, 386.
32. Barbara W. Grossman, *Funny Woman*, 33.
33. For more on Brice's "Sadie Salome," see Goldman, *Fanny Brice*, 37; Sobel, *Burlycue*, 150; Grossman, *Funny Woman*, 33.
34. On Brice's ability to simultaneously transcend and retain her Jewishness, see June Sochen, "Fanny Brice," 41–46. This excellent article ably compares Brice and Sophie Tucker.
35. On masked forms of Jewishness, see Sarah Blacher Cohen, ed., *From Hester Street to Hollywood*, whose essays chronicle Jewish contributions to popular culture.
36. Stephen J. Whitfield, *American Space, Jewish Time*, Chapter Three compellingly examines these sublimations. How then to contextualize Ellen Schiff's fine anthology, *Awake and Singing!*, which would argue that the "classic" Jewish-American repertory only began to be created at the point when these sublimations started? Her work ironically underscores the point I make here: that starting in the era I examine in this chapter, Jewish performances became more inscribed in the tradition of the serious drama, less rooted in the popular culture and mass mainstream which Jews were instrumental in creating. Many of Schiff's classic plays reached relatively small audiences and remain little-known even to Jews today, in contrast to other performances, such as the songs of Gershwin, the movies of the Marx Brothers, or the early plays of Arthur Miller. A related point may be that with the coming of O'Neill and a less commercial theater in the 1910s, film inherited much of theater's audience, lending credence to Schiff's suggestion that modernism liberated the stage Jew. For a cultural historian, therefore, the worlds of theater before and after 1920 may not fit comfortably into the same larger narrative.
37. On the cultural politics of African American representation, the work of bell hooks makes relevant reading. See *Black Looks*, for example, for a series of excellent critiques towards African American subjectivities not grounded in the old essentialism.

Appendix A

1. Frank Bush, *Pesock the Pawnbroker*. The author of this song is given as Allen De Mond.
2. Bush, *O! Moses*.
3. George Jessop, *Sam'l of Posen*, 157–158.

4. This monologue appears in the appendix to Distler, "Rise and Fall of the Racial Comics."
5. This is from the 1913 promptbook, in the Library of Congress, Manuscript Collection. I have made minor changes to the stage directions, to simplify for reading.
6. The sheet music is in the Harris Collection of Brown University.
7. Montague Glass, *Potash and Perlmutter*, 16–17.

SELECT BIBLIOGRAPHY

Key to Abbreviations on Rare Materials:

HH: Hay Library (Brown University)/Harris Collection
HT: Harvard Theatre Collection
LOCR: Library of Congress/Rare Books Division
LOCM: Library of Congress/Manuscript Division
NYPL: New York Public Library/Billy Rose Collection
NYPLM: New York Public Library/Manuscript Division

Plays and Sketches

Aldrich, Thomas Bailey. *Judith of Bethulia*. New York: Houghton Mifflin, 1904.

Alfriend, Edward M., and A. C. Wheeler. *The Great Diamond Robbery*. In *The Great Diamond Robbery and Other Recent Melodramas*, edited by Garrett H. Leverton. Princeton: Princeton University Press, 1940.

Barnett, Charles. *Dream of Fate; or, Sarah, the Jewess*. New York: Turner and Fisher, c. 1838. HT.

Baswitz, Charles. "Levy the Drummer; or, Life on the Road." Typescript, 1885. LOCM.

Belasco, David, and Henry C. De Mille. *Men and Women*. In *America's Lost Plays*, vol. 17, edited by Robert Hamilton Ball. Bloomington: Indiana University Press, 1940.

Bixby, Frank L. *The Little Boss*. Boston: Walter H. Baker, 1901.

Boucicault, Dion. *Flying Scud*. 1867. In *America's Lost Plays*, vol. 1, edited by Allardyce Nicoll and F. Theodore Clark. Princeton: Princeton University Press, 1940.

Brougham, John. "The Lottery of Life." Holograph, 1867. NYPL.

————. *Much Ado About A Merchant of Venice*. New York: Samuel French, 1868.

Carpenter, Edward Childs. *The Tongues of Men*. New York: Samuel French, 1913.

Chase, Frank Eugene. *The Great Umbrella Case*. Boston: W. H. Baker, 1881.

————[Abel Seaman]. *In the Trenches: A Drama of the Cuban War*. Boston: Walter H. Baker, 1898.

————. *A Ready-Made Suit*. Boston: Walter H. Baker, 1913.

Corbin, John. *Husband*. New York: Houghton Mifflin, 1910.

Curtis, M. B., and Ed Marble. "Sam'l of Posen as the Drummer on the Road (Spot Cash)." Typescript, 1883. LOCR.

Daly, Augustin. *Leah, the Forsaken*. New York: Samuel French, 1872.

Dreiser, Theodore. *The Hand of the Potter*. New York: Boni and Liveright, 1918.

Dunbar-Nelson, Alice. *Mine Eyes Have Seen*. 1918. In *Black Theater U.S.A.: 45 Plays by Black Americans*, edited by James V. Hatch. New York: Free Press, 1974.

Fitch, Clyde. *Beau Brummel*. 1890. New York: John Lane, 1908.

————. "The Woman in the Case." Typescript, 1905. NYPL.

Fitch, Clyde, and Edith Wharton. "The House of Mirth." Typescript, 1906. NYPL.

Forbes, James. *The Show Shop*. In *The Famous Mrs. Fair and Other Plays*. New York: George H. Doran, 1920.

Glass, Montague. *Potash and Perlmutter*. New York: Samuel French, 1913.

Hancock, C. W. *Down on the Farm*. New York: Samuel French, 1906.

Harrigan, Edward. "The Leather Patch." Typescript, [1886]. NYPLM.

————. "Mordecai Lyons." Typescript, 1882. LOCM.

————. "Reilly and the Four Hundred." Holograph, [1890]. NYPLM.

Hatton, Frederic, and Fanny Hatton. *Lombardi, Ltd*. New York: Samuel French, 1917.

Heermans, Forbes. *Down the Black Cañon*. Chicago: Dramatic Publishing, 1890.

Heijermans, Herman, Jr. *The Ghetto*. Adapted by Chester Bailey Fernald. London: William Heineman, 1899.

Jessop, George H. *Sam'l of Posen; or, The Commercial Drummer*. 1881. In *America's Lost Plays*, vol. 4, edited by Isaac Goldberg and Hubert Heffner. Bloomington: Indiana University Press, 1940.

————. "Isidore Plastrick ("Sam'l Plastrick")." Typescript, 1880. LOCM.

Klein, Charles. *Maggie Pepper*. New York: Samuel French, 1916.

Klein, Charles, and Lee Arthur. "The Auctioneer." Typescript, 1915. LOCM.

"The Larks." *The Shakespeare Water Cure*. 1883. New York: Dick and Fitzgerald, 1897.

Leah, the Forsaken: Costume Monologue, Pantomime or Tableaux for a Woman. New York: Reciter's Library, 1901.

Lewis, Leopold. *The Bells*. In *Laurel British Drama: The Nineteenth Century*. New York: Dell Publishing, 1967.

McCree, Junie. "Hebraic Types." Typescript, 1915. LOCR.

————. "Hebrewing and Shewooing." Typescript, 1909. LOCM.

McLellan, C.M.S. *Leah Kleschna*. New York: Samuel French, 1920.

Mahoney, Will. "The Hebrew Fireman and the Foreman." Typescript, 1908. LOCM.

Manners, J. Hartley. *The House Next Door*. Boston: W. H. Baker, 1912.

Mosenthal, Salomon Hermann von. *Argument of the Play Leah*, adapted by Albert Darmont. New York: Theatre Ticket Office, 1892.

————. *Deborah*. Dual English/German version. New York, 1867.

Newton, Harry Lee. *Dinkle and Pinkle*. Chicago: Will Rossiter, 1907.

————. *Izzy's Vacation*. New York: M. Witmark and Sons, 1913.

————. *The Second-Hand Man.* New York: Will Rossiter, 1901.

Newton, Harry Lee, and Aaron S. Hoffman. *All About Goldstein.* New York: Dramatic Publishing, 1902.

————. *Glickman the Glazier.* Chicago: T. S. Denison, 1904.

Nobles, Milton. *The Phoenix.* Chicago: Dramatic Publishing, 1907.

Norton, Charles. "The Hebrew Detective." Typescript, 1914. LOCM.

Quick, William A. "Cohen's Courtship." Typescript, 1907. LOCM.

Parker, Louis N. *Disraeli.* New York: John Lane Company, 1911.

Reid, James Halleck. "Israel Isaacs; or, A Jew's Gratitude." Typescript, 1904. LOCM.

————. "The Money Lender." Typescript, [1907] NYPL.

Rhode, Mary. "The Hebrew Business Woman." Typescript, 1908. LOCM.

Robyns, William, and Melvin Winstock. "Abram's Christmas." Typescript, 1908. LOCM.

————. "A Hebrew's Christmas." Typescript, 1909. LOCM.

Scribe, Eugene. *The Jewess.* New York: C. and D. Koppel, 1884.

Selwyn, Edgar. *The Country Boy.* New York: Samuel French, 1917.

Shelland, Harry. *The Great Libel Case.* New York: Dick and Fitzgerald, 1900.

————. *Two Wandering Jews.* New York: Fitzgerald Publishing, 1904.

Sherwood, Clara Harriot. *The Cable Car.* New York: T. H. French, 1891.

Smith, Winchell, and John E. Hazzard. *Turn to the Right.* New York: Samuel French, 1916.

Taylor, Tom. *The Ticket-of-Leave Man.* In *Plays by Tom Taylor*, edited by Martin Banham. New York: Cambridge University Press, 1985.

Thomas, Augustus. *As a Man Thinks.* New York: Duffield, 1911.

Thompson, Marshall. "The Jew Friend." Typescript, 1910. LOCM.

Townsend, Charles. *The Jail Bird.* New York: Dick and Fitzgerald, 1893.

Tullidge, Edward W. *Ben Israel; or, From under the Curse.* Salt Lake City, 1875.

Wilde, Oscar. *Salome.* Paris: Limited Editions Club, 1938.

Zangwill, Israel. *The Melting-pot.* New York: Macmillan, 1909.

Other Sources

Allen, Robert C. *Horrible Prettiness: Burlesque and American Culture.* Chapel Hill: University of North Carolina Press, 1991.

Altman, Sig. *The Comic Image of the Jew: Explorations of a Pop Culture Phenomenon.* Rutherford, N.J.: Farleigh Dickinson University Press, 1971.

Archer, Stephen M. *Junius Brutus Booth: Theatrical Prometheus.* Carbondale: Southern Illinois University Press, 1992.

Berkowitz, Joel. "'A True Jewish Jew': Three Yiddish Shylocks." *Theatre Survey* 37, no. 1 (May 1996): 75–98.

Bernhardt, Sarah. *Memories of My Life.* New York: D. Appleton, 1907.

Biale, David. "Zionism as an Erotic Revolution." In *People of the Body: Jews and Judaism From an Embodied Perspective*, edited by Howard Eilberg Schwartz. Albany: State University of New York Press, 1992.

Boelhower, William. *Through a Glass Darkly: Ethnic Semiosis in American Literature.* Venice: Edizioni Helvetia, 1984.

Bordman, Gerald. *American Musical Comedy: From Adonis to Dreamgirls*. New York: Oxford University Press, 1982.

————. *American Theatre: A Chronicle of Comedy and Drama, 1869–1914*. New York: Oxford University Press, 1994.

————. *The Concise Oxford Companion to American Theatre*. New York: Oxford University Press, 1987.

————. *Oxford Companion to American Theatre*. New York: Oxford University Press, 1984.

Brazin, Nancy Topping. "The Destruction of Lily Bart: Capitalism, Christianity, and Male Chauvinism." *Denver Quarterly* 17, no. 4 (Winter 1983): 97–108.

Brereton, Austin. *The Life of Henry Irving*. 2 vols. New York: Longmans, Green, 1908.

Brudno, Ezra S. "The Russian Jew Americanized." *The World's Work* (March 1904).

Bryant, William Cullen. "Shylock Not a Jew." Excerpted in *Stars and Sand: Jewish Notes by Non-Jewish Notables*, edited by Joseph L. Baron. Philadelphia: Jewish Publication Society of America, 1943.

Buelens, Gert. "The Jewish Immigrant Experience." *Journal of American Studies* 25, no. 3 (December 1991): 473–479.

Burns, Warren T. "The Plays of Edward Green Harrigan: The Theatre of Intercultural Communication." Ph.D. diss., Pennsylvania State University, 1969.

Bush, Frank. *Frank Bush's O' Moses Songster*. New York: Popular Publishing, 1878. HH.

————. *Frank Bush's Pesock the Pawnbroker Songster*. New York: Popular Publishing, c. 1880. HH.

Butler, Judith. *Gender Trouble: Feminism and the Subversion of Identity*. New York: Routledge, 1990.

Calisch, Edward. *The Jew in English Literature as Author and as Subject*. Richmond: The Bell Book and Stationery Company, 1909.

Chametzsky, Jules. "Beyond Melting Pots, Cultural Pluralism, Ethnicity: Or, Déjà Vu All Over Again." *Melus* 16, no. 4 (Winter 1989–1990): 3–17.

Cohen, Sarah Blacher. "Yiddish Origins and Jewish-American Transformation." In *From Hester Street to Hollywood: The Jewish-American Stage and Screen*, edited by Sarah Blacher Cohen. Bloomington: Indiana University Press, 1983.

Coleman, Edward D. *The Jew in English Drama*. New York: New York Public Library and Ktav Publishing, 1968.

Conquergood, Dwight. "Rethinking Ethnography: Toward a Critical Cultural Politics." *Communications Monographs* 58 (June 1991): 179–194.

Curtis, M. B. *The Legend of Sam'l of Posen from Early Days in Fatherland to Affluence and Success in the Land of His Adoption*. New York, 1884. HH.

Dell, Robert Merritt. "The Representation of the Immigrant on the New York Stage, 1881–1910." Ph.D. diss., New York University, 1960.

Dijkstra, Bram. *Idols of Perversity: Fantasies of Feminine Evil in Fin-de-Siècle Culture*. New York: Oxford University Press, 1986.

DiMeglio, John E. *Vaudeville, USA*. Bowling Green, Ohio: Bowling Green University Popular Press, 1973.

Dimock, Wai-chee. "Debasing Exchange: Edith Wharton's *The House of Mirth*." *PMLA* 100, no. 5 (October 1983): 783–792.

Diner, Hasia R. *A Time for Gathering: The Second Migration, 1820–1880*. Baltimore: Johns Hopkins University Press, 1992.

Dinnerstein, Leonard. *Anti-Semitism in America*. New York: Oxford University Press, 1994.

———*Uneasy at Home: Anti-Semitism and the American Jewish Experience*. New York: Columbia University Press, 1987.

Distler, Paul Antonie. "Ethnic Comedy in Vaudeville and Burlesque." In *American Popular Entertainment: Papers and Proceedings of the Conference on the History of American Popular Entertainment*, edited by Myron Matlaw. Westport, Conn.: Greenwood Press, 1977.

———. "Exit the Racial Comics." *Educational Theatre Journal* 18, no. 3 (October 1966): 247–254.

———. "The Rise and Fall of the Racial Comics in American Vaudeville." Ph.D. diss., Tulane University, 1963.

DuMaurier, George. *Trilby*. New York: Oxford University Press, 1995.

Eilberg-Schwartz, Howard. *People of the Body: Jews and Judaism from an Embodied Perspective*. Albany: State University of New York Press, 1992.

Erdman, Harley. "Two Booths and a Bard: *Julius Caesar* and Nineteenth Century Theatrical Ideals." *Centennial Review* 36, no. 3 (Fall 1992): 517–530.

Erenberg, Lewin A. *Steppin' Out: New York Nightlife and the Transformation of American Culture, 1890–1930*. Westport, Conn.: Greenwood Press, 1981

Ewen, Elizabeth. "City Lights: Immigrant Women and the Rise of the Movies." In *Women and the American City*. Chicago: University of Chicago Press, 1981.

Eytinge, Rose. *The Memories of Rose Eytinge*. New York: Frederick Stokes Company, 1905.

Felheim, Marvin. *The Theater of Augustin Daly: An Account of the Late Nineteenth-Century American Stage*. Cambridge, Mass.: Harvard University Press, 1956.

Felsenstein, Frank. *Anti-Semitic Stereotypes: A Paradigm of Otherness in English Popular Culture, 1660–1830*. Baltimore: Johns Hopkins University Press, 1995.

Fields, Armond, and L. Marc Fields. *From the Bowery to Broadway: Lew Fields and the Roots of American Popular Theatre*. New York: Oxford University Press, 1993.

Flaxman, Seymour L. *Herman Heijermans and His Dramas*. The Hague: Martinus Nijhoff, 1954.

Friedman, Lester D. *Hollywood's Image of the Jew*. New York: Frederick Ungar, 1982.

———. *The Jewish Image in American Film*. Secaucus, N.J.: Citadel Press, 1987.

Gabler, Neal. *An Empire of Their Own: How the Jews Invented Hollywood*. New York: Anchor Books, 1988.

Gandal, Keith Leland. "The Spectacle of the Poor: Jacob Riis, Stephen Crane, and the Representation of Slum Life." Ph.D. diss., University of California at Berkeley, 1990.

Gelle, Jay. "(G)nos(e)ology: The Cultural Construction of the Other." In *People of the Body: Jews and Judaism from an Embodied Perspective*, edited by Howard Eilberg Schwartz. Albany: State University of New York Press, 1992.

Gerber, David A. "Cutting Out Shylock: Elite Anti-Semitism and the Quest for Moral Order in the Mid-Nineteenth- Century Marketplace." In *Anti-Semitism in America*. Urbana: University of Illinois Press, 1986.

Gibson, Mary-Ella. "Edith Wharton and the Ethnography of Old New York." *Studies in American Fiction* 13, no. 1 (Spring 1985): 57–68.

Gilbert, Douglas. *American Vaudeville: Its Life and Times*. New York: Whittlesey House, 1940.

Gilman, Sander. *Difference and Pathology: Stereotypes of Sexuality, Race, and Madness*. Ithaca, N.Y.: Cornell University Press, 1985.

———. *Jewish Self-Hatred: Anti-Semitism and the Hidden Language of the Jews*. Baltimore: Johns Hopkins University Press, 1986.

———. *The Jew's Body*. New York: Routledge, 1991.

———. "Salome, Syphilis, Sarah Bernhardt, and the 'Modern Jewess.'" *The German Quarterly* 66, no. 2 (Spring 1993): 195–211.

Gilman, Sander, and Stephen T. Katz. Introduction to *Antisemitism in Times of Crisis*. New York: New York University Press, 1991.

Glenn, Susan A. *Daughters of the Shtetl: Life and Labor in the Immigrant Generation*. Ithaca, N.Y.: Cornell University Press, 1990.

Gold, Arthur, and Robert Fizdale. *The Divine Sarah: A Life of Sarah Bernhardt*. New York: Alfred A. Knopf, 1991.

Goldman, Herbert G. *Fanny Brice: The Original Funny Girl*. New York: Oxford University Press, 1992.

Goodale, Katherine. *Behind the Scenes with Edwin Booth*. New York: Benjamin Bloom, 1931.

Grant, Madison. *The Passing of the Great Race; or, The Racial Basis of European History*. New York: Charles Scribner's Sons, 1916.

Grimsted, David. *Melodrama Unveiled: American Theatre and Culture, 1800–1850*. Chicago: University of Chicago Press, 1968.

Gross, John. *Shylock: Four Hundred Years in the Life of a Legend*. London: Chatto and Windus, 1992.

Grossman, Barbara W. *Funny Woman: The Life and Times of Fanny Brice*. Bloomington: Indiana University Press, 1991.

Grossmann, Edwina Booth. *Edwin Booth: Recollections by His Daughter*. New York: Century, 1894.

Gunning, Tom. *Outsiders as Insiders: Jews and the History of American Silent Film*. Waltham, Mass.: National Center for Jewish Film. Undated.

Gutjahr, Paul. "'To the Heart of Solid Puritans': Historicizing the Popularity of *Ben Hur*." *Mosaic* 26, no. 3 (Summer 1993): 53–68.

Halberstom, Judith Marion. "Parasites and Perverts: Anti-Semitism and Sexuality in Nineteenth-Century Gothic Fiction." Ph.D. diss., University of Minnesota, 1991.

Hall, Prescott F. *Immigration and Its Effects upon the United States*. New York: Henry Holt, 1906.

Harap, Louis. *Creative Awakening: The Jewish Presence in Twentieth-Century American Literature, 1900–1940s*. Westport, Conn.: Greenwood Press, 1987.

————. *Dramatic Encounters: The Jewish Presence in Twentieth-Century American Drama, Poetry, and Humor, and the Black-Jewish Literary Relationship.* Westport, Conn.: Greenwood Press, 1987.

————. *The Image of the Jew in American Literature: From Early Republic to Mass Migration.* Philadelphia: Jewish Publication Society of America, 1974.

Hark, Ina Rae. "The Jew as Victorian Cultural Signifier: Illustrated by Edward Lear." In *Culture and Education in Victorian England*, edited by Patrick Scott and Pauline Fletcher. Lewisburg, Pa.: Bucknell University Press, 1990.

Hearn, Lafcadio. "The Jew upon the Stage." In *Occidental Gleamings*, vol. 2. New York: Dodd, Mead, 1925.

Hellie, Thomas. "Clyde Fitch: Playwright of New York's Leisure Class." Ph.D. diss., University of Missouri at Columbia, 1985.

Henderson, Mary C. *The City and the Theatre: New York Playhouses from Bowling Green to Times Square.* Clifton, N.J.: J. T. White, 1973.

Henderson, Robert M. *D. W. Griffith: The Years at Biograph.* New York: Farrar, Straus and Giroux, 1970.

hooks, bell. *Black Looks: Race and Representation.* Boston: South End Press, 1992.

Howe, Irving. *World of Our Fathers.* New York: Schocken Books, 1976.

Howells, William Dean. "An East-Side Ramble." In *Impressions and Experiences.* New York: Harper and Brothers, 1896.

Irving, Laurence. *Henry Irving: The Actor and His World.* London: Faber and Faber. 1951.

Isman, Felix. *Weber and Fields: Their Tribulations, Triumphs, and Their Associates.* New York: Boni and Liveright, 1924.

Jaher, Frederic Cople. *A Scapegoat in the New Wilderness: The Origins and Rise of Anti-Semitism in America.* Cambridge, Mass.: Harvard University Press, 1994.

Jasen, David A. *Tin Pan Alley: The Composers, the Songs, the Performers, and Their Times.* New York: Donald I. Fine, 1988.

Jenkins, Henry. *What Made Pistachio Nuts?: Early Sound Comedy and the Vaudeville Aesthetic.* New York: Columbia University Press, 1992.

Johnson, Claudia D. *American Actress: Perspective on the Nineteenth Century.* Chicago: Nelson-Hall, 1984.

Joselit, Jena Weissman. *The Wonders of America: Reinventing Jewish Culture, 1880–1950.* New York: Hill and Wang, 1994.

Kahn, E. J., Jr. *The Merry Partners: The Age and Stage of Harrigan and Hart.* New York: Random House, 1955.

Kanter, Kenneth Aaron. *The Jews on Tin Pan Alley: The Jewish Contribution to American Popular Music, 1830–1940.* New York: Ktav Publishing House, 1982.

Kaufman, Alan. "Foreigners, Aliens, Mongrels: Literary Responses to American Immigration, 1880–1920." Ph.D. diss., Indiana University, 1982.

King, Miriam, and Steven Ruggles. "American Immigration, Fertility, and Race Suicide at the Turn of the Century." *Journal of Interdisciplinary History* 20, no. 3 (Winter 1990): 347–369.

Klein, Marcus. *Foreigners: The Making of American Literature, 1900–1940.* Chicago: University of Chicago Press, 1981.

Koger, Alicia Kae. "A Critical Analysis of Edward Harrigan's Comedy." Ph.D. diss., University of Michigan, 1984.

Kosok, Heinz. "Dion Boucicault's 'American' Plays: Considerations on Defining National Literatures in English." In *Literature and the Art of Creation*, edited by Robert Welch and Suheil B. Bushrui. Totowa, N.J.: Barnes and Noble, 1988.

Kren, George M. "The Jews: The Image as Reality." *Journal of Psychohistory* 6, no. 2 (Fall 1978): 285–299.

Landa, M. J. *The Jew in Drama*. New York: Kennikat Press, 1926.

Laurie, Joe, Jr. *Vaudeville: From the Honky-Tonks to the Palace*. New York: Henry Holt, 1953.

Lears, T. J. Jackson. *No Place of Grace: Antimodernism and the Transformation of American Culture, 1880–1920*. New York: Pantheon Books, 1981.

Lelyveld, Toby. *Shylock on the Stage*. Cleveland: Press of Western Reserve University, 1960.

Levine, Lawrence W. *Highbrow/Lowbrow: The Emergence of Cultural Hierarchy in America*. Cambridge, Mass.: Harvard University Press, 1988.

Library of Congress. *Dramatic Compositions Copyrighted in the United States, 1870–1916*. 2 vols. Washington, D.C.: Government Printing Office, 1918.

Lindemann, Albert S. *The Jew Accused: Three Anti-Semitic Affairs (Dreyfus, Beilis, Frank), 1894–1915*. New York: Cambridge University Press, 1991.

Lockridge, Richard. *Darling of Misfortune: Edwin Booth, 1833–1893*. New York: Century, 1932.

Lutz, Tom. *American Nervousness, 1903: An Anecdotal History*. Ithaca, N.Y.: Cornell University Press, 1991.

McConachie, Bruce A. *Melodramatic Formations: American Theatre and Society, 1820–1870*. Iowa City: University of Iowa Press, 1992.

McLean, Albert F. *American Vaudeville as Ritual*. Lexington: University of Kentucky Press, 1965.

———. "United States Vaudeville and the Urban Comics." *Theatre Quarterly* 1, no. 4 (October–December 1971): 47–52.

Mankowitz, Wolf. *Mazeppa: The Lives, Loves, and Legends of Adah Isaacs Menken*. New York: Stein and Day, 1982.

Mann, Arthur. *The One and the Many: Reflections on the American Identity*. Chicago: University of Chicago Press, 1979.

Marcuson, Lewis R. *The Stage Immigrant: The Irish, Italians, and Jews in American Drama, 1920–1960*. New York: Garland Publishing, 1990.

Marker, Lise-Lone. *David Belasco: Naturalism in the American Theatre*. Princeton: Princeton University Press, 1975.

Marks, Edward B. *They All Sang: From Tony Pastor to Rudy Vallee*, as told to Abbott J. Liebling. New York: The Viking Press, 1934.

Marra, Kim. "Taming America as Actress: Augustin Daly, Ada Rehan, and the Discourse of Imperial Frontier Conquest." In *Performing America: Cultural Nationalism in American Theatre*, edited by J. Ellen Gainor and Jeffrey Mason. Forthcoming.

Mayor, Louise A. *The Ambivalent Image: Nineteenth-Century America's Perception of the Jew*. Rutherford, N.J.: Farleigh Dickinson University Press, 1988.

Menken, Adah Isaacs. "Shylock." *American Israelite* 2 (October 1857).

Michelson, Bruce. "Edith Wharton's House Divided." *Studies in American Fiction* 12, no. 2 (Autumn 1984): 199–215.

Minsky, Morton, et al. "Modern Burlesque." In *American Popular Entertainment: Papers and Proceedings of the Conference on the History of American Popular Entertainment*, edited by Myron Matlaw. Westport, Conn.: Greenwood Press, 1977.

Mitchell, Robert. "Recent Jewish Immigration to the United States." *Popular Science Monthly* (February 1903): 334–343.

Moody, Richard. *Ned Harrigan: From Corlear's Hook to Herald Square*. Chicago: Nelson-Hall, 1980.

Morris, Clara. *The Life of a Star*. New York: McClure, Philips and Company, 1906.

———. *Life on the Stage*. New York: McClure, Philips and Company, 1901.

Mullenix, Elizabeth Reitz. "Neither Fish, Flesh, Nor Fowl: Adah Isaacs Menken and the Politics of Transgression." Paper presented at Association for Theatre in Higher Education annual conference, San Francisco, 1995.

Murphy, Brenda. *American Realism and American Drama, 1880–1940*. New York: Cambridge University Press, 1987.

Nobles, Milton. *Shop Talk*. Milwaukee: Riverside Printing, 1889.

Odell, George C. D. *Annals of the New York Stage*. 15 vols. New York: Columbia University Press, 1927–1949.

Pearlman, Michael. *To Make Democracy Safe for America: Patricians and Preparedness in the Progressive Era*. Urbana: University of Illinois Press, 1984.

Pearson, Roberta E. *Eloquent Gestures: The Transformation of Performance Style in the Griffith Biograph Films*. Berkeley and Los Angeles: University of California Press, 1992.

Peiss, Kathy. *Cheap Amusements: Working Women and Leisure in Turn-of-the-Century New York*. Philadelphia: Temple University Press, 1986.

Phelan, Peggy. *Unmarked: The Politics of Performance*. New York: Routledge, 1993.

Prell, Riv-Ellen. "Why Jewish Princesses Don't Sweat: Desire and Consumption in Postwar American Culture." In *People of the Body: Jews and Judaism from an Embodied Perspective*, edited by Howard Eilberg Schwartz. Albany: State University of New York Press, 1992.

Quoyeser, Catherine. "The Antimodernist Unconscious: Genre and Ideology in *The House of Mirth*." *Arizona Quarterly* 44, no. 4 (Winter 1989): 55–79.

Reynolds, Kirk Mallory. "A Stage History of *The Merchant of Venice*, 1596–1982: A Study Based on Selected Promptbooks." Ph.D. diss., University of South Carolina, 1987.

Richardson, Joanna. *Sarah Bernhardt and Her World*. New York: G. P. Putnam's Sons, 1977.

Riegel, Christian. "Rosedale and Antisemitism in *The House of Mirth*." *Studies in American Fiction* 20, no. 2 (Autumn 1992): 219–224.

Riis, Jacob A. *The Children of the Poor*. 1892. Reprint, New York: Arno Press and the New York Times, 1971.

———. *How the Other Half Lives: Studies Among the Tenements of New York*. 1890. Reprint, Williamstown, Mass.: Corner House Publishers, 1972.

Riis, Thomas L. *Just before Jazz: Black Musical Theater in New York, 1890–1915.* Washington, D.C.: Smithsonian Institution Press, 1989.

Ripley, William I. *The Races of Europe.* London: Kegan, Paul, Trench, Trubner, 1899.

Rischin, Moses. *The Promised City: New York's Jews, 1870–1914.* Cambridge, Mass.: Harvard University Press, 1962.

Rood, Arnold. "Henry Irving's Tours of North America." In *Theatrical Touring and Founding in North America*, edited by L. W. Conolly. Westport, Conn.: Greenwood Press, 1982.

Rosenberg, Edgar. *From Shylock to Svengali: Jewish Stereotypes in English Fiction.* Stanford: Stanford University Press, 1960.

———. "The Jew in Western Drama: An Essay." In *The Jew in English Drama.* New York: New York Public Library and Ktav Publishing, 1968.

Rosenfeld, Lulla. *Bright Star of Exile: Jacob Adler and the Yiddish Theatre.* New York: Thomas Y. Crowell, 1977.

Ruggles, Eleanor. *Prince of Players: Edwin Booth.* New York: W. W. Norton, 1953.

Said, Edward W. *Orientalism.* New York: Vintage Books, 1979.

Sandrow, Nahma. "'A Little Letter to Mama': Traditions in Yiddish Vaudeville." In *American Popular Entertainment: Papers and Proceedings of the Conference on the History of American Popular Entertainment*, edited by Myron Matlaw. Westport, Conn.: Greenwood Press, 1977.

———. *Vagabond Stars: A World History of Yiddish Theater.* New York: Harper and Row, 1977.

———. "Yiddish Theater and American Theater." In *From Hester Street to Hollywood: The Jewish-American Stage and Screen*, edited by Sarah Blacher Cohen. Bloomington: Indiana University Press, 1983.

Sarna, Jonathan D. "The 'Mythical Jew' and the 'Jew Next Door' in Nineteenth-Century America." In *Anti-Semitism in America*, edited by David A. Gerber. Urbana: University of Illinois Press, 1986.

Schickel, Richard. *D. W. Griffith: An American Life.* New York: Simon and Schuster, 1984.

Schiff, Ellen. *From Stereotype to Metaphor: The Jew in Contemporary Drama.* Albany: State University of New York Press, 1982.

———. Introduction to *Awake and Singing: Seven Classic Plays from the American Jewish Repertoire.* New York: Mentor, 1995.

———. "Shylock's *Mishpocheh*: Anti-Semitism on the American Stage." In *Anti-Semitism in America*, edited by David A. Gerber. Urbana: University of Illinois Press, 1986.

Schultz, Alfred P. *Race or Mongrel.* Boston: L. C. Page, 1908.

Senelick, Laurence. "Variety into Vaudeville: The Process Observed in Two Manuscript Gagbooks." *Theatre Survey* 19, no. 1 (May 1978): 1–15.

Shapiro, James. *Shakespeare and the Jews.* New York: Columbia University Press, 1996.

Showalter, Elaine. Introduction to *Trilby.* New York: Oxford University Press, 1995.

———. *Sexual Anarchy: Gender and Culture at the Fin de Siècle.* New York: Viking, 1990.

Singerman, Robert. "The Jew as Racial Alien: The Genetic Component of American Anti-Semitism." In *Anti-Semitism in America*, edited by David A. Gerber. Urbana: University of Illinois Press, 1986.

Skinner, Cornelia Otis. *Madame Sarah*. Boston: Houghton Mifflin, 1967.

Slobin, Mark. "Some Intersections of Jews, Music, and Theater." In *From Hester Street to Hollywood: The Jewish-American Stage and Screen*, edited by Sarah Blacher Cohen. Bloomington: Indiana University Press, 1983.

Smith, Joe. "Dr. Kronkite Revisited." In *American Popular Entertainment: Papers and Proceedings of the Conference on the History of American Popular Entertainment*, edited by Myron Matlaw. Westport, Conn.: Greenwood Press, 1977.

Smith-Rosenberg, Carroll. *Disorderly Conduct: Visions of Gender in Victorian America*. New York: Alfred M. Knopf, 1985.

Snyder, Robert W. *The Voice of the City: Vaudeville and Popular Culture in New York*. New York: Oxford University Press, 1989.

Sobel, Bernard. *Burlycue: An Underground History of Burlesque Days*. New York: Farrar and Rinehart, 1931.

———. *A Pictorial History of Vaudeville*. New York: The Citadel Press, 1961.

Sochen, June. "Fanny Brice and Sophie Tucker: Blending the Particular with the Universal." In *From Hester Street to Hollywood: The Jewish-American Stage and Screen*, edited by Sarah Blacher Cohen. Bloomington: Indiana University Press, 1983.

Sollors, Werner. *Beyond Ethnicity: Consent and Descent in American Culture*. New York: Oxford University Press, 1986.

Sonnenfeld, Albert. "The Poetics of Anti-Semitism." *Romantic Review* 75, no. 1 (January 1985): 76–93.

Sorin, Gerald. *A Time for Building: The Third Migration, 1880–1920*. Baltimore: Johns Hopkins University Press, 1992.

Stallybrass, Peter, and Allon White. *The Politics and Poetics of Transgression*. Ithaca, N.Y.: Cornell University Press, 1986.

Staples, Shirley. *Male-Female Comedy Teams in American Vaudeville*. Ann Arbor, Mich.: UMI Research Press, 1984.

Stern, Charles W., ed. *American Vaudeville, As Seen by Its Contemporaries*. New York: Alfred A. Knopf, 1984.

Stoker, Bram. *Personal Reminiscences of Henry Irving*. 2 vols. New York: Macmillan, 1906.

Taylor, George. "Svengali: Mesmerist and Aesthete." In *British Theatre in the 1890s*, edited by Richard Foulkes. New York: Cambridge University Press, 1992.

Timberlake, Craig. *The Bishop of Broadway: The Life and Work of David Belasco*. New York: Library Publishers, 1954.

Toll, Robert C. *Blacking Up: The Minstrel Show in Nineteenth-Century America*. New York: Oxford University Press, 1974.

Trachtenberg, Alan. *The Incorporation of America: Culture and Society in the Gilded Age*. New York: Hill and Wang, 1982.

Veidemanis, Gladys V. "Reflections on 'The Shylock Problem.'" In *Censored Books: Critical Viewpoints*. Metuchen, N.J.: Scarecrow Press, 1993.

Watermeier, Daniel J., ed. *Between Actor and Critic: Selected Letters of Edwin Booth and William Winter.* Princeton: Princeton University Press, 1971.

West, Shearer. "The Construction of Racial Type: Caricature, Ethnography, and Jewish Physiognomy in Fin-de-Siècle Melodrama." *Nineteenth Century Theatre* 21, no. 1 (Summer 1993): 3–40.

Wharton, Edith. *The House of Mirth.* New York: New American Library, 1964.

Whitfield, Stephen J. *American Space, Jewish Time.* Hamden, Conn.: Archon Books, 1988.

———. "Movies in America as Paradigms of Accomodation." In *The Americanization of the Jews,* edited by Robert M. Seltzer and Norman J. Cohen. New York: New York University Press, 1995.

Who Was Who in the Theatre, 1912–1976. 3 vols. Detroit: Gates Research, 1978.

Wiese, Roberta J. "Racism in the Progressive Era: The Anglo-Saxon Myth." Ph.D. diss., University of Texas at Austin, 1970.

Williams, Raymond. *The Sociology of Culture.* New York: Schocken Books, 1981.

Wilmeth, Don B. *Variety Entertainment and Outdoor Amusements: A Reference Guide.* Westport, Conn.: Greenwood Press, 1982.

Wilson, Garff. *Three Hundred Years of American Theatre.* Englewood Cliffs, N.J.: Prentice-Hall, 1973.

Winter, William. *Life and Art of Edwin Booth.* New York: Macmillan, 1894.

———. *The Life of David Belasco.* 2 vols. New York: Jefferson and Winter, 1925.

———. *Shakespeare on the Stage.* Vol 1. New York: Yard, 1911.

Young, Wiiliam C., ed. *Famous Actors and Actresses on the American Stage.* New York: R. R. Bowker, 1975.

Zangwill, Israel. *Children of the Ghetto: A Study of a Peculiar People.* New York: Macmillan, 1926.

Zeidman, Irving. *The American Burlesque Show.* New York: Hawthorn Books, 1967.

INDEX

"Abie, Dot's Not a Business for You"
(song), 142
Abie's Irish Rose (Nichols), 159
"Abie the Sporty Kid" (song), 140
Addams, Jane, 139, 148
Addison, Thomas, 139
Adler, Jacob, 10, 114–116
Adler, Julia, 115
African Americans, 121; as characters,
xi, 17, 76, 90, 160, 199n37; as
performers, 91, 94; situation of,
symbolized by Jewish characters,
188n5
Aldrich, Thomas Bailey, 52–53, 57,
189n24
Alfriend, Edward, 58
Ambivalent Image, The (Mayor), 5
American Society for the Suppression
of the Jews, 67, 70
Angels in America (Kushner), xii
Anti-Defamation League of the B'nai
B'rith, 150
anti-Semitism, 114, 119; and British
theater, 2, 5, 31–32; and Jews in
entertainment industry, 93–99, 105–
112; in "Isaacs-Crummels Boom,"
74–75; in *Life* magazine, 93–96, 99;
and Manhattan Beach incident, 67–
71; as reflected in racialism, 123–
127; and theater boycotts, 150–153,
159; usage of term, 12–13; in

Victorian America, 66–67, 125,
190n3. *See also* philo-Semitism
Anti-Semitic Stereotypes (Felsenstein), 5
Anti-Stage Ridicule Committee, 150
Arliss, George, 147, 183n1
Arthur, Lee, 108, 194n41
As a Man Thinks (Thomas), 145–149,
198n6
assimilation, 137–138, 150. *See also*
Jews, and immigration; melting pot;
racialism
Associated Rabbis of America, 150
Auctioneer, The (Klein and Arthur),
108–113, 109fig., 120, 194n41;
mentioned, 116, 134–135, 153, 154,
197n49, 198n22; scene from, 167–
168
audiences, 11, 81–82, 186n20. *See also*
Jews, in audiences
Awake and Sing! (Odets), 159
Awake and Singing (Schiff), 8, 199n36
Ayrton, Edith, 134

Bateman, Kate, 46, 47fig., 49, 188n7,
189n16
Bayes, Nora, 157–158
Beau Brummel (Fitch), 123, 128, 195n5
Belasco, David, 99–101, 135, 153,
196n24; and *The Auctioneer*, 108–
113, 194n41; and *The Merchant of
Venice*, 115–117

belle juive, *see* Jewess, as belle juive
Bells, The (Lewis), 186n37
Ben Hur (Wallace), 52
Ben Israel (Tullidge), 146
Benneaux, W., 188n5
Berlin, Irving, 8, 96, 140, 157–158
Bernard, Barney, 153–154
Bernard, Sam, 104, 106, 108
Bernhardt, Sarah, 12, 48–51, 50fig., 70,
    188–189n10, 189n16
Bert and Leon, 76
Beyond Ethnicity (Sollors), 134, 137,
    139, 196n31, 196n33, 196–197n37
biblical plays, 52–53, 146
Biograph Studios, 54–55
Boelhower, William, 6, 196n33
Booth, Edwin, 70, 174, 189n24; as
    Shylock, 21–28, 24fig., 29, 31,
    186n20
Booth, John Wilkes, 22
Booth, Junius Brutus, 22
Boucicault, Dion, 31
Braham, David, 89
Brice, Fanny, 8, 157–159
British theater, *see* anti-Semitism, and
    British theater
Broadway, *see* Jewish characters (male),
    in entertainment industry; Jews in
    entertainment industry; musical
    comedy
Brougham, John, 31–32, 35, 39, 59
Bruening, Albert, 128, 196n24
burlesque (genre of nineteenth-century
    parody), 17–18, 31–32, 43
burlesque (genre mixing music,
    comedy, and chorus girls), 99–100,
    102–108, 144, 193n23
Bush, Frank, 65–66, 75–83, 77fig.,
    79fig., 91; lyrics to songs, 163–164;
    mentioned, 102, 105, 107
Butler, Judith, 6

Cahill, Marie, 105
Calisch, Edward, 6
"Callahan the Detective" (Harrigan and
    Hart), 76

Campbell, Bartley, 90
Cantor, Eddie, 8, 159
Capra, Frank, 137
Carr, Alexander, 153–154
Casino Company, 106–107
Caught in a Corner (Shaw), 91
Central Conference of American
    Rabbis, 150
Chanfrau, Frank, 70
Chase, Frank Eugene (Abel Seaman),
    39, 187n61
Child of the Ghetto (film), 55–57,
    190n30
Children of the Ghetto (Zangwill), 134–
    135, 196n34
Cincinnati, Jewish community of, 48,
    70–71
Cohen's Courtship (Quick), 133
Cohen's Fire Sale (film), 58
Cohen's Luck (Arthur), 103fig.
Coleman, Edward D., 5, 198n20
"College Girls Show" (revue), 157
comedy, *see* burlesque; Jewish characters
    (male), trend toward comedy of;
    variety theater; vaudeville
Conquergood, Dwight, 7
"Construction of Racial Type, The"
    (West), 5
Cooper, Harry, 153
Corbin, Austin, 66–69, 89, 131, 160
Corbin, John, 116, 118, 131–133, 137
Crane, Stephen, 127–128
Cumberland, Richard, 146
Curtis, M. B., 65, 71, 83–92, 102, 105,
    185, 192n48; scene from *Sam'l of
    Posen*, 164–165

Daly, Augustin, 43, 46, 52, 188n5,
    188n6, 188n7, 189n16
Dandy, Jess, 102, 104, 106, 153
Darwin, Charles, 123–124, 126, 131
Davidge, William, 72
Deborah (Mosenthal), 43, 46
Dickens, Charles, 32–33, 146
Dijkstra, Bram, 53
Diner, Hasia R., 184n11

"Dinkle and Pinkle" (Newton), 93
Dinnerstein, Leonard, 96, 190n3
"Dion Boucicault's 'American Plays,'"
    (Kosok), 184n15
Disraeli (Parker), 145–147, 149, 198n5,
    198n6
Distler, Paul Antonie, 102, 105, 112,
    149, 155, 184n10
Dodson, J. E., 187n48
Donnay, Maurice, 139, 197n49, 197n50
Down on the Farm (Hancock), 33
Down the Black Cañon (Heermans), 33,
    39
Dracula, 187n45
Du Maurier, George, 98, 193n34
Dumont, Frank, 90

Eloquent Gestures (Pearson), 190n30
emotionalism, 46–47
English Notebooks (Hawthorne), 40
entertainment industry, *see* Jewish
    characters (male), in entertainment
    industry; Jews in entertainment
    industry
Erckmann, Emile, 186n37
Erlanger, Abe, 96
ethnicity, performance of, 6–7
Eytinge, Rose, 70

Fagin (character, *Oliver Twist*), 2, 32–
    33, 37–39, 100
Fairchild, H., 124
Fast Life in New York (Woods), 153
fellowship, meanings of, 63–66
Felsenstein, Frank, 5
Fiddle-Dee-Dee (Smith), 107
Fields, Armond and Marc, 99
Fields, Harry and Sadie, 102
Fields, Lew, 99–100, 101, 107–108,
    111–112, 149, 155
Fisher, Charles, 31, 37
Fiske, Minnie Maddern, 54
Fitch, Clyde, 123, 127–131, 135
Flying Scud (Boucicault), 31, 37
Freund, Ernest, 151
Friedman, William S., 150

Frohman, Charles, 96, 196n24, 198n22
From Shylock to Svengali (Rosenberg),
    5, 193n34
From Stereotype to Metaphor (Schiff),
    183n4
Furnace, Horace, 26

Gabler, Neal, 97
Gandal, Keith Leland, 25
gender, 11; differences between Jewish
    women and men, 40–41, 110, 156;
    intersection of ethnicity and
    femininity, 46, 157–158; and
    marriage roles, 58, 131–132; and
    masculine ideals, 63–66, 86, 100,
    125, 127, 131, 155; and the New
    Woman, 57, 131–132; performance
    of, 6; in racialism, 127; and
    Victorian womanhood, 49–50, 94.
    See also Jewess (character type);
    Jewish characters (male), sexuality of
Gerber, David A., 35
German ("Dutch") characters, xi, 76,
    99–100, 149
German Jews, 9, 48, 66–70, 152,
    184n11
Gérôme, Jean Léon, 24
Gershwin, George, 8, 199n36
Ghetto, The (Heijermans), 120, 135,
    196–197n37
Giacommetti, Paolo, 53
Gilbert, Douglas, 76
Gilbert and Sullivan, 17
Gilman, Sander, 4, 6, 125
Girl from Kays, The (Caryll), 104
Glass, Montague, 153–154
Glickman the Glazier (Newton and
    Hoffman), 118–120, 119fig., 142
Goodwin, Nat, 187n48
Gordin, Jacob, 196n36
Gorman, Dick, 90
Grand Army Man, The (Belasco), 113
Grant, Madison, 124–125, 127
Great Diamond Robbery, The (Alfriend
    and Wheeler), 58–59, 190n36,
    196n25

Griffith, David Wark, 41, 51, 54–57, 190n30

Gross, John, 5, 185n7

Grossman, Barbara W., 158

Halévy, Jacques Fromenthal, 42, 70

Hall, Prescott F., 123–124

Hancock, C. W., 33

Harap, Louis, 6

Harrigan, Edward, 76, 89, 196n36

Hart, Tony, 76

Hawthorne, Nathaniel, 40–41

Hayman, Abe, 96

Hebraic Types (McCree), 104, 193n31

"Hebrew Glazier, The" (Bush), 81

Hebrewing and Shewooing (McCree), 133

Heermans, Forbes, 33

Heijermans, Herman, 120, 135

Helter Skelter (Smith), 107

Hilton, Henry, 66, 87

Hines, William, 105, 157

Hoffman, Aaron, 104, 118, 193n31

Hoffman, Dustin, 20

Horniman, Roy, 139

Houdini, Harry, 159

House Next Door, The (Manners), 139

House of Mirth, The (Fitch), 128

House of Mirth, The (Wharton), 122–123, 195n4; as Broadway play, 128

Howard, Sammy, 97

Howard, Willie, 144–145, 153

Howe, Irving, 96–97

Howells, William Dean, 25

How the Other Half Lives (Riis), 58

Hurly Burly (Smith and Stromberg), 107

Husband (Corbin), 118, 131–133, 137

Ibsen, Henrik, 131, 135, 137, 196n36

Idols (Horniman), 139

Image of the Jew in American Literature, The (Harap), 6

"I'm a Yiddish Cowboy" (song), 140–141; lyrics to, 169

immigration, *see* Jews, and immigration

Immigration and Its Effects Upon the United States (Hall), 123–124

In Gay New York (McLellan), 106–107

intermarriage, *see* Jews, and intermarriage

In the Trenches (Chase), 39, 58, 63

Irish Americans: as characters xi, 63–64, 76, 78, 81–82, 89, 120, 136, 149; as playwrights, 31, 84

Irving, Henry, 12, 187n45; as Shylock, 17, 22–23, 28–31, 30fig., 89, 114, 115, 186n37, 187n48

Irving, Laurence, 29

"Isaacs-Crummels Boom, The" (Nobles), 74–75

Isadore Plastrick (Jessop), 84

Isman, Felix, 100

Israel Isaacs; or, A Jew's Gratitude (Reid), 104

"It's Tough When Izzy Rosenstein Loves Genevieve Malone" (song), 141

Ivanhoe (Scott), 42, 48

Jail Bird, The (Townsend), 33–37, 39

James, Henry, 29

Janauschek, Fanny, 46, 58–59, 190n36, 196n25

Jazz Singer, The (film), 159

Jessica (character, *The Merchant of Venice*), 41, 115

Jessop, George H., 84

Jew, The (Cumberland), 146

Jewess, The, see Juive, La

Jewess (character type), 13, 60, 66, 70–71, 146; as belle juive, 40–60, 120, 132–133, 156; in comedy, 105; gentile perspective on, 42–43, 47–50, 54, 57–60; invisibility of, xii, 156–157; and the Jewish actress, 46–50; and the Jewish American Princess, 60; as the Jewish mother, 60, 110; as masculinized hag, 41, 58–60, 74–75, 110; and racialism, 127, 132–133

Jew in Drama, The (Landa), 5, 192n48

Jew in English Drama, The (Coleman), 5
*Jew in English Literature as Author and
    as Subject, The* (Calisch), 6
Jewish characters (male): as admirers of
    Christianity, 101, 110, 150; class
    issues with, 11, 36, 66, 81, 89, 149;
    "cleaning up" of, 99–101, 144–146,
    149–159; connections to money, 34–
    36, 73–74, 80; effeminacy of, 36–38,
    74, 129–130; in entertainment
    industry, 34, 65, 75, 98–101; as
    exemplary, 145–149; exoticism of,
    25–27; and fellowship with gentiles,
    63–66; and fin-de-siècle sensibility,
    53, 98, 158; increasing invisibility
    of, 159–161, 199n36; legitimation of
    as sympathetic, 65–66, 80–88, 108–
    113; as moneylenders, 122–123; in
    motion pictures, xi, 54–57, 58;
    physical traits of, 1–2, 33, 73, 84–
    86, 104, 112, 144–145, 154–156; as
    played by gentiles, 3–4, 10, 76–78,
    104–105, 114; recent reemergence
    of, xi–xii; in romantic relationships
    with gentiles, 118–123, 128–143,
    147–148, 155; sexuality of, 36–37,
    129–130; speech of, 33–34, 73, 79–
    80, 84; studies on, 5–6, 8, 183n4,
    184n10; trend toward comedy of,
    38–39, 71–91; unusual variations on,
    105; in vaudeville and variety
    comedy, 71–91, 101–113, 133, 144–
    145, 149–153; verbal humor of,
    154–155; as victims of violence, 81–
    83, 90; as villains, 1–2, 31–39, 63–
    66; in Wild West, 90, 140. *See also*
    Fagin; Jessica; Jewess; Leah;
    Shylock
Jew of Malta, The (Marlowe), 185n8
Jews: as actresses, 46–50; in audiences,
    70–71, 87–89, 90, 97, 110, 111, 114,
    192n8; boycotts of shows by, 150–
    153, 159; definitions of, 7–8;
    described by gentiles, 25–26, 35; in
    early American theater, 70–71; and
    immigration, 8–9, 21–22, 55, 90,
    111–112, 121, 139, 150, 184n11,
    196n29; and intermarriage, 120–
    121, 133, 138, 140–143, 155–156;
    less ethnic stage names of, 83–84,
    157, 183n2; and racialism, 123–127;
    response to *The Melting-pot*, 138,
    151; as Shylock, 114–117; as targets
    of anti-Semitism, 66–70; terms for,
    13
Jews in entertainment industry, 64, 93–
    97, 117, 151, 190n1, 192n7;
    aesthetic implications of, 97;
    invisibility of, xii, 99–101, 145, 160;
    in nineteenth century, 70–71
Jew Trouble at Manhattan Beach
    (Stout), 68, 190n7
John Russell's Comedians, 106
Jolson, Al, 8
Judith (Giacommetti), 55
Judith of Bethulia (Aldrich), 51–54,
    146, 190n30
Judith of Bethulia (film), 55–57
Juive, La (Scribe and Halévy), 42, 51

Kallen, Horace, 138
Katz, Stephen, 4
Kean, Charles, 22
Kean, Edmund, 22, 70, 185n13
Kern, Jerome, 96
Klaw, Marc, 96
Klein, Charles, 108, 139, 153, 194n41,
    197n49, 198n22; scene from *The
    Auctioneer*, 167–168; scene from
    Potash and Perlmutter, 170–171
Kosok, Heinz, 184n15

Lackaye, Wilton, 98, 134, 196n34
Landa, M. J., 5, 7, 183n4, 192n48
Laurie, Joe Jr., 153
Lawrence, Florence, 55–56
Leah (character, *Leah, the Forsaken*),
    see *Leah, the Forsaken*
Leah Kleschna (McLellan), 54
Leah, the Forsaken (Daly), 43–46, 48–
    51, 53–54, 56, 57, 66, 188n5, 188n6,
    189n16

Leah, the Forsook (Setchell), 43
Leather Patch, The (Harrigan), 89
Lederer, George W., 106–107, 113
Lessing, G. E., 146
Levi, Julius, 68–70
"Levinsky at the Wedding" (Rose), 102;
   text of, 165–167
Levy Cohn (play), 90
Levy the Drummer; or, Life on the Road
   (Baswitz), 90
Levine, Lawrence, 11
Lewis, Leopold, 186n37
Life magazine, 93–96, 95fig., 99
Little Boss, The (Bixby), 36, 37–38, 39
Loew, Marcus, 96, 117
London, Jack, 127–128
Lottery of Life, The (Brougham), 31–32,
   35, 36, 37, 38–39

McConachie, Bruce A., 186n20
McCree, Junie, 104, 133, 193n31
Macklin, Charles, 20, 22, 26, 187n48
McLean, Albert, 97
McLellan, C.M.S. (Hugh Morton), 54,
   106, 189n28
Macready, William C., 20, 22
Manhattan Beach incident, 67–71, 89,
   91, 131
Mann, Arthur, 134, 137
Mannners, J. Hartley, 139, 142
Mansfield, Richard, 71, 114, 195n5
Marble, Ed, 84
Marks, Edward B., 76–77, 140
Marlowe, Christopher, 146, 185n8
"Marry a Yiddisha Boy" (song), 140
Marx, Groucho, 87, 140, 155
Marx Brothers, 8, 155, 159, 199n36
Mason, John, 148
Maugham, William Somerset, 184n16
Mayor, Louise, 5, 34, 183n16
Mazeppa (Milner), 48
melodrama, 1–2, 31–39, 58–59, 63–65,
   89, 187n47
Melodramatic Formations
   (McConachie), 186n20
melting pot, 121–143, 145, 155, 158, 160

Melting-pot, The (Zangwill), 134–139,
   148, 151, 155, 184n16, 196–197n37,
   197n44, 198n6
Melting-pot Mistake, The (Fairchild),
   124
Men and Women (Belasco and De
   Mille), 101, 110
Menken, Adah Isaacs, 22, 48–49, 70,
   189n24
Merchant of Venice, The (Shakespeare),
   17–31, 41, 88, 114–117, 185n11.
   See also Jessica; Portia; Shylock
Merry World, The (Smith), 106
Meyer and Son (Addison), 139
Miller, Arthur, 199n36
Mississippi Masala (film), 197n44
Mitchell, Robert, 25, 125
Money Lender, The (Reid), 104
Mordecai Lyons (Harrigan), 89, 191n40
Morris, Clara, 47, 70–71
*Morris Cohen, the Commercial
   Drummer* (play), 90
Morton, Hugh, *see* McLellan, C.M.S.
Mosenthal, Salomon Hermann von, 43,
   46, 70, 188n6, 189n16
*Moses, a Dealer in Second-Hand
   Clothing* (play), 75
Moses Levy (play), 90
"Moshe from Nova Scotia" (song), 140,
   156
motion pictures, 9, and D. W. Griffith,
   54–57, 190n30; Jewish characters in,
   xi, 54–57, 58; Jewish presence in,
   xii, 97, 117, 190n1, 199n36;
   mentioned, 159, 197n44
Much Ado About a Merchant of Venice
   (Brougham), 31–32
multiculturalism, 121
Muni, Paul, 10
musical comedy, 9, 11, 104–105, 149–
   150, 189n28
Music Master, The (Klein), 113, 153
My Hebrew Friend (Dumont), 90

Nair, Mira, 197n44
Nathan the Wise (Lessing), 146

New Lamps and Old (Leonard), 196n34
Newton, Harry Lee, 93, 104, 118
New Woman, *see under* gender
Nixon, Sam, 96
Noah, Mordecai Manuel, 70
Nobles, Milton, 65, 71–75, 83, 190–191n12
Nordau, Max, 126
Norris, Frank, 127–128
"Northern Exposure" (TV series), xi
Norworth, Jack, 157

Object, Matrimony (Glass and Goodman), 154
Oliver Twist (Dickens), 32–33, 70, 100
O'Neil, Nance, 51–53, 57
O'Neill, Eugene, 93, 199n36
On the Bowery (Stephens), 83
opera, 42
Orientalism, 25–26, 29–30, 53

Pam, Judge Hugo, 151
Parisian Widows' Show (revue), 102
Parker, Louis, 145
Passing of the Great Race, The (Grant), 124
Passion, The (play), 101
Pastor, Rose Harriet, 121
Pastor, Tony, 68, 76, 102, 107–108
Pearson, Roberta E., 190n30
Peddler, The (Reid), 104
philo-Semitism, 42, 43, 126, 189n16
Phoenix, The (Nobles), 71–75
Pinero, Arthur, 184n16
Pit, The (Pollock), 196n34
Plastrick, Sam'l (character, *Sam'l of Posen, Spot Cash*), 65, 84–91, 85fig., 102
Po-ca-hon-tas (Brougham), 32
"Poetics of Anti-Semitism, The" (Sonnenfeld), 183–184n9
Polish Jew, The (Erckmann), 186n37
Poponoe, Paul, 126
Portia (character, *The Merchant of Venice*), 9–10, 23, 65
Potash and Perlmutter (Glass), 146, 153–156, 197n49
Potter, Paul, 98
Prince of Pilsen, The (Luters and Pixley), 106
Puck, 68–70

Quick, William A., 133
Quiz Show (film), xi

Race or Mongrel (Schultz), 124
Rachel (Éliza Félix), 47–48, 70
racialism, 51–52, 121–122, 123–127, 131–132, 137, 142–143, 160, 196n29
realism, 135, 198n6
Rebecca (character, *Ivanhoe*), 42, 48
"Rebecca" (song), 140
Reid, Hal, 104
Reigel, Christine, 195n4
Reilly and the Four Hundred (Harrigan), 89
Remington, Earle, 105, 157
Return from Jerusalem (Donnay), 139, 197n49, 197n50
Return of Peter Grimm, The (Belasco), 113
Reynolds, Abe, 105
Reynolds, Kirk Mallory, 26
Rice, Andy, 153
Rich Mr. Hoggenheimer, The (Smith), 104
Riis, Jacob A., 25, 58
"Rise and Fall of the Racial Comics, The" (Distler), 184n10
Ristori, Adelaide, 53
Romance of a Jewess (film), 54–56, 190n30
Romanticism, 22, 42
Roosevelt, Theodore, 125, 127, 134, 139, 148, 195n15
Rose, Julian, 102, 106, 113, 152, 153; monologue from, 165
"Rosedale" (Riegel), 195n4
Rosenberg, Edgar, 5, 98–99, 146, 193n34
Rosenfeld, Monroe, 96

Ruggles, Eleanor, 26
Russian characters, 90, 135–138, 154–155

"Sadie Salome, Go Home" (song, Berlin), 157–158
Said, Edward, 26
Sally in Our Alley (Hobart), 105
Salome, 53, 158, 189n27
Sam'l of Posen (Jessop), 71, 83–90, 85fig., 102, 110; scene from, 164–165
Sandrow, Nahma, 184n12, 196n36
Schiff, Ellen, 8, 183n4, 199n36
Schultz, Alfred P., 124, 126, 127
Schwartz, Alonzo, 72
Scott, Walter, 42
Scribe, Eugène, 42
Second-Hand Man, The (Newton), 104
"Seinfeld" (TV series), xii
Seligman, Joseph, 66
Setchell, Dan, 43
Shakespeare, William, 17, 19, 20–21, 27–28, 34, 41, 88, 114–115, 145, 195n4. *See also* Jessica; *Merchant of Venice*; Portia; Shylock
Shakespeare and the Jews (Shapiro), 185n7
Shakespeare Water Cure, The (play), 17–18
Shapiro, James, 185n7
Shatchen, The (Dickson), 91
Shaw, George Bernard, 135, 137, 184n16
sheenies, *see* Jewish characters (male), as villains
Shelland, Harry, 104
Shop Talk (Nobles), 74–75
Showalter, Elaine, 98
Shylock (character, *The Merchant of Venice*), 17–36, 71, 94, 114–117, 185n3, 185n5, 185n7, 185n8, 187n45, 187n48, 195n4; mentioned, 40, 41, 43, 45, 63, 65, 89, 98, 105, 115, 153
Shylock (Gross), 5, 185n7

Siberia (Campbell), 90
Singerman, Robert, 125
Sobel, Bernard, 144
Sollors, Werner, 134, 137, 139, 196n31, 196–197n37
song-publishing industry (Tin Pan Alley), 9, 11, 96, 140–142; lyrics to songs, 150–151, 169–170
Sonnenfeld, Albert, 7, 22, 183–184n9
Spot Cash (Curtis and Marble), 63, 84, 85fig., 90–91, 191n44
stage Jews, *see* Jewess (character type); Jewish characters (male)
Stoker, Bram, 187n45
Stokes, James Graham Phelps, 120–121
Stowe, Harriet Beecher, 18
Svengali (character, *Trilby*), 98–99, 143, 192–193n15, 196n34
Sweet, Blanche, 57
Syndicate, The, *see* Theatrical Syndicate, The

Taming of the Shrew, The (Shakespeare), 21, 23
Tannehill, F. A., 72
Taylor, Tom, 1–2
television, xi, 96, 160
Terry, Ellen, 28
"That's Yiddisha Love" (song), 141
theatrical design, 23–25, 29–30
Theatrical Syndicate, The, 93–94, 96, 99–100, 192n3, 194n41, 198n22
Third Degree, The (Klein), 198n22
Thomas, Augustus, 145–149
Through a Glass Darkly (Boelhower), 6, 196n33
Ticket-of-Leave Man, The (Taylor), 1–2, 12, 36, 106
Time for Gathering, A (Diner), 184n11
Tin Pan Alley, *see* song-publishing industry
Townsend, Charles, 33, 187n50
Tree, Herbert Beerbohm, 98, 184n16
Trilby (Potter), 98–99, 184n16, 196n34
Tucker, Sophie, 8, 159
Turner, Frederick Jackson, 134

Two Wandering Jews (Shelland), 104

Uncle Tom's Cabin (Stowe), 19
"Under the Matzos Tree" (song), 140

Vagabond Stars (Sandrow), 184n12,
   196n36
Variety, 192n7
variety theater, 73–83, 190n7, 192n10
vaudeville, 11, 83, 96–97, 118–120,
   133, 192n10; decline of Jewish
   comics in, 149–159; rise of Jewish
   comics in, 101–106
Victorian era, 12, 66–67, 125, 184n13,
   190n3

Wallace, Lew, 52
Walsh, Blanche, 129, 196n25
Walthall, Henry, 56, 57
Wandering Jew, The, 99, 105, 106,
   193n34
Warfield, David, 7, 106–113, 109fig.,
   115–117, 144, 156, 183n1; debut
   story told by, 1–4; ethnic heritage of,
   3, 112, 183n2; mentioned, 10, 95,
   100, 104, 152, 153, 158, 159; scene
   from *The Auctioneer*, 167–168
Weber, Joe, 99–100, 107–108, 111, 149,
   155
Weber and Fields, *see* Fields, Lew;
   Weber, Joe
Wehman, Henry J., 96
Weininger, Otto, 36–37

Welch, Ben, 102, 113
Welch, Joe, 102–104, 103fig., 106, 113,
   152, 157, 193n34, 198n20
Welcome Stranger (Hoffman), 193n31
West, Dorothy, 56
West, Shearer, 5
Wharton, Edith, 122–123, 128, 195n4
Wheeler, A. C., 58
"When Mose with His Hand Leads the
   Band" (song), 141–142
Whitfield, Stephen, 97
Wilde, Oscar, 128
Winter, William, 17, 25, 26, 27, 29, 30–
   31, 71
Woman in the Case, The (Fitch), 128–
   131, 142
Woods, Al H., 153

"Yiddisha Luck and Irisha Love"
   (song), 141; lyrics to, 169–170
"Yiddisha Nightingale" (song), 140
Yiddish theater, 10–11, 71, 114–115,
   184n12, 196n36
"Yiddle on Your Fiddle" (song, Berlin),
   140, 142
"Yonkele the Cowboy Jew" (song), 140

Zangwill, Israel, 134–139, 142, 148,
   184n16, 196–197n37, 197n44
Zimmerman, J. F., 96
Zionism, 126, 139, 195n20
Zukor, Adolf, 190n1

About the Author

Harley Erdman is an assistant professor in the Department of Theater at the University of Massachusetts at Amherst, where he teaches dramaturgy and theater history. His work has appeared in *Theatre Annual*, *Theatre Journal*, and *Centennial Review*.